The Year Without Christmas

The Year Without Christmas

A Novel

by

John M. Wills

Edited by Kate Lehman

Oak Tree Press Hanford, CA

Oak Tree Press
Publishers Since 1998

THE YEAR WITHOUT CHRISTMAS, Copyright 2013, by John M. Mills. All rights reserved. Printed in the United States of America. No part of this book may be used or reproduced in any manner whatsoever without written permission except in the case of brief quotations used in critical articles and reviews.

For information, address Oak Tree Press, 1820 W. Lacey Boulevard, Suite 220, Hanford, CA 93230.

Oak Tree Press books may be purchased for educational, business, or sales promotional purposes. Contact Publisher for quantity discounts.

First Edition, November 2013

ISBN 978-1-61009-075-9
LCCN 2013940709

For my deceased uncle, James Callahan.

Acknowledgments

My thanks to the critique group of the Riverside Writers. Our regular Monday night meetings have proven to be an invaluable aid in developing my writing skills.

My editor, Kate Lehman, continues to guide me in the right direction when my prose fails to live up to expectations.

Thank you to Elizabeth Willman, a dear friend who dedicates her life to helping others. Her volunteer efforts with the Night Ministry for the homeless in Chicago led me to include that wonderful resource in my book.

My former colleague and good friend, Tony Riggio, agreed to read my manuscript. His keen eye spotted a few things that I overlooked. Thanks, Tony.

Finally, to my best friend and confidant—my wife of 43 years, Christine—thanks for your patience and love.

1

Men's hearts are cold. They are indifferent.
  —Marry Harris Jones

The ice cold wind assaulted him, stinging his exposed skin like thousands of needle pricks. The approaching night would definitely be colder than the ones before, challenging him to survive an hour at a time. If he didn't find a spot near the exhaust grate beneath the city streets, tonight might finally bring about what had been worrying him: he might die in a strange town. Alone. At least his ordeal would be over If that happened.

Eric Doyle, who was born and raised in a small town in Michigan, had been homeless for almost a year. His choice. Well, kind of. The original plan was to leave his hometown of Websterville and start a new life with a new identity in a big city, lost among millions of people where no one from his previous life might find him. That was the plan. But as was the case with many plans, the end result rarely resembles the intent and hoped for outcome. And if the truth be known, as each day slowly passed, the will to create a new life dripped slowly from his soul like the last drops of water from a sprinkling can.

With only a spark remaining in his once fiery will to live, he nevertheless set about making preparations to ensure his spot with the others huddled next to a heat exhaust, deep in the bowels of one of Chicago's myriad skyscrapers. That is, if the cops didn't chase them away. Theirs was a constant cat and mouse game—the homeless and the cops—each trying to outwit the other. To their credit, the police seemed more sympathetic toward the numerous nomads when Chicago's weather turned deadly. The city's infamous winters invariably claimed the lives of a few people who dared not fear it.

Eric was accustomed to cold weather. Michigan winters were legendary, with their bountiful snowfalls blanketing the landscape to the delight of skiers and snowmobilers. Temperatures often dipped below zero, turning the countless ponds and lakes into mirror-like skating rinks. But that was different; Eric was clothed properly and sheltered from the elements. In this new life, he had neither the appropriate clothing nor a place to escape from the brutally cold conditions.

And Chicago's climate, although similar to Michigan's winters, was different in one very distinct regard—the wind. The city of Chicago bears many different nicknames: "Second City, City of Big Shoulders, Chi-Town," and, "The City That Works." But the most popular and perhaps most appropriate moniker is, "The Windy City." The architecture in downtown Chicago, with hundreds of towering buildings, creates giant wind tunnels for the gales that sweep off Lake Michigan. The vortex created is such that the wind seemingly comes from all directions, creating eddies and swirls, sometimes resembling mini-tornadoes. This weather phenomenon is particularly harsh in wintertime, causing the wind chill to sometimes drop as low as thirty degrees below zero.

That's exactly what it felt like to Eric as he walked into a tempestuous headwind on Wacker Drive. He glanced over the edge of the concrete railing that paralleled the street and saw huge chunks of ice floating in the Chicago River, like so many translucent stepping stones scattered on top of the water. It was late afternoon and the darkness had yet to steal the daylight. There was still enough time to search for just the right piece of cardboard to sleep on and create a barrier between his body and the cold concrete that would be his bed this night, just as it had been on countless other nights.

He knew of several places to search that regularly discarded large cardboard boxes. Most times the boxes were cut up and placed in a neat stack to await the disposal company pickup in the early morning hours. But every once in a while, Eric would get lucky and find a box that had not been sliced. On an arctic day like today, an intact box created the perfect shelter against the wind. And if he lucked out and found a spot next to the heat exhaust grate, he could turn the opening of the box toward the grate and have a heated shelter. But that was the exception rather than the norm, particularly if other street denizens had searched before him and found what he was seeking.

THE YEAR WITHOUT CHRISTMAS

Good boxes were in high demand in the homeless sub-culture. People who live on the street have the same singular mindset—stay alive. Everyone searches for the same things to get them through another day. Having a shelter at night was a necessity people often battled for. It wasn't unusual to see fights break out as one homeless person tried to take another's cardboard box. It was quintessential Charles Darwin, survival of the fittest, as each individual struggled to prevail.

A strong gust of wind shouldered him toward the alcove of a coffee shop, like a big brother bullying a younger sibling with superior size and strength. In his old life, Eric could have withstood that quick shove from Mother Nature. Now, his once muscular frame and considerable strength had vanished like a magician's trick on stage. He knew he'd lost weight, eating only when he could find food, but he was barely recognizable as he stared at his reflected image in the café's window. He was the "after," in the typical before and after photo of people losing unwanted weight.

Standing sheltered from the "Hawk," the nickname Chicagoans gave the wind in their town, he took in the deep aroma emanating from freshly brewed coffee grounds inside the shop. Breathing deeply, his thoughts drifted back home to where his wife brewed fresh coffee each morning, a ritual that marked the beginning of their day. He liked his coffee black; she preferred just a touch of cream. Whether real or imagined, that daily jolt of caffeine energized them both and jumpstarted their day. More importantly, sharing that morning cup together served to strengthen their bond of love.

Still lost in the reverie of home, he was suddenly knocked off balance as the door to the restaurant swung open and struck him. A patron leaving the café stood before Eric. "Oh, pardon me," the stranger quickly blurted. "I didn't mean to . . ." Getting a better look at the individual who had impeded his exit from the coffee shop, the man's tone quickly changed. "Hey, get the hell out of the doorway, bums aren't welcome in here." The stranger pushed Eric aside and allowed the door to close.

"Sorry, Sir, I was just trying to get out of the wind for a moment. It's so cold." Hoping the man might understand his predicament, Eric wondered if the customer might be compassionate and perhaps buy him a cup of coffee.

"Go stand somewhere else, you're not welcome here. And besides, you need a bath. People don't appreciate your kind stinking up the place."

Eric sank into himself. "Hey, I'm sorry, I didn't mean to get in your way," Eric offered in supplication. "I wonder if I might have a couple of dollars for a cup of coffee."

"Yeah, right," the man replied as he turned up his collar and buttoned the top button of his long wool overcoat. "I know how the game is played. I give you a handout and you head right to the liquor store for a bottle of cheap wine—you're a worthless drunk."

"But . . ."

"Save it, I've got a train to catch. I still have Christmas presents to buy for my family. Putting on his gloves, the man stepped out into the loud, frigid wind and shouted. "Why don't you do yourself a favor? Quit living in the bottom of a bottle, get a life and quit feeling sorry for yourself." And with that the man was gone.

A single tear crawled down Eric's cheek as he stood wounded from the verbal assault. As his warm breath formed mini-vapor clouds in the cold air, he thought about his family and what the stranger had called him . . . a worthless drunk, a bum. But one word stood out from all the others, a word he had been whispering to himself for hundreds of days, a word that seemed inadequate to account for what Eric had done. Sorry. I am so sorry.

2

Mistakes are the portals of discovery.
  —James Joyce

One year earlier . . .

As the police cruiser rocketed forward toward the silent alarm, emergency lights and siren activated, Officer Eric Doyle snatched the mic from the dash and replied, "10-4, Sector 3 on the way." Eric replaced the mic and looked over at his partner, Officer Alberto (Al) Giordano. The two had a combined total of thirty-five years on the job and had worked this sector of Websterville for years.

"Sounds like the old clinic building," Al offered.

"Yeah, it's only been closed a couple of weeks and already the vultures want to pick it clean."

"Well, you know night time is the right time for break-ins," Al remarked, while cracking a sharp right turn off of Main Street and guiding the blue and white onto Pine. Eric braced himself against the centrifugal force created by the maneuver while checking his equipment belt. He pulled out his flashlight and flicked it on and off several times. "I don't know if the power in the building is totally off yet," he said. "Sometimes they cut everything off but the alarm system."

"Doesn't matter, Eric, we're not turning on the lights anyway. I don't want to lose our advantage of working in the dark. If they bolt when we get inside, they're liable to run into something or trip over whatever's left in the way of furniture."

"Agreed." Satisfied that his light was operational, Eric put it back in its place. "Same plan partner, once we get through the door you go left; I go right."

A block from the scene, Al killed the emergency equipment, and as they neared the location of the break-in he quietly guided the unit and parked discreetly near a stand of pines. "Mostly dark inside," Eric whispered, as he looked through a window and saw the red glow from an exit sign above a stairwell door. "Let's do a check of the exterior and find the entry point."

A minute later they crept next to a rear exit door, its safety glass shattered into miniscule pieces and lying on the ground like a cache of diamonds. The two cops held their ground, listening. Seconds later they heard muffled voices. "Sounds like two of them," Eric said, pressing his face close to his partner's ear.

"Yeah, must be in the room through this door—you ready?"

Eric nodded. Guns drawn, the partners made their entry into what appeared to be a large treatment room with a storeroom adjacent to it. The voices were coming from the storeroom. Eric, using hand signals, motioned that he would take the lead as they approached the room. Measuring each step and controlling each footfall as they made their way around cots and other furniture, the pair moved stealthily, closing the distance. When they were about twenty feet from the doorway, Al stepped on the remains of a broken light bulb, the glass crunching beneath his shoe and immediately causing a stir in the room ahead. Suddenly, a figure appeared in the darkened doorway.

"Stop! Police!" Both cops shouted in unison.

The unknown burglar displayed an object in his hand. "Drop the gun!" Al shouted at the man as both officers focused on the sights of their weapons.

Eric spotted movement just past the man with the weapon. "Al, we've got another subject just behind our guy."

"Last time—drop the gun!"

With that, the subject behind the figure in the doorway tried to get by the other man. All Eric saw was that the first man's arm, the one holding the gun, had begun to rise up toward the officers. Eric fired his Glock .40 caliber pistol. The explosion from the round was deafening in the still of the night, and the muzzle blast in the cave-like room momentarily blinded the cops like the flash on a camera. Seizing the opportunity, the second subject bolted toward the stairwell.

"Eric, we got a runner! Can you get him? I'll keep this guy covered."

"Yeah," Eric shouted, already in mid-stride. "Call it in, Al."

The stairway door banged loudly against the wall as the fleeing suspect threw it open and disappeared up the staircase. Chasing as quickly as he could, Eric was thankful for his daily runs and workouts. This moment was exactly why he trained.

Passing by the first landing, Eric could hear the sound of his prey still working his way upward. He knew the time to worry was when he no longer heard those sounds. It meant the suspect was ready to ambush him. Eric took the stairs evenly, concentrating on his target, waiting for the next piece of the puzzle to unfold.

Three floors scaled, one to go. Then all at once, silence. Eric immediately stopped and listened. Controlling his breathing, he nevertheless felt his heart pumping against his ballistic vest. He willed his heart rate to slow as he waited for the suspect to make the next move.

The crash of another door ricocheting off the wall launched Eric up the final set of stairs. He felt the rush of winter air sweep across his face as he mounted the last landing and realized he had chased his prey onto the roof of the clinic. The cloudless November night allowed the moon to cast a fluorescent glow that washed over the tarred roof, turning it into a murky looking black pool. Rushing through the door, Eric took cover behind the first object he found—an air conditioning unit. Silence. Hunkered down, gun at the ready, Eric held his position, not wanting to make the first move. The clinic was an unattached structure with no fire escape, and except for several similar air conditioning units, there was nowhere the suspect could hide.

Waiting and scanning the roof top, Eric heard the sirens approach. Assist units, two of them. The exhausted burglar heard them as well. As Eric continued to maintain cover, the offender stood up and moved out from behind his hiding place.

"Okay, you got me," the man yelled over the din of the sirens.

As he kept his weapon trained center mass on the suspect's body, Eric shouted commands. "Keep your hands up. Turn away from me. Now, slowly walk backward toward my voice."

Eric finished cuffing and searching the prisoner just as two other officers came through the doorway leading to the roof. "You okay, Doyle?" asked one of the cops.

"Yeah, thanks, he's secure. No ID on him, but he had a dime bag of weed in his jacket along with a medium-size folding knife."

Just then the night watch commander joined the group on the roof. Walking up to Eric, the lieutenant's face was resolute. "Doyle, any other suspects?"

"No, our guy here tells me it was just him and his friend downstairs. Said they were looking for pills that may have been left behind after the clinic closed down."

Expressionless, the supervisor replied. "Okay, good job. Turn the prisoner over to the Sector One car," he said, nodding toward the two other officers, "and then follow me out to my car."

Making their way down to the ground floor, Eric saw an EMS team working on the wounded burglar. His partner, Al, was kneeling next to the man and appeared to be whispering in his ear. As the handcuffed prisoner was led from the building, Eric turned to walk over to where the emergency team was feverishly working on the motionless suspect. Before Eric could take a step in that direction the lieutenant grabbed Eric's coat sleeve. "No, come out to my vehicle."

"But, Lew, I just want to . . . "

"Follow me, that's an order!"

The normally easy going watch commander's actions seemed totally out of character and Eric began to worry that something was wrong. *Was this a good shoot or not? The guy refused to drop his gun after being ordered to do so.* Reaching the supervisor's car, the lieutenant extended his hand. "Let me have your weapon, Officer."

Taken aback, particularly by the impersonal nature of the order, Eric hesitated. "Officer Doyle, I said hand over your weapon."

Reaching into his holster, Eric drew his pistol and handed it to his boss. "This is routine, you know whenever we have an officer involved shooting we test the weapon's ballistics."

"Yeah, I know, Lew, it's just that . . . something else is going on here. I mean, the guy had a gun and wouldn't drop it and . . ."

"Don't say another word until you are asked to give an official statement," the lieutenant quickly interjected. "As of this minute you are on administrative leave until the shooting team conducts an investigation of the incident."

Shoulders sagging at the hint that he had not acted properly, Eric made a request. "Can I just go inside and see how Al is doing? I mean, we were just involved in a shooting. And anyway, I'd like to take a look at the gun the guy had."

The watch commander shook his head and glanced downward. "I don't know any other way to say this than to just tell you the truth. There was no gun; it was a small paint scraper he was using to pry open cabinets."

Eric felt his knees go weak and his pulse begin to race. Fumbling to find some way to explain, Eric offered, "Okay, maybe it wasn't a gun, but in the dark and the heat of the moment it looked like one. Even Al shouted to the guy to drop the gun." Eric started to catch his breath as he sensed his body going into a fight or flight mode. He couldn't believe what was happening. Just minutes ago he had faced down and shot an armed felon, or at least he thought the man was armed, and then chased another suspect up three flights of stairs. Great police work, or so he thought.

"Lew, check the history on the guy on the floor in there, I bet he has priors for breaking and entering. The guy is probably an ex-con— I'd bet on it."

The lieutenant stood stone-faced, the red and blue emergency lights from the squad cars reflecting off his skin like some bad 3-D movie effect. Turning slowly, he opened the trunk of his vehicle and placed Eric's service pistol inside. Looking over the top of the car he stared at Eric. "No need to do a record check on him."

"Why?"

"The person you shot is a 17-year-old kid. His name is Gene . . . Gene Giordano . . . your partner's son."

3

Grief is the agony of an instant, the indulgence of grief the blunder of a life.
—**Benjamin Disraeli**

More than three weeks had passed since Eric last reported for work. Thanksgiving was quickly approaching, but in his mind he had little to be thankful about. His administrative leave had done nothing to assuage his guilt over shooting his partner's son. The young man had died on the way to the hospital.

Without anything to occupy his time, each moment away from his job became a slow, torturous journey just to reach the day's end. Unable to find the key to unlock the door of boredom, Eric regularly found himself at Christy's Tap, a local bar on Main Street. His visits began earlier and earlier. At first he went to have a drink to de-stress after dinner, but as the interminable days and nights wore on, the after-dinner drink soon became the after-lunch drink.

The fact that his drinking had increased did not go unnoticed by Eric's wife, Sharon. She feared for her husband, worrying that his increased alcohol consumption might lead to bigger problems in the future. The couple had been married twenty-seven years and had weathered many storms along the way, always relying on each other to see their way through. Although Sharon was a small woman, standing a mere 5'3", and weighing only 105 pounds, she was the family's pillar of strength. She recalled when Eric's mother, Patricia, committed suicide. Eric's father, Marvin, a retired Websterville police officer, was inconsolable and blamed himself for his wife's death. He felt he should have seen the danger signs and if he had, could have prevented her passing. Those closest to her were aware that Patricia had slipped into a deep depression because of her cancer treatment. Nevertheless, her death from a drug overdose surprised everyone.

Patricia had been Marv's one and only love. The two had grown up together and knew no other love beyond the one they had created together. They did everything as a couple and were frequently seen at the local park, holding hands while they took their daily walk.

After the funeral, Marv began drinking heavily and Eric told Sharon he feared his father might be so lost without his wife that he might want to follow in his wife's footsteps and end it all. As his dad's drinking progressed, Eric tried to comfort him, explaining how much everyone loved and needed him. Despite the visits by family and friends, Marv continued to mourn his wife's death and soon began drinking first thing in the morning.

That destructive behavior continued until one night while Eric was on duty, he stopped in to visit his father. Walking in the front door Eric found the house was eerily quiet. "Dad . . .?" No answer. Searching each room he found no sign of his father and began to worry. His dad's car was parked in the driveway. *Could he be out for a walk?* Beads of sweat born from fear popped out on his forehead as he bounded the steps to the second floor bedrooms. "Dad!" Eric shouted, now fearful that he *would* find his father.

His parents' bedroom was at the end of a long hallway that separated the three other bedrooms and bathroom from the master bedroom. *No way he'd be anywhere else but in the master bedroom.* Rushing through the doorway, Eric saw what he had feared he might find—his father lay sprawled across the bed, an empty glass in one hand and his service revolver in the other. "Dad! Dad!" Eric prayed: *Please, Lord, not again. Don't take another loved one from me.*

Snatching the gun from his father's hand, Eric quickly examined the man's body. No wounds. Gathering himself, Eric, assessed his dad's situation quickly—shallow breathing and faint pulse—his beloved father was alive.

"Sector One, emergency; Sector One, emergency." Eric shouted into his police radio.

"Go ahead with your emergency," the dispatcher replied.

"I need an EMS Unit at 450 Grove Street for a non-responsive older male."

"10-4, Sector One."

Eric opened the cylinder on his father's gun and found it fully loaded with six live rounds—none had been fired. *Thank you, Lord,* he prayed.

Sharon arrived at the hospital shortly after her father-in-law was stabilized. The doctor told them that Marvin had nearly died from alcohol poisoning, and in his stupor he was unable to fire the weapon. He added that Eric's father would likely have died had Eric not discovered him when he did. That near-death experience changed Marvin.

After detoxing, he checked himself into an outpatient rehab facility and made Alcoholics Anonymous part of his daily routine. He reconciled to his wife's death, realizing he had no culpability in the matter. Furthermore, he recognized that as much as he grieved for her, he had to move on and focus on himself and his family. Grateful to be alive, he found a new mission in retirement: he became a volunteer in the cancer unit at Websterville General Hospital.

Hoping her husband would not repeat what happened to his father, Sharon dialed Eric's cell phone. After several rings the call went to voicemail. She quickly hung up and dialed again, hoping Eric would see the caller ID and realize she was trying to reach him—again no answer—this time she stayed on the line and left a voicemail. "Eric, honey, it's dinner time. Bridget's home from practice and we're waiting to sit down to eat. Can you come right home? We love you, Sweetheart."

As Sharon hung up, their daughter, Bridget, walked into the kitchen. "He's not coming home again, is he?" The thin, young girl sighed and filled her glass with water at the kitchen sink. "What's wrong with him, doesn't he care about us?"

Exhausted and frustrated by repeated attempts to explain to her seventeen-year-old that her father's world had turned upside down, Sharon simply hugged her. "He cares about us, Bridget, he's just lost right now."

Tears formed in the girl's eyes. "Mom, I know Dad's been through a lot with the shooting and all, but he hardly even talks to me. He was supposed to pick me up after my track practice today at school but he never showed up. I had to have one of my friends give me a ride. It's like he doesn't care about whether I get that track scholarship or not."

Sharon pulled her daughter closer and whispered in her ear. "He loves us, Honey. He just has to find a way to love himself . . . again."

~~~~~~~~~~

The phone rang a second time and Eric grudgingly pulled it from his pocket. He didn't intend to answer the call but checked the screen anyway and saw it was from Sharon. *I can't, Hon* . . . A few seconds later his phone chimed, alerting him that she had left a voicemail. Peggy, the bartender at Christy's, looked at Eric curiously. "Aren't you going to see who keeps calling you?"

Eric shrugged. "I already know."

"So do I," Peggy threw back at him. "It's your wife and she's probably worried, tired and desperate, wondering why you're sitting at a bar instead of at home where you belong." She turned away from Eric and moved toward the far end of the long bar where another patron signaled for a refill. "Men," she mumbled, "they just don't get it."

Eric took another sip of his drink and looked at himself in the mirror behind the bar. He was disgusted at the man who stared back at him, seemingly boring a hole through his head with such intensity that he thought perhaps the image had hidden powers. *How long are you going to continue down this road of self-destruction?* The man in the mirror had no answer.

Eric was torn between staying at the bar and going home. If he stayed, he was close to where the pain in his soul was numb enough so that he no longer cared what happened. If he went home, he'd have to answer a barrage of questions from his wife and daughter, questions that would rekindle the fire of guilt and remorse. He brought the glass to his lips to drain the remainder of his drink and made his decision.

"Peggy, can I get another?"

4

Death is not the greatest loss in life.
The greatest loss is what dies inside us while we live.
   —Norman Cousins

The fresh gravesite stood in marked contrast to the surrounding graves. Wreaths and once fresh flower arrangements lay frozen and withered in the cold November chill. Dirt, rather than grass, announced to all that the latest inhabitant had arrived. The neighboring plots had melded into a uniform patchwork of dormant fescue and ornamental weathered headstones. It would be spring before Gene Giordano's resting place would mirror those of his neighbors.

Websterville's cemetery was nearly 100 years old and had no restrictions on markers and headstones. And although the venue represented great sorrow, the beauty of its grounds was undeniable. Al Giordano stood at the foot of the stone where his only child, Gene, now forever slept. Al's reflection on the four foot highly polished granite was that of a man desperate for hope. He had so many plans for his son . . . The daily drive here drained him of what little energy he had left, but his visits to the cemetery were his only remaining connection to the boy he loved so dearly.

Being on bereavement leave from the police department was both a blessing and a curse. He needed the time off to gather himself. His grief had been more intense than he'd ever imagined it would be. Just when he thought he had cried his last tear, his heart ached again and squeezed out a fresh torrent that threatened to drown him in despair. But the time away from work, which he gladly accepted, had not gone quite as he had planned. Without his job, he had too much time to think about Gene. Why hadn't his son listened to his advice and stayed away from the older crowd? Al had warned him that he was involving himself with kids who had records. Didn't Gene realize that hanging with that group would bring him nothing but trouble?

When his mind mercifully wandered away from thinking about his boy, his thoughts took him to a place where Al didn't want to go—thoughts about his partner, Eric. After the shooting and subsequent investigation the incident was ruled a justifiable homicide. Al and his partner had acted according to department policy, and were within the boundaries of the Websterville PD's use of deadly force guidelines. All very sanitary and proper . . . and emotionless.

The report said nothing about how Al had cautiously approached the fallen figure Eric had shot. It didn't mention a word about how once Al was sure the wounded subject was not a threat, he directed his flashlight at the man and discovered the person he thought was a felon was actually his son.

The report didn't say one word about the abject terror and grief Al suffered as he tried in vain to revive the boy he affectionately called, "Little Geno." As he knelt over the body of the child he had loved from the moment he'd first heard the infant's cry in the hospital, Al tried everything he could remember from his training to revive him. Despite all the massaging and breaths he administered, his precious Geno remained unresponsive.

When the paramedics arrived, he refused to give ground to them, afraid to lose contact with his son. In his panic he felt if he somehow continued to have physical contact, his boy would know Dad was there. He'd know his Daddy would save him. Al feared if he let go, Geno would be gone. So while the EMTs administered drugs and oxygen, he made sure he held his son's hand. He bent over and whispered in his boy's ear, "It's me, Daddy, I won't leave you, Son . . . you're going to be okay." Even as the emergency personnel loaded the critically wounded youngster on a stretcher and placed him in the back of the ambulance, Al persisted in holding on to Little Geno. Father and son were one as the vehicle screamed through the night, its siren warning the hospital to be ready. It wasn't until the boy was in the hands of the ER doctors that he finally relinquished his hold on the most precious thing in his life. When he released that fatherly touch he realized his son was gone—forever.

As Al stared down at the scarred earth, his thoughts turned to Eric. *Why did he shoot? Why?* A cold wind whipped a dusting of light snow across the frozen ground and blew down one of the wreaths propped up against the headstone. *He should have given Geno a second chance.* Al stepped carefully around the grave and picked up the wreath that had fallen over. Bending over, he replaced it against the granite marker and read the inscription on the wreath's banner: **Beloved Son**. Standing, he shouted at his Creator: "Why! . . . Why?" He didn't expect an answer. He hung his head and began to make his way back to his car. He was torn, not wanting to leave his little boy, but knowing deep inside that his son had already left him.

~~~~~~~~~~

"You're home. Why?" Al said to his wife, Sandy, as he hung his coat in the front hall closet. She was seated at the kitchen counter, her coat thrown over the back of her chair.

"I just came home for a sandwich and a cup of coffee. Is that okay with you?

Lately, the couple had been extremely curt with each other. One word answers were becoming the norm, as each turned deeper into themselves in an effort to somehow escape the pain of losing their son. Their twenty-year marriage had not been without its ups and downs, but the death of their only child was a crisis they never could have foreseen.

"What, you can't eat at work? You've got all kinds of food there."

Sandy stood and went over the trash, dumping the remaining half of her lunch. She took a long drink from her coffee, put the cup on the counter and took a deep breath. "It's a catering business, Al, not a cafeteria. I'm the owner, not a customer. Besides, I can't stay there all day; I can't concentrate. I just wanted to get away from there for a while." Pouring the remainder of the coffee in the sink, she gathered her coat from the back of the chair. "Listen, the trays for that catering job at the hotel are just about done. Would you like me to bring home some pasta for dinner?"

Al stood staring at the family portrait hanging over the fireplace in the family room. The painting had been made from a photo taken on Gene's sixteenth birthday. It depicted their son standing between his parents, an arm around each of their waists, and Gene's long, thick black hair falling into his eyes. Al kept threatening to handcuff the boy and take him to the barbershop for an old school haircut, but Gene knew his father was bluffing. It was their constant friendly jab at each other. Al secretly liked his boy's hairstyle, simply because Gene did, but Al pretended to make it an issue saying their Italian heritage meant only girls in the family had long hair.

"Al . . . Al, did you hear me?"

"What?"

"Do you want the pasta or not?"

"What pasta?"

"Forget it." Sandy put on her coat and walked past Al without a word. In an instant she was out the door.

Moving to his recliner in the family room, he collapsed into it, still staring at the portrait. Later, he didn't know how long he sat there, but it was daylight when he sat down. It was now dark.

5

*Children are the hands by which
we take hold of heaven.*
   —**Henry Ward Beecher**

As Sharon placed the garlic bread on the table, her son Mark set his four-year-old son in the booster seat while his wife Bridget held the boy's chair.

"Dad, can you pass me a piece of bread for Brian so he can keep himself busy?" Mark asked.

"Here you go," said Eric, handing a slice to Mark. "When you're done with that, Bri-Bri, Papa's got some more for you."

Brian was Eric and Sharon's only grandchild and the little tyke quickly proved to be the star of the family. With his fiery red hair and light blue eyes, probably inherited from Sharon, he was the center of attention at every family gathering and was showered with toys and clothing by his doting grandparents. Mark and his wife, Erin, had to plead constantly with the older couple, asking them to please stop buying gifts as their house began to resemble a toy store.

Eric blessed the meal and Sharon began passing the dishes around the table. Placing a modest helping of pasta on her plate, she handed the serving dish to her daughter-in-law. "So, Erin, tell me more about the doctor's visit. What do they think is wrong with Brian?"

Taking the dish from her mother-in-law, Erin explained. "Well, you know I told you that we noticed little Brian's appetite had decreased and he was losing weight. At first I thought maybe he had the flu or a stomach virus, but he wasn't vomiting so I ruled that out." She placed a small portion on her son's plate and cut it up for him. The boy simply stared at the plate of food. "So we decided to take him to the pediatrician to find out what was wrong. The doctor ran some preliminary tests and performed a general checkup, but she wasn't able to come up with a diagnosis."

Eric took a sip of water. "So what's next? There has to be a reason for Brian's reluctance to eat."

"I know, Dad, that's why we have an appointment next week at Children's Hospital in Detroit," Erin answered. "I know it's a long drive, and I'm kind of scared travelling to the big city, but if they can find out what's wrong with Brian it will be worth it."

"Dad, I'm taking that day off so I can be with them," Mark added. "No need to worry."

Eric bit his lip as he thought about his family travelling to Detroit. "Listen, I'm still on leave. Why don't I drive you guys down there? You know, Detroit is a dangerous place, they have one of the highest homicide rates in the nation."

"Thanks, Dad, but we'll be okay," Mark said. "Bridget and I will make sure Brian thinks he's on an adventure and we'll bring plenty of toys to keep him busy. Besides, it's liable to be an all day affair. You'd be bored."

Sharon got up and retrieved a bowl of fresh pasta sauce from the stove and placed it on the table in front of Mark. "Here, this is nice and hot. Take some more pasta, Son."

"Thanks, Mom."

"You're welcome. It's nice of your boss to allow you to take the time off. I know you said you are buried with work with the new account and all."

Mark poured the sauce on his pasta. "Yeah, that John Deere account will be keeping me busy for a long time, but I've got a couple of junior accountants helping me so taking a couple days off won't do any harm. Besides, I have lots of vacation time coming."

"Make sure you use every day of it," Eric added. "I've lost so many days off that I wasn't able to take because of overtime that I've lost track of the number."

"That's why I'm glad he's not a cop," said Erin, as she leaned over and kissed her husband on the cheek.

"Me too," Sharon chimed in.

Eric's daughter, Bridget, sat quietly as the family discussed little Brian. She ran her fingers through her long blonde hair, a habit she'd developed lately as a coping mechanism whenever she felt left out of things. She loved Brian dearly, but since his birth she felt her family often ignored her. Well, maybe ignored isn't the right word, but she sure wasn't getting the attention she used to enjoy. She was competing soon in a big track meet at the Websterville Arena and no one had said a word about it. Heck, her dad probably doesn't even remember that the meet will be the determining factor as to whether she gets an athletic scholarship. She had already been accepted in the Criminal Justice program at the University of Illinois Chicago, but she needed that scholarship. *If he forgot to pick me up at practice, he probably has forgotten about the track meet.* Since her dad began drinking more she saw a change in him. He wasn't warm, didn't hug her and ask her about school. When she questioned him about why he'd changed, he simply shrugged his shoulders and walked away. Didn't he know she needed him?

Sharon looked over at her daughter. "Bridge, more pasta?"

"No thanks, Mom."

"Suit yourself, but you're the one always telling me the carbs in pasta give you the energy you need to run. You have a big meet soon, right?"

"Yeah." Bridget glanced over at her dad, hoping her mother's remarks would remind him that the upcoming competition was very important to her. Sadly, it appeared Eric had not absorbed what had just been said. He poured himself a glass of wine.

Here we go again, Bridget thought. *Once he starts drinking there's no talking to him.* She used to be so proud of her father, the cop, always bragged about him to her friends. Since "the incident," all that changed. She no longer talked about what her dad did for a living, and if her friends asked about what happened she simply refused to discuss the matter. Her dad's mistake had changed everything. *I won't let it beat me. I'll get that scholarship with or without his support.*

"Dad, when do you think you'll be going back to work?" Mark asked.

Eric took a sip of wine before answering his son. "Soon, I hope. I heard the investigation is finished, so if there are no disciplinary issues I should be getting a call."

Sharon silently wished for that call to come as soon as possible. Her husband was not doing well with all the free time on his hands.

He needed to go back to work; she needed him back there as well. She feared for their marriage if Eric didn't return soon. More than anything, she knew her husband needed to move forward and put the shooting behind him. She wasn't convinced he would be able to do that, but she had been praying every night that he would. What she was sure of was that their life had changed and only time would tell if that change would make or break them.

6

Police officers may drive black and white cars, however what goes on in their job is a lot of gray.
—Arik Matson

"You can go inside, he knows you're here," said the chief's secretary to Al as he sat in one of three wooden chairs in the room. Al had been staring at the FBI Top Ten Fugitive posters that adorned the wall opposite of where he sat, and which served as part of the décor for the anteroom. The adjacent wall held photos of Websterville's police chiefs, including the current occupant of the office, Chief Jimmy Williams.

Officer Al Giordano made his way into the modest office of the city's chief law enforcement official. "Mornin' Chief."

"Good morning, Al," the chief replied while motioning for his officer to sit down. "What brings you here? I thought you were still on bereavement leave?"

"Well, Sir, I'm ready to go back on duty."

"Are you sure? I told you to take as much time off as you needed. I don't want you back on the street if your head isn't fully in your job."

"Chief, believe me, I'm ready. The time off has been nice but I need to get back to work to keep my mind occupied." Al leaned forward in his chair. "I appreciate the fact that you said I could take all the time I wanted, but believe me, I'm ready to go back."

Chief Williams jotted down a note before looking up at Al. "Okay, tell you what . . . I'll advise your lieutenant that you'll be returning to duty effective tomorrow on the day watch—early roll call."

"Great."

"Now, that brings us to the issue of who you'll be working with. Your old partner, Eric, is still on admin leave, but just between you and me, he'll be returned to duty shortly. My sense is that perhaps you may want to wait awhile before you two work together again."

Al squirmed a bit. "Uh, Chief? If it's possible, I'd like to work alone."

"Listen Al, I know what happened was tragic—for both of you—but I don't want this to impact your work. I don't want you working alone the first few weeks back on the street, but I don't have a problem teaming you up with another partner."

"Thank you, Sir."

The chief folded his hands on his desk. "I know there may be some difficult days ahead for you and Doyle. You may never have the relationship you both enjoyed before the shooting, but the fact remains that whether or not you two are partners, you're both still on the same department. We are a small force and every officer depends on each other. I don't want an adversarial relationship forming, one that will endanger you, Eric, or any of my other officers. Is that clear?"

"Yes, Sir."

Leaning back in his oversize chair, the chief continued. "Remember, the department will provide counseling for you and your family if you want it."

Al relaxed. "I know, you told me that before. We'll be okay."

The chief paused. "I hope so, Al. Just remember that the offer will remain on the table for you if you find things beginning to go south. And believe me, no one will think any less of you if you decide you'd like to talk with a professional."

"Okay, Chief. I'll keep that in mind."

Nodding, the chief stood and went to the cabinet behind his desk. He unlocked one of the drawers, opened it, and retrieved Al's gun and badge. "Here you go, consider yourself officially back on the job."

As he affixed the holstered weapon to his belt and put his badge back in his ID case, Al replied. "Thanks, Chief."

"You're welcome, and remember Al, my door is always open if you need to talk."

Turning to walk out the door, Al replied, "I appreciate it."

~~~~~~~~~~

The next few days were mostly a blur for Eric. As much as he wanted to drive Mark and Erin down to Detroit to have Brian examined at Children's Hospital, he read between the lines and realized that they didn't want him to go. The kids didn't explain why, but Eric sensed that his drinking may have played a role in their decision. His daughter and wife seemed to be standoffish lately as well, Sharon telling him that his drinking was becoming a problem, and Bridget barely talking with him. *Hey, what am I supposed to do, walk around as if I don't have a care in the world? I killed my partner's kid! You don't just forget something like that.*

What made things even worse, thought Eric, was that Gene was Al and Sandy's only child. Not that having another child or two would have eased the couple's pain, but the void wouldn't be as pronounced. *Or . . . would it? What am I thinking? It's a horrible situation regardless.* Eric replayed that regret-filled night over and over in his head until he could stand it no longer. Thinking about how it would feel if the roles were reversed caused him to grieve even more. *Oh, God, I couldn't survive if Mark or Bridget was gone . . . or for that matter, Baby Bri Bri.*

When the heartache became too much, Eric made his way to Christy's Tap and medicated his soul with alcohol and solitude. The last stool at the far end of the bar was becoming Eric's personal domain. It seemed the other patrons recognized that somehow Eric had marked that territory as his own and no one had better invade that space. The only time Eric spoke was when he had to ask the bartender for another drink.

Late nights quickly became the norm rather than the exception. At first, Sharon waited up for him in case he wanted to talk. She would fall asleep on the couch while reading or watching television, unable to stay awake. But when Eric finally came home, she quickly discovered he had locked his feelings away and was not about to share them with anyone. Eric knew how bad he felt. However, he had no idea how his pain and refusal to share his grief with Sharon caused her to feel even worse. A wall was growing between the once inseparable pair, one that grew higher each day. Sharon feared it would eventually become so tall that she would no longer be able to see Eric. For his part, Eric sensed the wall was just what he needed.

7

*It is the working man who is the happy man.
It is the idle man who is the miserable man.*
    —**Benjamin Franklin**

Stumbling downstairs to the kitchen, Eric spotted a note on the counter. He poured himself a cup of coffee from the carafe that was always full and then read the message.

The chief left a voicemail for you on the phone—call him.

"Sharon?" Eric shouted. Looking at the clock he noticed it was close to noon. Not getting an answer, he guessed she was with a friend eating lunch somewhere. Eric picked up the house phone and dialed the chief's number.

"Websterville Police Department, Chief Williams' office, how may I help you?"

"Hi, this is Officer Doyle. I had a message to call the chief."

"Yes, can you hold, please? I'll see if he is available to speak with you." Seconds later Eric was transferred to the chief.

"Eric, how are you?"

"I'm okay, Chief. Kind of bored—I need to get back to work."

"Exactly, that's why I called first thing this morning. Your wife said you were up early doing some chores at your dad's house." *Sharon must have covered for me*, Eric thought. He remembered coming home from the bar well past midnight last night, but that's about all he remembered. "Uh, yeah, Chief, I was busy and didn't take my cell phone with me."

"Okay," sighed the chief. "I wanted to see you this morning about returning you to duty, but since you didn't get back with me right away it will have to wait until tomorrow morning. I have a meeting with the village board this afternoon."

"Sorry, Chief." *Crap, now I have to wait another day.*

"Be in my office in the morning at 0900; we'll talk about your future."

"Yes, Sir. Thank you." Eric heard the line go dead and had a sinking feeling in the pit of his stomach. *Talk about my future? What does that mean?* He poured himself another cup of coffee and moved toward the corner cabinet where the liquor was kept. As he reached for the whiskey bottle, intending to give his coffee a bit more of a jolt, he hesitated. *Probably need to cut back if I'm going to return to work.*

Sitting at the kitchen table, he opened the newspaper that was laying there. After about ten minutes of trying to get interested in the news around town he gave up and folded the paper closed. Finished with his coffee, he brought the cup over to the sink and looked out the window. It had snowed a couple of inches last night. He saw the tire tracks leading from the garage to the street. Sharon must have driven Bridge to school, he concluded. *I should have been up early to shovel the driveway for them. I have to get my act together.*

Anticipating tomorrow's meeting with the chief, and feeling a sense of purpose for the first time in three weeks, Eric went back upstairs to get dressed. *Gotta get that driveway shoveled.*

An hour later the driveway and walks were clear, just in time for Sharon's return. Eric brought the shovel to the garage as Sharon got out of her car and closed the door. "Good morning," she said, facetiously.

Eric sheepishly looked at his watch. "Yeah, I know, it's almost one-thirty. Sorry."

Stopping just outside the garage onto the newly cleared driveway, Sharon took a deep breath. "Eric, this has to stop. Your behavior and your drinking are tearing this family apart. Bridget was in tears this morning . . . didn't want to go to school. She told me she thinks you hate her. She wouldn't eat breakfast; I'm worried about her."

"What?" Eric answered, his mouth falling open. "Why would she think that? I haven't done anything to her."

"Exactly. You haven't done anything . . . with her. Ever since the shooting you've ignored her. You don't talk to her or ask her about school or track. You even forgot to pick her up after practice."

Cocking his head sideways, Eric replied. "I did? When?"

"See?" Sharon shot back. "You don't even remember what you've done. It's as if you have forgotten you have a family. You come home drunk every night, sleep late, maybe eat dinner with us if we're lucky, and then you're off to the bar."

Eric hung his head and mindlessly scraped a patch of snow with his boot. He knew his wife was right about everything, but didn't she know what he was going through? Before he could respond she cut in.

"The chief called here this morning. Not his secretary . . . the chief himself. I was embarrassed because I had to lie to him about where you were."

"Sharon, I . . ."

"No, Eric, don't say a word. Maybe I should have told him the truth—that you were sleeping off another drunk and that's why you couldn't come to the phone."

Standing with widespread arms, Eric tried to reason with his wife. "Listen, Honey, I'm meeting with him in the morning. I'm guessing he's going to tell me to report back to work. Everything will be okay."

Sharon looked at her husband through teary eyes; his blurred image seemed to reflect what she felt. She no longer had a clear idea of who her partner was. She sensed they were at a crossroad, about to take a wrong turn that would take them off course where they would be forever lost. She turned and made her way to the house.

~~~~~~~~~~

Her shower finished, Bridget wrapped the towel around her lean torso and walked back to her locker to get dressed. Track practice had been grueling, the coach challenging each of her athletes in anticipation of the coming regional championship meet. As she began putting on her clothes a team member walked over. "Hey, Bridge, Coach Julie asked me to tell you to stop by her office when you're dressed."

"What's up, Lindy?"

"Don't know," the girl responded. "Maybe it's something about the meet. Since you're the team captain maybe she has something she needs to go over with you about the competition."

"Okay. Thanks."

Bridget's teammate turned and disappeared around the row of

lockers.

Hmmm . . . strange. A few minutes later Bridget knocked on the coach's office door and went inside. "You wanted to see me?"

The coach sat at her desk surrounded by paperwork and framed by a wall filled with ribbons and plaques won by her athletes over the years. "Yes, Bridget, I did." The woman pointed to a chair off to the side. "Have a seat."

The young girl put her backpack on the floor and all but collapsed into the chair. "So, what's up, Coach?"

"What did you think about today's practice?"

Smiling, Bridget quickly replied. "It was one of your toughest, I'm fried."

Without returning the smile, the woman answered. "That's what I thought. Granted, today's workout was tough but it wasn't anything we haven't done in the past. I wanted to challenge each of you in preparation for the regional meet without risking injury to anyone, but you were obviously working at your max. You were exhausted after several sprints; what's going on?"

Bridget felt the heat rise from her neck and spread to her cheeks. She was not about to talk to her coach about her dad and how bad she'd felt these past few weeks. The fact was she had been coping the only way she knew how—she had been cutting back on her food. She rationalized that if she couldn't get her dad to be the father she used to know, at least she'd be in control of something. Even if that something was her weight. "Uh, Coach, why do you think something's wrong?"

"You're performance is declining rather than peaking as we approach one of the most important meets of the season. You came in third on the last five sprints we did—a sophomore beat you—then you darn near collapsed after the last set of stair repeats." The coach slid forward on her chair and stared directly into her runner's eyes. "I know something's going on. What is it?"

Bridget shifted in her seat, trying to avert her gaze away from the woman. Unsure of whether she should share her secret, she hesitated answering her coach's question. As her eyes slowly filled with tears she thought about how much she still loved her dad and resolved that she wasn't willing to besmirch his reputation. "Coach, I just haven't been feeling like my usual self lately. I don't have the energy it seems."

"Really, Bridget? Low energy is why you're about to cry?" The woman continued. "How's your diet? Are you taking in enough carbs?"

"Oh yeah," she joked, trying to quickly hide her despair. " You know my mom makes sure I get everything I need."

"Okay," the coach said, "What about you head? You know I always encourage our team to be mentally tough. Any problems at home or in your relationships that I can help you with?"

Bridget hesitated. *Any problems at home? If you only knew.* "No, it's all good."

Sitting back in her chair, Bridget's coach had not missed the fact that her young athlete was on the verge of breaking down. She tried one more time. "Bridget, you're sure nothing's impacting your performance? If you're under some emotional stress we need to fix it immediately. Now is not the time for you to allow any distraction to deter you from winning that meet. This competition is not only important for our school, but for you personally. You need to get that scholarship."

Bridget reached for her backpack and stood up from her chair. "Coach, I told you, everything's cool. Look, I have to catch a ride home. Okay?"

"Yeah, sure. Eat a good meal and get to bed early tonight. I don't like what I saw on the track today. We need to get your energy level back up. I'll see you at practice tomorrow."

Bridget walked out and shut the door behind her. *I don't need a meal, Coach. I need my dad.*

8

Rest when you're weary. Refresh and renew yourself, your body, your mind, your spirit. Then get back to work.
—**Ralph Marston**

Yesterday's snow had been cleared from the Websterville Police Department's parking lot, but the sub-freezing temperatures made walking across the macadam a dangerous balancing act. Eric took baby steps to carefully make his way to the main entrance. Without his employee ID and card key, he was unable to use the employee entrance in the rear of the station. Entering the station through the front made him feel like a visitor rather than a member of the force.

"Hey, Sarge!" Eric waved and shouted to the desk sergeant seated behind the ballistic glass, then made his way down the corridor toward the chief's office. Walking through the open glass door, he saw the chief was pouring himself a cup of coffee in the secretary's office.

"Ah, Eric, good morning."

"Hi, Chief."

"Care for a cup of coffee?"

"That would be great; thanks." Eric grabbed a plastic cup and filled it.

"Shelley is over at City Hall running an errand for me," the chief said, making his way back to his office. "C'mon in; shut the door behind you."

Eric followed the chief into his office and waited.

"Have a seat, Eric," said the chief, pointing to a chair in front of the desk. As the chief sat down in his high back arm chair behind his mahogany desk, he set his coffee cup down and began. "So, Eric, do you think you're ready to return to work?"

"Yes sir," Eric replied immediately.

"You know . . . the reason we put officers involved in shooting incidents on administrative leave is so we can give them ample time to think about their actions. Traumatic incidents happen in an instant, and our brains take a while to fully comprehend exactly what happened before, during and after the event." The chief sipped his coffee and continued. "Years ago, we required the officer involved in any shooting to immediately give a statement regarding his actions. We've subsequently learned that's not the best way to conduct the investigation, since it takes several days for the brain to recall details about what happened.

Eric nodded. "I know, Chief, I appreciate the time off and the fact that the detectives allowed me to take some time before giving my official statement."

"Right. Based on your statement and that of your partner, as well as the evidence at the crime scene, the shooting team concluded you acted within the parameters of our deadly force policy. Consequently, your actions were deemed appropriate and the shooting has been ruled a justifiable homicide. No action will be taken against you."

"Does that mean I can return to work now?"

"Technically, yes." The chief rolled his chair backward a bit. "How is your relationship with your partner, Officer Giordano?"

Shifting in his seat, Eric answered. "Well, Chief, we haven't spoken since that night. I didn't attend the funeral for his son; I didn't think it was appropriate for me to be there. And I haven't called him, just because I really don't know what I'd say, other than I'm sorry."

"Just so you know, Al is back at work. He asked me to assign him a new partner."

Eric paused before answering. "Chief, he's probably right about us not working together. After what happened it would be difficult for us to be partners again. Did he say anything about me?"

The chief shook his head. "No, but I'm telling you exactly what I told him. We have a small department here, which means both of you are going to cross paths frequently. You may not be partners, but you will probably answer some of the same calls and have to back each other up. I don't want there to be any problems that might endanger any of our officers' lives."

"I completely understand, Chief. You won't have any problems from me."

"I hope not, that's why I have to ask you something."

Uh-oh, is this the part about my future? Eric thought.

The chief's phone rang. He checked the caller ID and let it go to voicemail. "I've had a couple people tell me they've seen you drinking rather frequently at one of the bars downtown. I won't tell you who told me, they want to remain anonymous. But if you are having any problems putting the shooting behind you I need to know. I am prepared to provide you with counseling from our Employee Assistance Program (EAP). The process is confidential, no one need know."

"No, Chief, I'm fine; I don't have a problem. I just need to get back to work."

The chief stared at Eric as if he were trying to read Eric's mind. After an uncomfortable few seconds of silence the chief continued. "Okay, Eric, but if you find yourself having any problems whatsoever, the EAP program is there for you."

"Yes, Sir."

Swinging around in his chair, the chief opened a credenza drawer behind him and retrieved Eric's gun and badge. Standing, the chief leaned forward and handed them to Eric. "Here you go, Officer, you are back on duty effective tomorrow on the afternoon watch."

Eric gladly took his gun and badge from the chief. "Thank-you, Sir."

"You're welcome," said the chief, sitting down and reaching for his phone.

As Eric made his way toward the door to leave, the chief called out to him.

"Eric, by the way, that was a good bit of police work that night. It was unfortunate that one of the offenders was the son of one of our own. Don't let the incident ruin your future. You have to move on."

"Thanks, Chief." *Right now I need something to settle my nerves,* Eric thought.

~~~~~~~~~~

"Where have you been? Why didn't you answer your phone?" Sharon stood at the stove stirring a pot of homemade chicken soup as Eric walked through the kitchen door from the driveway.

"I stopped off for a couple of drinks. Any law says a man can't have a drink?"

Sharon turned around and put her hands on her hips. "No, there's

THE YEAR WITHOUT CHRISTMAS

no law against having *a drink*, if one drink is all you're going to have. But there are laws against drunk driving. You should know that since you're a cop." She turned away from him and resumed cooking.

"Yeah, yeah, I know all that. For your information, I'm not drunk."

"Whatever," Sharon threw at him, disgustedly. "Did you meet with the chief today, or did you forget about that too?"

Pouring a cup of coffee from the carafe on the kitchen counter, Eric took the cup over to the table and sat down. "Yes, I saw him. I'm reinstated; start back to work tomorrow afternoon."

Sharon covered the pot on the stove and then joined her husband at the table. "Oh, I get it—you figured you had until tomorrow afternoon to get sober so you thought today was a great time to get drunk. Why didn't you think about spending your last day off with me?"

"Hey, I'm here aren't I?"

"Wait a minute. You spend the whole day in a bar and then come home in time for supper. How is that spending the day with me?"

Eric sipped his coffee, buying some time, and then pushed on. "Listen, Sharon, don't start anything, okay? After tomorrow things will be back to normal."

"Really?" she asked. "And just how are things going to be normal? Are they going to be normal between you and me? We haven't even slept together in the last few weeks. How about things being normal with Bridget? What are you going to do, wave a magic wand to fix the hard feelings and hurt you've caused her?"

"What are you talking about? We're all going to be fine."

Sharon stood and pushed her chair into the table. Walking over to the sink, she turned on the faucet and began to rinse the dirty dishes and place them in the dishwasher. "We're going to be fine, huh? Tell that to Mark and Erin who didn't want you to go with them to the hospital in Detroit because Mark thought you might embarrass them with your drinking. Tell that to our friends who've stopped calling here."

Eric absentmindedly played with the salt shaker on the table as he listened to his wife's harangue. "I think you're exaggerating, Sharon."

"Am I? I went shopping this afternoon at the supermarket. I saw Sandy Giordano there and decided I wanted to tell her how sorry I was for what happened. As soon as she saw me she turned and walked away."

"Well . . . uh . . ."

"Damn it, Eric. Are you blind as well as drunk? Can't you see what you've done? Wasn't it bad enough you killed our friends' child, but you decided you have to punish your family by becoming a drunk?"

Slamming the salt shaker down, Eric bolted upright. "Wait a minute. I'm not a drunk. So I've had a few drinks while I'm off from work, so what? That doesn't make me a drunk."

Sharon closed the dishwasher. "Save your breath, I've heard it all before and, frankly, I don't have the patience or the time to listen. Believe it or not, I'm still a part of this family and your daughter is at school waiting to be picked up. It's obvious you've forgotten about her again."

"Wait a minute, Sharon, I'll go get her."

"The hell you will—go have another drink." As she grabbed her jacket from the hook near the door she turned and looked at her husband. "Where's the man I used to love so much?" She opened the door and seconds later he watched the car back out of the driveway.

Eric placed both hands on the kitchen table. Resting his weight on the table he hung his head. *Sharon, I honestly don't know where that man is, but I need him as much as you do.*

9

You don't choose your family. They are God's gift to you, as you are to them.
—**Desmond Tutu**

Bridget got into her mother's car and shut the door. "Thanks, Mom. I figured it would probably be you picking me up." Fastening her seatbelt, she asked her mother, "So, what's new?"

Still hurting from her exchange with Eric, Sharon nevertheless tried to be the glue holding her family together. She answered her daughter's question without emotion. "Your father goes back to work tomorrow. He'll be on the afternoon shift so I'll be picking you up after practice for the time being. Thought I may as well start today."

Glancing sideways at her mother, Bridget hesitated before answering. "Mom, c'mon, we both know Dad probably forgot about coming to get me. He's not even home, is he?"

Sharon chewed her lip. She tried to hide her husband's problems from their daughter as best she could, but lately the tension had become so obvious that her efforts were futile at best. "He's home. He got there late so I told him I'd come for you."

"Is he drinking?"

Not wanting to lie, Sharon replied. "Yes. He said he stopped for a few drinks after meeting with the chief."

"I knew it," the girl said, pounding her fist on her leg. "Mom, what's going on? Why is Dad acting like this? Can't he see how much he's hurting us?"

Sharon stopped for the red traffic light and then turned toward her daughter. "I don't think he realizes how much damage he's doing to those who love him. The shooting that night shook him to his core, causing him to question himself." The light turned green and Sharon continued her drive home. "He hasn't shared very much with me about that night, except he's uncertain about how he might handle his job once he returns to duty."

"I can kind of understand that, I guess. I mean . . . having to shoot someone? That has to mess you up."

A light snow had begun to fall and Sharon turned on the wipers. "You're right, Bridge, it's a traumatic event for a police officer. But your dad didn't shoot just anyone, he shot a friend's son."

"Yeah, I know." Bridget replied, taking a tube of lotion from her gym bag and rubbing some on her hands. "Some of the kids at school said they knew Gene was headed for trouble. He was hanging out with the wrong crowd and cutting school. A few kids even said Gene deserved what he got."

Sharon looked at her daughter. "What do you think?"

"I feel terrible about the whole thing. Gene was wrong, but the shooting was an accident—Dad thought Gene had a gun." Brushing her hair from her face, Bridget continued. "It's kind of Gene's own fault. What was he doing breaking into that place anyway? And besides, Dad didn't know it was Gene."

Turning into their driveway, Sharon hit the remote, opening the garage door. She saw that Eric's car was gone.

"I thought you said Dad was home?"

"He was. I guess we're eating alone again."

Mother and daughter got out of their car and went through the back door to enter the kitchen. Bridget set her backpack and gym bag on the floor while she hung her coat on the hook near the door.

"Mom?"

"What, Sweetheart?"

"Do you think our family will ever be normal again?"

The question from her daughter pierced her heart like a hunter's arrow. *How do I handle this?* "Honey, we'll have to wait and see what happens after your father returns to work. Hopefully, once he gets back to his regular routine things will get better and he'll be his old self. In the meantime, we have to try and be patient with him. He's been through a lot."

Bridget picked up her bags and headed for her room. Sharon began to prepare dinner. Before she walked out of the room, her mother called to her. "Bridge?"

"Yeah, Mom?"

"I need a favor."

"Sure, what is it?"

"Please pray for your dad. I think that's what he needs more than anything else."

Setting her bags down, she walked over to her mother and hugged her. "Mom, I've been praying . . . for both of you."

~~~~~~~~~~

Business was slow. Not many customers at the bar tonight. A couple of guys from one of the offices nearby stopped for one drink after work and left. *How does anyone have just one drink?* Eric had intended to kill some time at the bar after his argument with Sharon. She was changing. She no longer understood him. *Sharon, I killed a kid! What the hell, am I just supposed to forget what happened and not let it affect me?*

He finished his two fingers of whiskey and then slid the empty glass toward the back of the bar. Seconds later the bartender appeared. "Hit me again," Eric ordered.

"Sure thing."

At least Peggy wasn't tending bar tonight. She was becoming as annoying as Sharon, nagging him about spending too much time at the bar. He didn't need that—what he needed was for the pain to stop.

The bartender placed a fresh drink in front of Eric, then took several dollars from the stack of cash Eric had placed on the bar. As he took a drink, his mind flashed back to "that night." *Why did I shoot? Why?* Try as he might, he couldn't erase the image of his partner, Al, leaning over his wounded son. Sometimes, when Eric's dreams were particularly haunting, it was no longer "Little Geno" lying on the ground. Instead, it was Eric's son, Mark. On those nights Eric would bolt upright and have to get out of bed. He'd go downstairs to the kitchen and soothe himself with a couple of drinks, hoping to get beyond the horrible nightmare he'd just witnessed. Tears would come, washing waves of despair over him, drowning him in guilt and regret. *If only . . .*

He held his silent cry deep inside, not wanting his wife and daughter to know the anguish he was experiencing. His gut ached from the tension and pain. *How long can this go on?* He felt God was punishing him for what he did. He hoped God would show him mercy and end his ordeal soon.

Eric finished his drink and found the bartender standing in front of him, bottle in hand. "'Nother one?"

Remembering that he was going back to work tomorrow, Eric answered. "No, I'm good." He left a five-dollar tip on the bar and walked out to the parking lot. His was the only car parked there, all alone in the corner space. All alone, just like Eric.

10

The greatest weakness of all is the great fear of appearing weak.
—Jacques Benigne Bossuel

Sharon heard her daughter coming down the stairs and looked up from the newspaper she had been reading at the kitchen table. Bridget walked into the room and set her gym bag and backpack on the floor by the back door.

"Morning, Hon."

"Hi, Mom."

"Standing, Sharon moved toward the refrigerator. "Can I fix you breakfast?" The woman asked as she opened the door and grabbed a couple of eggs.

Bridget glanced down at her phone and texted as she went to the cabinet and grabbed a glass. "No thanks. I'll just have a glass of orange juice. Jessica is on her way to pick me up."

Frowning, Sharon replaced the eggs. "Bridge, I think you need to eat something. You barely touched your dinner last night, and now, no breakfast?" Sharon closed the door and stood facing her daughter, her hands on her hips. "I think we need to talk. You have to eat, particularly since your big meet is coming up. You need energy."

Bridget continued to focus on her phone, her thumbs dancing on the keys as she held a silent conversation with someone in cyberspace. "Mom, I'll grab something quick at school."

"Like what?"

The girl closed her phone and poured herself a glass of juice. After taking a long drink, she set the glass on the counter and walked over to where she had placed her school bags. "I'll get something out of the machines. Plenty of kids do that. It's no big deal."

"That's not nutritious food. You're an athlete; you need to eat a healthy diet. Breakfast is . . ."

Before Sharon could finish her thought, a car pulled up in the driveway.

"Gotta go, Mom. Jessica's here. Don't bother picking me up, Jess said she'd drive me home. Love you."

Bags in hand, Bridget was out the door and into her friend's car before Sharon could even say good-bye. Lately, she had spotted a pattern in her daughter's behavior. It seemed Bridget was slowly cutting her food intake to the point of only eating a couple of mouthfuls at dinner. Sharon had no idea how much Bridget ate while at school, but she suspected the girl's eating habits were much the same there as they were at home. With the regional meet close at hand, Sharon knew her daughter would be at a disadvantage at the meet if she continued her Spartan eating regimen. *How do I get through to her?*

~~~~~~~~~~

"Hey girlfriend! How was the weekend?"

Bridget got into her friend's car and fastened her seatbelt as Jess backed out of the driveway. "The weekend was good. I went for a long run both days."

Driving toward school, Jessica remarked, "Wow. Coach told us to get plenty of rest on our days off cuz this week was going to be tough."

"Yeah, I know, but I'm trying to cut some weight before regionals."

"Too late for that. Now's the time to be getting stronger, not weaker. Besides, you're looking thin enough—maybe too thin."

Not wanting to get involved in a discussion about her weight, Bridget deflected her friend's conversation. "Hey, I heard Melissa and Ron broke up."

For the rest of the ride to school, their classmates' breakup became the topic of conversation, rather than Bridget's weight. Things were going her way . . . for the time being.

~~~~~~~~~~

Eric sat in the squad car with his new partner, Tommy Small. They were parked in the lot at the discount store. The pair had just finished refereeing a dispute between a customer and one of the store employees. "They're both wrong," offered Tommy. "One's a fool; the other's a stubborn ole mule."

Eric nodded. "Yeah, it's not really worth writing a report about, but if the guy comes back later and causes trouble at least there'll be something on file." He signed his name on the case report, folded it, and then put it in the visor. "Hey, feel like grabbin' a couple of coffees over at the drive-thru?"

"Yeah, good idea." His partner swung the car around and headed in that direction. A few minutes later they were cruising their beat sipping their drinks.

"So, how was your time off?"

"Terrible." Eric balanced his coffee cup as his partner turned off Main Street into one of Websterville's subdivisions. "I'm glad it's over."

Eric had avoided the subject of the shooting the first couple of hours into his tour of duty. Now it seemed his colleague wanted to put it front and center. "That right?" Tommy answered. "I'd think three weeks bein' at home would be kind of relaxing."

Eric didn't know how to take that remark. Was his partner being sincere or facetious? Either way, it seemed this discussion was headed down the wrong road.

"Yeah," Eric answered. "You'd think not working for three weeks would be nice . . . but you'd be wrong. Too much time to think about things."

"Guess you had a lot to think about. Shootin' somebody can't be easy, particularly if it's a kid." Tommy took a slow ride around the local elementary school, shining the car's spotlight at the doors to ensure they were closed and not damaged.

"Listen, Tommy, I don't know what you're gettin' at, but if you have a problem with me, spit it out."

His partner finished his inspection of the school and headed back toward the subdivision entrance. "I got no problem with you Doyle. I just think you're a little too quick on the trigger. Seems to me you coulda waited a bit longer before you shot the kid."

"Really?" Eric finished his coffee and tossed the empty cup at his feet. "I didn't see you inside the building that night. You have no idea what went down—don't try to second guess what happened." Eric felt his blood pressure rising. "Besides, the shooting team ruled it justifiable."

"Yeah, Doyle, I know. That don't make it right."

"You got a problem working with me?"

Before Eric's partner could answer, the radio barked: "Sector one, we have a report of a man with a gun—224 Main Street—Bilford's Discount."

"Damn, we just came from there. That fool must be back." Eric keyed the mic and answered. "Sector One, 10-4, on the way."

Minutes later Eric and his partner pulled into the lot just in time to see the man they had previously warned to stay away from the store. As the man was about to get into a car, both officers got out of their patrol car and took positions behind the doors of their vehicle. Officer Small, gun in hand, shouted commands at the man.

"Stop! Police!"

Eric stood behind the passenger door of the police car, his hand on his holstered weapon. At that moment, a flood of memories from the break-in at the old medical building washed over him. His partner, Tommy Small, quickly morphed into his old partner, Al Giordano.

"Put your hands up and turn away from me. Start walking backward toward my voice." As the man obeyed and neared the police car, everything became a blur and Eric thought that somehow it wasn't the man they had dealt with earlier. It was Al Giordano's son, Gene.

"Stop. Get down on your knees." When the man complied, Tommy continued. "Don't move." Looking over at Eric, Tommy said, "Cuff him."

Eric moved forward carefully and cuffed the subject. Searching the man, Eric discovered a small automatic in the right hand pocket of the man's coat. After a more thorough search, the arrestee was placed in the cage in the back of the patrol car. The two officers, who were joined by another assist car, searched the man's vehicle.

"It's clear," shouted one of the officers.

"Thanks," replied Small. "Doyle, come here for a second." Standing out of earshot of the others, Small asked Eric, "Why didn't you have your gun out on that guy; why didn't you cover me?"

"What?"

"Your gun—you kept it in your holster the whole time. What if the guy went for his gun?"

"I didn't have my gun out?" Eric asked, with a puzzled look on his face. "I thought I did."

Officer Small took a step forward, his face just inches from Eric's. "You thought you did? Are you trying to get us killed?"

"No, Tommy, I . . ."

As he backed away, Small said, "Let's transport this guy to the lockup, then I need to talk with the watch commander. I can't work with somebody who's afraid to pull his gun."

11

Alcohol is a very patient drug. It will wait for the alcoholic to pick it up one more time.
  —**Mercedes McCambridge**

Eric spent the rest of the shift working behind the front desk. He answered a few phone calls and took several walk-in reports, none of which helped the time pass any quicker. After completing the arrest report and booking the man he and Tommy Small had arrested, they met with the watch commander. Tommy had briefly explained the arrest at the discount store. And while the lieutenant didn't take either side of the discussion, he nevertheless felt it was best for Eric to finish his tour inside, particularly after Tommy told the boss he refused to work with Eric.

As he sat at one of the computer terminals behind the desk printing lookout messages for the next shift commander to distribute, the watch commander walked out of his office and signaled for Eric to join him. Eric walked through the door and hesitated after entering. "C'mon in, Doyle; shut the door behind you."

Both men sat down. Eric felt an awkward pause before the lieutenant began. "Doyle, I'm not going to pass judgment on you over this one incident. The fact is you were tactically correct, taking cover and eventually cuffing and searching the subject and finding the gun. I don't know if you had your own weapon out or not—Small said you didn't—you say you don't remember."

Eric breathed a sigh of relief. "Thanks, Lew."

The lieutenant picked up the car assignment sheet and continued. "I don't have another car for you to work tonight, and since Officer Small refuses to work with you the only place I can put you is behind the desk."

"Not much goin' on there tonight, Lew."

THE YEAR WITHOUT CHRISTMAS

Nodding, the lieutenant agreed. "Right. Why don't you put in a slip for a couple hours vacation time and call it a night. I'll team you up with Gandurski tomorrow night on Sector 4."

"Sounds good," Eric responded. "And just so you know, that situation out there was under control. Small had the guy covered; I was ready in case the guy broke bad on us."

"Okay, I'm not going to make a big deal out of it. Maybe Small is having a bad night . . . who knows. In any case, just do your job and things will work themselves out."

Eric stood and reached across the lieutenant's desk. "Hey, thanks, Lew. I appreciate it."

The two cops shook hands. "No problem. Just don't over analyze this thing, Doyle. My advice to you is to let go of the shooting and move on—it's downrange, there's nothing you can do about it now."

"Yeah, Lew, you're right. Good night." Eric walked out, completed his leave slip and headed for Christy's Tap.

Four hours later Eric parked his car in his driveway and let himself in the back door. He crept up the stairs to the bedroom trying not to disturb his wife and daughter. In doing so, he miscalculated one of the steps and crashed sideways against the wall knocking down one of the family pictures. *Damn.* Bridget ran out of her room to see what had caused the noise and saw her father bending over picking up the photo that now had a broken frame.

"Who is it?" Sharon asked, as she joined her daughter at the top of the stairs, protectively wrapping her arms around Bridget.

"It's just Dad. He's drunk. I'm going back to bed."

"Honey . . ." Sharon didn't want her daughter to go back to bed before she could talk with her and help her understand what was going on. Although Sharon hardly understood her husband's behavior herself, she didn't want Bridget to have to worry about it. But before she could say anything, Bridget was in her room, slamming the door behind her.

"I slipped," Eric said, trying to act as if things were normal. He picked up the few pieces of broken glass on the stairs and placed them on top of the picture frame. Walking up the final few steps, he placed the damaged photo on the hallway table and followed Sharon into their bedroom. She let him walk inside and then closed the door behind him.

"I thought you worked tonight. How did you find time to get drunk?"

As he pulled off his shirt, he noticed a blood stain. "Crap, I'm bleeding." He walked into the bathroom to tend to his cut, hoping it would buy him some time. Sharon followed him.

"What's going on, Eric, were you working or not?"

Rinsing his cut finger under the tap, he looked in the mirror above the sink. His eyes were bloodshot; his face tired. "Yeah, I was at work but I got out early so I thought I'd relax and have a couple of drinks. I figured you and Bridge would be in bed anyway . . . what's the problem?" Eric didn't want to get into the reason he didn't work the whole night. He didn't want his wife to know that one of his fellow cops didn't think he was safe.

"What's the problem? Are you serious? You're telling me that you don't think that spending the last few weeks drinking most of the day is not something to worry about?"

Eric wrapped a washcloth around his finger to stop the bleeding. "Sharon, c'mon you know what I went through. I couldn't talk about it with anybody." He walked into the bedroom and sat on the bed.

She followed him. "You couldn't talk about it with anybody? Who am I, Eric, just someone who's here to fix your meals and sleep with?"

"No, you've got it all wrong. That's not what I meant."

Standing directly in front of him, she responded. "No, I don't have anything wrong. You're the problem here, Eric, the one who's upset this family's well-being. Ever since the shooting you've been distant. Instead of coming to me you shut me out. Don't you think I might be able to help you with what you're going through? Damnit, Eric, I'm your wife! I love you."

He hung his head and looked down at the floor, not saying a word.

"You think this is going to help—keeping things inside? If you're not going to talk with me, go and get help from the department. Get the counseling they offer." Sharon knelt down in front of her husband, putting her hands on his thighs as he sat there dejectedly. His body trembled as his teardrops crashed to the floor in front of her. She desperately wanted him to see what was unfolding, the damage that was already done to their once happy life.

As she began to shed her own tears, Eric raised his head and looked at his wife. "Sharon, I can't help it . . . I just can't get past what happened. Every time I think about it I want to die. I killed a kid; I killed Al's son."

Looking into his eyes she saw that his despair mirrored hers. She didn't want the damage to continue, but she didn't know how to stop it either. "Honey, listen. Let's get help; let's go see a counselor. I'll go with you, we're both hurting but if we face this together we'll get through it. It's not too late."

Eric ran his fingers through his hair. "I don't know . . ."

Sharon held his head with her hands. "Look at me—if you continue behaving this way you'll destroy what's left of our marriage. You need to get help, to talk this out. If you're not going to talk about it with me, fine, but you have to let this thing out."

"You're right. Let me think about it."

She let go of him, stood and wiped her eyes. "Don't take too much time thinking about it. The longer you wait to get help, the harder it will be to fix."

~~~~~~~~~~

Bridget turned to the wall, wrapping herself tightly in the blankets. As her stomach growled she thought of only one thing. *Bring my Dad back. Please.*

12

Children will not remember you for the material things you provided but for the feeling that you cherished them.
—**Richard L. Evans**

Sharon felt faint and pulled out a kitchen chair. Hardly believing what she had just heard, she asked her daughter-in-law to repeat it.

"The doctor thinks Brian has leukemia."

With one hand, Sharon held her phone, her other hand held her head as she tried to understand the implications of the horrible news. "Erin . . . how . . . why?"

"Mom, I don't know how and I can't understand why. How does a four-year-old get leukemia? The doctor said the blood test confirmed it, but he already suspected as much based on Brian's symptoms—not wanting to eat and the swelling under his arms."

"What about the fever Brian keeps getting?" Sharon asked. "Is that part of it too?" She switched her phone to speaker mode while she went to the sink for a glass of water.

"Yes, apparently the infections Brian keeps getting are due to a lack of normal white blood cells. Without them the doctor said Brian's body can't fight off infection."

As she continued her phone conversation, Eric came into the kitchen. He was on his way to work the afternoon shift. Hearing bits and pieces of his wife's call he became alarmed when he heard his grandson's name. "What's going on? Is that Erin on the phone?"

"Hi, Dad, yes it's me. I was just telling Mom about Brian's blood test results. It's not good."

Eric leaned against the counter and listened as the conversation continued on speakerphone.

"What's next?" Sharon asked.

"Well, we'll have to bring Brian in for some more testing. The doctor said he'll need to do another blood test to get a complete blood count so he knows how many of each blood cell is present in the blood. He wants us to come back in two days for an MRI to get a better look at Brian's swollen lymph nodes, as well as his spine and brain."

As the two women talked, the little boy began crying in the background. "The doctor told us to be prepared to have Brian admitted when we go back. He wants to start treatment immediately. Mom, I gotta go," Erin said. "Brian's crying; I need to see what's wrong."

"Okay. Erin, keep us informed. We're here for you."

"I will, Mom. Thanks."

Sharon ended the call and sat with a dazed look. "Oh my God, how can this be happening?"

"There must be some mistake," Eric offered. "You know, doctors are always screwing things up . . . and, well, blood tests get mixed up. I mean, it could be anything . . . like maybe a bad virus or something." He stood with his back to the kitchen counter, both hands firmly on the counter holding him steady. "Let's not jump to conclusions."

Sharon shook her head. "Not jump to conclusions? Eric, it all makes sense—the fevers, the swelling, not wanting to eat. At least now we know what we're up against."

Eric crossed his arms. "I still don't believe it. He's just a baby. How can he have leukemia?"

"I don't know, but one thing is certain—we have to be strong for Mark and Erin. I need to find out more about what's going on, but it sure looks our baby is going to be hospitalized. From the little I know about leukemia, the earlier the treatment the better. They're going to need all the support we can give them to get through this." Sharon stood and moved toward her husband.

"You're right," Eric replied.

Sharon wanted some type of stronger reaction than that. She wanted Eric to take her in his arms and hold her tight, reassuring her that everything would be okay. Unfortunately, that didn't happen. "Eric, are you with me on this?"

He stood stunned, as if the information about their grandson had just sunk in. "What?"

"I said, are you with me? Can I depend on you to help us get through this crisis?"

"Sure, uh, I've got to get to work. I'll see you tonight." He turned and went toward the back door, but Sharon grabbed his jacket and stopped him. "What?" He asked.

She looked into her husband's eyes looking for a connection. "Eric, I'm serious. We need you—all of you—not the man you've been lately, but the caring husband and father that you used to be." As her eyes welled with tears, she said, "Eric, promise me you'll come right home from work tonight . . . I need you now more than ever. If we lose our grandchild . . ."

Eric pulled her close and held her head against his chest, while stroking her hair. "I promise." He kissed her and walked out the door.

Lord, help us, she thought as the door closed.

~~~~~~~~~~

Mark walked into the kitchen and gave his wife and son a kiss. "Sorry honey, I tried to get out early but one of the junior accountants called in sick today."

"That's okay, "Erin replied. "There isn't much you could have done around here anyway. Brian and I have just been chillin' on the couch watching cartoons."

Erin sat at the table attempting to feed their son, but was not having much success. "I thought I'd make his favorite food tonight, mashed potatoes. He ate a couple of mouthfuls but now it looks like he's finished."

Mark pulled a chair next to where his son was sitting in the booster seat. "C'mon, Brian, you have to eat if you want to be big and strong like Daddy." Mark held a spoonful of potatoes and was bringing it close to his son's mouth but the little boy was having none of it and turned away. "He's not going to eat for me either."

Getting up from the table, Erin went to the stove. "Are you ready to eat? Dinner's still warm; I already ate with Brian."

"Yeah, sure. Thanks." He moved his chair as she set a plate down in front of him. "Did you call Mom?"

"Yep."

"Was Dad there?"

"He was," she answered. "Your Mom had me on speaker and your

THE YEAR WITHOUT CHRISTMAS

Dad joined in."

Mark swallowed a bite of food and asked, "Was my Dad drinking?"

Erin came back to the table with a glass of water for her husband. "It didn't sound like it, but then he didn't say a whole lot so I really can't be sure."

"He was probably on his way to work. He's on afternoons. Speaking of work, I spoke with HR today. I wanted to give them a heads up about Brian. I checked on my vacation and sick days. Beginning in a couple of days, Brian's treatment will probably mean a lot of our time will be spent at the hospital. It looks like I have about six weeks vacation time coming and about seventy sick days."

"I hope that's enough," she replied. "I hope our insurance covers most of the costs."

"That's the least of my worries," Mark said.

Trying again to get Brian to eat a bit more, she gathered a spoon of potatoes and tried to coax him into eating but he was adamant and refused. "Mark, why did you have me call you Mom about the test results? Why didn't you call?"

Hesitating, he finally answered. "I didn't want to talk with my Dad if he answered. Particularly if he was drinking. I don't know whether to be upset with him or sorry for him."

"Such a shame," she replied. "How long do you think it will it take for your dad to get over the shooting?"

Moving his food around on his plate with his fork, Mark answered. "Soon, I hope. I don't think my Mom can take much more."

Erin took Brian out of the booster seat and held him while her husband ate. The day they received the news about their little boy had been the worst day of their lives. That night as they lay in bed they cried themselves to sleep and wondered if their son would survive this battle—and if they would be strong enough to make sure he did.

~~~~~~~~~~

"Jackson."

"Here, Sir."

"Sector Three with Thornton."

"Gandurski."

"Here, Sir."

"Doyle."

"Here, Sir."

"Sector Four with Gandurski."

"Yes, Sir."

The lieutenant looked up from his assignment sheet. "Doyle, unless you have court in the morning you're scheduled for fourth quarter firearms qualification. Report to the range at 0900."

"Yes, Sir."

Finishing up the assignments, the watch commander shared the latest lookouts and stolen vehicles with the afternoon shift. "One more thing. Next week is Thanksgiving. If you haven't already put in a request to take the day off, you're S.O.L. I tried to accommodate everyone but a couple of you will have to work. If it's any consolation, Sally's Diner left a message that they will stay open until 1900 hours. They'll have a full Thanksgiving menu to offer."

"You hear that, Jackson. You won't have to eat PB & J that night," remarked one of the officers.

"Screw you," Jackson shot back.

"All right, guys, hit the street. Hey, we're supposed to get a couple of inches of snow tonight so be careful, we've got two units in the shop already from fender benders. You crack up any more cars and you'll all be on foot patrol."

As the officers filed out of the roll call room and gathered their equipment, Eric went out to the parking lot to find the patrol car he and Gandurski had been assigned. Walking out the door, he spotted his old partner, Al Giordano, who had just parked his squad and was coming inside to check off and go home. Eric felt himself tense up and his mouth become dry. He wanted to talk with Al in the worst way; wanted to tell him how sorry he was. As Al neared, Eric began. "Al, I . . . "

Without acknowledging him, Al continued inside. *I guess that says it all*, Eric thought. *How do I put this all behind me and get back to normal when Al won't even talk to me?*

Eric walked down the row of parked police vehicles and found the one he'd be working tonight. He got in and started it up, checked the emergency equipment and back seat. A minute later, Gandurski walked up with the shotgun and placed it in the rack between them.

"Ready to roll partner?"

"Uh, yeah. Let's go." Minutes later the cruiser rolled by Christy's Tap on Main Street, on the way to a domestic disturbance call. As Eric drove past, the flashing red neon "Open" sign beckoned to him like a lighthouse in a foggy harbor.

13

Every man has his secret sorrows which the world knows not; and often times we call a man cold when he is only sad.
—Henry Wadsworth Longfellow

Eric came downstairs just as his daughter was walking out the back door to catch her ride to school. "Bye, Bridge," he called out, as the door closed. He watched as she got into her friend's car and it backed slowly out of the driveway. "Must not have heard me," he said to his wife who was sitting at the table.

He went to the counter and poured himself a cup of coffee. "I've got range this morning so I'm on the day shift today."

Sharon put down the paper she was reading. "Nice way to prepare for it."

"What?" Eric moved over and sat down.

"I asked you to come right home from work last night. Instead you went drinking."

He took a quick sip of the hot coffee, hoping it would help soothe his headache. "I stopped for a couple drinks with Gandurski," he told her. "I was home before the bar even closed."

Sharon sat bewildered, not knowing how she could make him understand that their relationship was on the verge of collapse. "Am I supposed to give you some kind of medal because you didn't close the place? Eric, you're drinking every day—it controls you and you can't even see it." She shook her head as he sat staring. The silence between them roared until finally he answered.

"Listen, Sharon, I'm doing the best I can. It just seems like everything is hitting me all at once. First, the shooting, and now our grandson's health problem . . . it's too much." Eric placed both hands around his coffee cup and stared at it. "I can't get away from it."

She softened, looking at him and thinking about how broken he'd become. Her husband used to be a pillar of strength, able to solve problems and get the family through the rough patches in their lives. Now she didn't know if he'd be able to climb out of the hole he'd fallen into. "Eric, for the last time, please, go for help before it's too late."

All Eric heard was, "too late." He got up and went to the drawer by the sink and grabbed two aspirins from the bottle, popped them in his mouth, and grabbed his jacket. "I've got to get to the firearms range for qualification. I'll see you tonight."

It seemed that once again her plea had fallen on deaf ears. Sharon's soul was deeply troubled. Her life was falling apart and she feared for her family. She went upstairs to take a shower and as the water covered her in its warm embrace, she lifted a prayer to the only One who could salvage what was left.

~~~~~~~~~~

"Mornin', Eric."

"Hey, Ed. Long time no see. How's the family?"

Handing Eric a box of ammo, the range master replied, "Everyone's good, my oldest will be heading off to Michigan State next year. Then the fun begins, trying to figure out how we're going to pay for it."

Eric took the ammo and began filling his magazines with the .40 caliber rounds. "Good luck with that one. When our son, Mark, went to State I wound up working more overtime than I care to remember."

The instructor smiled. "Well, I guess I'm in trouble. We'll have another one following him to State in two years. I'm going to be in the poor house."

Finished loading his magazines, Eric grabbed a set of ear protection and safety glasses and headed into the range. "What lane do you want me in?"

"Go ahead and set up in lane three," the instructor answered. "Same routine. We'll fire a thirty round warm up course, no time limit, and then the timed fifty round qualification course."

Eric hung his target and Ed sent it downrange from the instructor's control booth. The target turned and faced away from the firing line. "Okay, Eric. Eyes and ears in place?"

Eric gave the instructor a thumbs up.

The speakers boomed. "Is the line ready? The line is ready. Watch your target."

Three seconds later the target turned, facing Eric. He drew his pistol, got into a comfortable shooting stance and brought the gun up to his eyes. As he focused on getting a good sight picture, something odd happened. The faceless silhouette began to change. It suddenly resembled a familiar image—Gene Giordano! Eric's finger moved to the trigger, as he felt his now wet palms begin to slip on the grip of the gun. He tried to focus and maintain steady rearward pressure on the trigger, but as he looked through his sights at the target he couldn't bring himself to fire and lowered his weapon.

The instructor's voice boomed through the range loud speaker system. "Shooter, do you have a weapon malfunction? If not, go ahead and fire your first round."

Bringing the gun up once again, Eric tried to focus. He felt his heart pounding against his vest, and his shooting glasses began to fog as perspiration dripped down his forehead into his eyes. As he moved his finger back around to the trigger, he began to squeeze it. Before the weapon discharged, Eric dropped his point of aim to just below the target. The muzzle flash quickly brought him back to the warehouse, back to the moment when he had fired his gun at the boy. And although he was wearing ear protection, the concussion and noise from the explosion was enough to cause his body to tremble.

"Shooter on the line—cease fire; cease fire! Lay your weapon on the bench in front of you." Seconds later the range master was standing behind Eric. "Is your gun malfunctioning? You completely missed the target."

Eric turned to face the instructor. "No, Ed, it's working fine."

The instructor sized Eric up. "You feeling okay? You're sweating."

"Uh, not really."

"What's the problem? Are you ready to shoot today, or not?"

Eric hesitated. "I don't think I can."

"You sick?"

"No, it's not that."

Frustrated that Eric was wasting his time, Ed hoped he could persuade Eric to just fire the qualification. "Listen, if you're not feeling well let's just shoot the qual course and then you can get out of here. I've got another shooter coming in at ten."

Eric looked at his pistol lying on the bench, and then at the target hanging down range. "Sorry, Ed, I don't think I can shoot today. Something's wrong."

"Is it the shooting last month?"

"Yeah, pretty much."

"Come out to the staging area with me." The instructor grabbed Eric's weapon as the two cops left the range. Once outside, Ed emptied Eric's pistol and placed it on his desk. "Sit down for a second. I need to explain something to you." Eric sat on the bench along the wall; Ed sat on the edge of his desk. "We've had a couple of guys involved in shootings while I've been in charge of the range. Everyone reacts differently to their own particular incident. Some guys don't miss a beat after the smoke has cleared, while others take a while to get their head back on straight."

Eric listened, his head down.

"You may need some more time to work this out," Ed explained. "But here's the problem. If you don't qualify with your weapon, I can't authorize you to carry it. If you're not authorized to carry, you can't work the street."

His mind and his heart both racing a mile a minute, Eric weighed the consequences of what the instructor had just told him. He knew that if he didn't meet the department's firearm standard, it would ultimately jeopardize his job. Yet, how could he operate as a cop if he didn't have the ability to use his weapon if it came down to that? His future rested on the answer he was about to give so he took his time weighing his decision.

"Eric?"

Standing, Eric gave his answer. "Ed, sorry to waste your time this morning but I can't do it. I can't seem to focus." He turned and walked out the door and up the steps to the lot where his car was parked. The sun glistened off a coating of fresh snow that had fallen overnight, resting in the boughs of the evergreen trees surrounding the parking area. The picture it created was almost Hallmarkish, but it all escaped Eric who felt he was inching toward his own hell on earth.

Back inside the range, Ed placed Eric's pistol in the range vault.

He went to his desk and dialed the chief's number.

An hour later, Eric was in the chief's office seated across from his boss. "Ed Ramirez called me about your range appointment. He said you failed to qualify."

Eric looked at his boss, sensing the chief was about out of patience. "Yeah, Chief, I couldn't get into it . . . flashbacks. With the gun in my hand and finger on the trigger it brought it all back."

"I should have seen this coming, Doyle." He handed Eric a piece of paper. "Here's the address for the therapist we contract with for our Employee Assistance Program matters. They are expecting you to report at 0900 hours tomorrow."

Eric took the paper. "Yes, Sir."

"As of this moment, you are on light duty which means when you're not in counseling you'll be working admin duties somewhere in headquarters."

"Yes, Sir."

"One more thing. You're still a cop, but you will not work the street—no off-duty arrests or carrying an off-duty gun. Is that clear?"

"Yes, Sir."

The chief's intercom came to life. "Chief, Councilman Harris is here."

Chief Williams pressed the talk button and responded. "Okay, I'll be right out." Standing, he gestured to Eric that their meeting was over. "Doyle, my advice to you is to work with the EAP folks and get your problems taken care of. If you're having this much conflict at work, I know it must be affecting you family as well."

If you only knew, Eric thought. As he left the chief's office, he couldn't help but feel like an outsider. With the rest of the day to kill, he could only think of one place to spend it.

14

*When you get to the end of your rope,
tie a knot and hang on.*
  —**Franklin D. Roosevelt**

"This is the big weekend, Bridge, are you ready?" Sharon asked as she took a travel mug from the cabinet for her daughter.

"Ready as I'm going to be, I suppose. I don't know why they insist on holding the meet on Thanksgiving weekend, it seems dumb." Bridget took the mug from her mother and filled it with coffee.

Remembering her daughter's usual excitement about upcoming track events, Sharon couldn't help but sense some impending problem. She broke off a banana from a bunch on the table and offered it to Bridget. "I know you're in a hurry to get to school," she said, as Bridget's ride appeared in their driveway. "Here's something quick and easy for breakfast."

"Thanks, Mom . . . no time. Gotta go."

"But, Bridge . . ." Sharon stood holding the piece of fruit as her daughter hurried out the door and hopped into her friend's car.

"Hey, Jess. Let's go."

Jessica backed the car out and headed toward the high school. "Last day of school, girlfriend, Thanksgiving break is finally here!" The young girl gyrated to her own beat as she sang the observation to her friend.

"For you, maybe, you're not on the track team. I've got the regional meet on Saturday," Bridget quickly added.

"I know, and I'm going to be there cheering for you from the bleachers. Are you excited?"

Bridget sipped some coffee from her mug and stared out the window. Before the incident with her father had happened, she was confident she would win her event and lock in the scholarship she had almost taken for granted. Now she wasn't so sure. Things at home were stressful. Her relationship with her Dad was almost non-existent. She rarely saw him, and when she did neither one of them spoke to each other. She was avoiding her Mom, not wanting to get into the whole eating thing. She's not dumb; she must know what's going on.

"Earth to Bridget—did you hear me?"

Turning her head toward her friend, Bridget turned down the volume on the radio. "Uh, I guess not, the music was too loud."

"I asked if you were excited about the meet."

"Oh, yeah. Biggest track event of the season . . . can't wait."

Jessica reached over and cranked the volume back up on the radio, quickly moving to the music as she drove. Bridget turned her gaze out the window, watching the scenery pass by in a blur. Everything was passing her by. Everything was a blur.

~~~~~~~~~~

"Welcome, Mr. Doyle. Please, come in and make yourself comfortable. The middle-aged woman was pleasant enough, thought Eric. Glancing around the room, he saw it was not unlike some attorneys' offices he had been to—lots of diplomas and mementos. As was his custom as a cop, he sized up the woman. She wore her hair swept back from her face, which he noticed had aged quite well, unlike his own that displayed years of stress and worry. Eric noticed a rocker and several easy chairs in the room, causing him to comment, "No couch?"

"No, contrary to what people perceive, therapists conduct their practice like most other professionals." She motioned toward the easy chairs. "Take a seat, please."

After Eric opened his jacket, he sat down in the middle chair. The woman sat across from him in the rocker. "Mr. Doyle, my name is Dr. Sally Lake. I've been a counselor for almost twenty years, the last ten of which I've specialized in treating returning military veterans and public safety personnel. Your department has asked me to see if there is anything I can do to help get you healthy again." Reaching to the table next to her she grabbed a clipboard.

"In order for me to understand you better, I'd like you to complete this questionnaire." She handed the clipboard to Eric. "It's a standard diagnostic tool, nothing elaborate, and contains only a few pages. The questions are check box type and shouldn't take you more than twenty minutes. I'll be in the adjoining office; just knock on the door when you're finished."

Eric took a quick look at the forms, thumbing through the pages. It was as she explained. Nothing complicated. "Okay, Doc."

"By the way," she said, as she started toward the office, "there's coffee on the table by the window. Help yourself."

"Thanks."

The woman disappeared into her adjoining office, closing the door behind her so as not to distract Eric. He began filling in the background information, name, age, the usual stuff. Halfway down the page the questions caught his attention. *Have you ever witnessed an incident that was life-threatening to you or someone else? Have you had disturbing thoughts, memories or nightmares of the trauma you experienced?* He was surprised that many of the questions related directly to what he was experiencing. He was torn between answering truthfully and not wanting to open himself to a stranger. Heck, he hadn't even opened up to his wife. Despite his internal struggle, he plodded through the questions. When he had finished he walked over to the therapist's partially opened door and knocked. Dr. Lake appeared.

"Finished," Eric said, handing the clipboard to the woman.

Smiling, she replied. "Thank you. If you'll just relax for a few minutes, I can quickly review this questionnaire and then we can get started."

They moved back to the chairs they had previously occupied. Eric studied the woman as she perused his answers. She was attractive and kept good care of herself. Her legs seemed toned and her body was thin, yet shapely. *Must be a runner*, he thought.

"Okay, Mr. Doyle. Based on your answers to the diagnostic questionnaire, I think I have a good idea about what might be bothering you. But perhaps it might help if we took some time right now and you can tell me everything you remember about the night you were involved in the shooting incident."

Eric nodded and then awkwardly began explaining what had occurred that night, almost as if he were testifying in court. "On the night in question, my partner and I, Officer Giordano were responding to a call at an abandoned warehouse. Upon arrival, and according to proper police procedure . . . "

"Mr. Doyle," she interrupted, "we won't need any official-type language. Just tell me in your own words, as if you and I were having a conversation, what led up to the shooting, the incident itself, and then what has happened afterwards."

For the next thirty minutes, Eric explained everything he could remember about that night. When he got to the actual shooting, he started and stopped several times, needing to compose himself. Several times Dr. Lake had to gently persuade him to relate the rest of the events. He told her about his perceived alienation from his colleagues, and the despair he felt in having killed his partner's only child. He went on to explain his problems with his own family, including his grandson's leukemia. When he was finished, the doctor finally spoke.

"You've been through a tremendous amount of stress, Mr. Doyle. The shooting, in and of itself, was a critical incident of tremendous proportions. Your grandson's illness has only added to your burden. One of the ways to rid ourselves of stress is to do exactly what we're doing now—to get it out in the open—to discuss our feelings and concerns."

Eric shifted in his seat, feeling somewhat uncomfortable after having revisited that night with the counselor. He was anxious to end this session and get some fresh air.

The doctor sensed his anxiety. "I think we've had a good first meeting. Since this is Thanksgiving week, why don't we schedule our next meeting at the end of next week. Say, Friday morning . . . same time?"

"That's fine," he replied, as he got out of the chair.

"Are you having any problem sleeping? If so I can give you a prescription."

"Uh, no. I'm fine." *All I need is Christy's Tap,* he thought.

"Okay. I'll see you next week. Have a wonderful holiday. Enjoy your family."

~~~~~~~~~~

Chief Williams picked up his desk phone as it rang. "Hi, Chief. It's Dr. Lake."

"Hi, Doctor, how are you?"

"Fine. I just wanted to inform you that I met with Officer Doyle this morning."

The chief pushed back from his desk and looked out his office window. "How did it go?"

"It went well. He was cooperative and, I think, forthcoming in his answers."

"And . . ." Tapping his fingers on the arm of his chair, the chief was anxious to hear what she had to say.

"Well, based upon our earlier conversation, particularly, regarding the incident at the firing range, it's as you suspected. Officer Doyle is suffering from Post Traumatic Stress Disorder."

Nodding, the man quickly realized he had a problem on his hands. "Okay, Doctor, thanks for getting back with me so quickly on this. When's his next appointment?"

"Friday, the week after Thanksgiving."

"Very well. I'll make sure he's there. Have a nice holiday, Ma'am."

"Thank-you, I will. Chief, I wasn't sure when you asked me before about Officer Doyle's ability to function on the street. After our visit this morning, I'm convinced he should not be on full duty. I think your officer is going to need a lot of psychotherapy to get past this."

"Whatever it takes, Dr. Lake, I'm prepared to ensure he gets it. Thank-you, again. Good-bye."

The chief hung up the phone and leaned back in his chair. "I have some decisions to make," he thought.

15

*If pleasures are greatest in anticipation,
just remember that this is also true of trouble.*
   —**Elbert Hubbard**

As Sharon carried the roasting pan from the sink, the back door opened and her daughter walked in. "Ah, just in time. Bridge, will you open the oven door for me so I can get the turkey started?"

"Sure thing, Mom."

Sharon put the bird in the oven. "Should be done around five," she said, as she set the temperature and time. "Might as well start preparing the other dishes for tonight's Thanksgiving dinner." She looked over at Bridget. "How was your run?"

Taking off her hat and gloves, Bridget laid them on the table and went to the sink for a glass of water. "Pretty good, some icy spots here and there but the streets are clear for the most part. At least there's no new snow."

"Seems you were gone a long time," Sharon remarked as she began to cut the vegetables.

Finishing a long drink of water, Bridget wiped the sweat from her brow. "Yeah, well, I figured we'd be pigging out tonight at dinner so I should burn some extra calories beforehand." The girl removed her running jacket and put it on one of the kitchen chairs and then refilled her water glass. As she did, Sharon examined her daughter.

Trying not to be obvious about it, she stole glances at the teen girl whose skin hugging top and tights exhibited her form perfectly. It seemed Bridget had lost weight, her torso seemed lean and her breasts noticeably smaller. Not that they were large before, but they were no longer as prominent as they had been. Discussing weight loss seemed counterproductive to their present relationship. Sharon knew from experience that such conversations only served to drive mother and daughter apart. She didn't want that to happen—not now—not with the turmoil she was going through with Eric. So she said nothing about her concern.

"Two more days, Sweetheart. Are you excited about the meet?"

Bridget pulled out a chair and sat down. "I just want it over with," she answered calmly. "It's become more of a distraction than anything else. I'm really worn out; it's been a long season."

Worried about her daughter's frame of mind going into the biggest event of the year, Sharon knew to tread lightly and not damage her daughter's fragile psyche. She continued to concentrate on cutting the vegetables. "I'm sure you're tired, Honey. It has been a long, hard season, but after this weekend you'll have plenty of time to rest and recuperate."

Not getting a response from her comment, Sharon looked up from her task and saw her daughter staring into space. "Bridge, did you hear me?"

Startled, the girl turned toward her mother. "Uh, yeah, right. I am tired. Guess I'll hit the shower and take a nap before Mark and Erin get here." She walked out of the room.

Turning back to her meal preparation, the woman wondered. *This final high school track meet would be either a blessing or a curse.*

~~~~~~~~~~

Eric had not requested the holiday off and thus was scheduled to work. Headquarters was closed for the holiday, so he reported to the station. However, if he had known he would be working administrative duties behind the desk, he surely would have put in for the holiday. Filing case reports and keeping tabs on the fax machine and other tasks kept him busy. But the veteran officer wanted to be on the street with his fellow cops where he'd been his entire career. It seemed fate was working against him. He had his badge and gun back for a day, and now the department had his gun again. He couldn't blame them. A cop who doesn't qualify at the range is a liability. *That's what I am, a liability.* Even some of his colleagues refused to work with him.

He was like a fish out of water working inside, particularly since he was unarmed, a fact that stood out like a fireman not wearing his boots. His only consolation was that he'd finish his shift at four and be home in time for a cocktail before the Thanksgiving dinner. He was excited about seeing his little grandson, Brian. The boy was going to the hospital soon for tests and treatment and Eric wanted to smother him with love and attention today.

"Hey, Doyle, give me the key for an interview room."

Hearing a familiar voice Eric turned around from where he was sitting at the desk—it was his old partner, Al Giordano. "Okay, Al." Eric walked over to the key box on the wall and grabbed one of the keys for the interview rooms. "Here you go, Interview Room One."

The officer took the key and without looking at Eric began filling in the required information on the prisoner log. That done, he turned to walk away.

"Hey, Al, I've been meaning to . . ."

"No time to talk—my partner's in the back babysitting our prisoner," the man said over his shoulder. "I need to open the room." Giordano walked down the hall out of sight.

Having failed in another attempt at trying to speak with Al, Eric felt his Thanksgiving holiday spirit deflate. He had hoped to somehow find a way to apologize to his former partner today, considering it was a special day. However, nothing seemed to be going his way in his efforts to get his old partner to hear Eric's take on what happened that night. *If he'd only let me tell him how sorry I am . . .*

~~~~~~~~~~

Two hours later Eric was home and in his civvies. He walked into the kitchen and grabbed a bottle of whiskey from the cabinet. As he poured himself a drink, Sharon came into the room to check on the turkey. "Smells good, babe."

She opened the door and began basting the bird. "Yes, and it's about ready. I wonder why the kids aren't here yet?" She closed the oven door and turned to her husband. "Eric, please go easy with that tonight," she cautioned, watching him take a sip. "Please don't ruin our Thanksgiving."

How could I? "Yeah, yeah, I'm just having one to relax before Brian gets here."

"I think I'll just give the kids a call to see if they're on their way." Sharon went over to the counter and picked up the house phone and dialed her son's cell number.

THE YEAR WITHOUT CHRISTMAS

"Hello. Hey, are you guys on the way?"

Eric watched his wife's smile disappear. "Oh . . . uh huh . . . I understand. Poor little guy. I'll call later tonight . . . love you too."

Sharon hung up the phone. "Mark said Brian's running a fever. It's up around 102. They've been on the phone with the pediatrician who is talking them through a couple of things to get the temperature down. Obviously they won't be coming over."

"Damn," Eric muttered. Seeing his little grandbaby was going to be the highlight of his day *.He's the only one who doesn't judge me. What else can go wrong in my life?* As Sharon turned the oven off, Eric finished his drink and went to the cabinet for a refill. *Thanksgiving? Grateful? Yeah, right.*

16

When a man is in despair, it means that he still believes in something.
—Dmitri Shostakovich

Al Giordano came home to an empty house after his shift. His wife had left a message on his cell phone that she would try to be home by eight pm and that he should go ahead and eat without her. Sandy explained she had several catering clients who would be serving Thanksgiving dinner around 6pm, meaning she would miss celebrating the holiday with Al. Not that there was anything to celebrate.

Going to the refrigerator, Al got a bottle of beer and moved into the family room. Reflexively, he reached for the TV remote as he collapsed in his easy chair, but stopped short of turning the set on as the family portrait once again caught his eye. *Gene . . .son . . .* His mind drifted back to Thanksgiving last year when the family started their holiday by going to church and then enjoyed a big breakfast at a local restaurant. Sandy's catering business had flourished by that time and so she went to work right afterward. Nevertheless, Al and Gene didn't waste the day off. They spent it together watching football games on their big screen TV. Later that night, Sandy surprised them by bringing home a complete Thanksgiving dinner. He smiled as he remembered Gene eating a huge drumstick.

Taking a sip of beer, he thought about seeing Eric today at the station. Obviously the man had problems. Assigned to desk duties after being cleared in the shooting meant he was probably seeing a shrink. *Too bad, pal. I'm sure you're going through a rough spot, but put yourself in my shoes.* Al thought about turning on the football game, but instead put the recliner back and closed his eyes. *Gene, I miss you so much.*

~~~~~~~~~~

THE YEAR WITHOUT CHRISTMAS

Sharon let out a sigh as she surveyed the dinner table. A fifteen-pound turkey yielded a full platter of meat that had hardly been touched. The three adults should have put a sizable dent in the offerings, instead it was as if the meal was about to begin rather than having just been completed. Without Mark, Erin and the baby to help celebrate, the meal and all of Sharon's preparation were wasted. Bridget barely touched her plate and Eric seemed to be on a liquid diet. "C'mon you two, you can't be finished , you've hardly eaten anything."

Eric poured another glass of wine. "No more for me, but thanks, it was a great meal."

Sharon looked at her husband. *Yeah, not as great as the wine.* "Bridge, how about you? More turkey or rolls?"

"No, Mom. I'm stuffed."

Disappointed about how the holiday had turned out, Sharon made a decision. "Bridget, give me a hand. We're going to wrap the leftovers and that pumpkin pie and take it all to the soup kitchen downtown. There's too much food here to keep in the fridge. I know there are plenty of homeless people who will be grateful for a full course meal."

"Okay, Mom. Good idea."

"How about you, Eric, feel like brightening the day for the disadvantaged?"

He took another sip of wine. "Nah, they probably have enough to eat already. Thanksgiving brings a lot of do-gooders out of the woodwork."

Sharon didn't care to give that answer a response. All she knew was that her holiday was ruined and that she had to salvage it somehow. She went to the cabinet and began to line up some plastic containers to transport the uneaten meal.

Fifteen minutes later she and Bridget had the food ready to take to the shelter. "Are you coming with?" She asked her daughter while putting on her coat.

"Sure. I think it's nice that you're thinking of the people who are less fortunate than the rest of us." Bridget helped her mother put the containers in a couple of bags and the two went out to the garage and loaded the meal in the car. Twenty minutes later they were at the shelter helping the employees set a table with a mouth-watering meal.

"You folks saved the day," said the facility manager. "We ran a bit short of donations and had to ration the portions. This will ensure no one goes to bed hungry."

"Glad to do it," Sharon replied. Mother and daughter stayed for more than an hour, helping to serve the residents and visiting with families. Afterward, on the ride home, Sharon reflected on how her disappointment had turned into something good. "Bridge, we are so blessed to have a home."

"Yeah, I know, Mom."

"Some of those kids there seemed so lost," Sharon remarked. "I think I'm going to make that a regular part of my life. Volunteering at the shelter is a way I can show my gratitude for how much God has given us."

As they turned into their driveway, Sharon's cell phone rang. "Mom, it's Mark. We're in Detroit at Children's Hospital. The doctor wanted us to bring Brian in right away to prepare him to begin chemo. He's afraid Brian's immune system has been weakened to the point where even a tiny infection could be life-threatening."

"No," Sharon answered, her eyes filling with tears.

"What is it, Mom? Who's on the phone?"

"It's your brother. Little Brian is in the hospital, he needs chemotherapy."

17

*Success is not final, failure is not fatal:
it is the courage to continue that counts.*
    —**Winston Churchill**

Websterville Arena was packed for the Midwest High School Championship Track and Field Meet. Eric and Sharon sat in the stands watching each event unfold, waiting anxiously for their daughter's race. The Thanksgiving weekend was the perfect time to hold the track meet because of the break from school and work. People seemed relaxed and in a good mood after celebrating the holiday with family and friends.

"I don't care, Eric, I'm going to Detroit in the morning whether you go with me or not."

"But, Sharon, it's such a long drive and I told you it's not safe in that city. Besides, we're supposed to get some snow tomorrow—the roads will be slippery."

She shook her head and turned to look at her husband. "Who are you? Your family is down there—your only son and his wife with your grandson who is battling a disease that may take his life, and you're giving me excuses why I shouldn't go?"

"No, I didn't mean it like that," Eric pleaded. "I meant, let's wait till Mark calls with more news about Brian's condition. Then we can keep an eye on the weather too."

As the crowd around her cheered on their favorite runners, Sharon sat stunned by her husband's apathy. "I can't understand you anymore, Eric. You're not the man I married. Your family is in trouble; they need you. They need us. Yet all you can do is make excuses about why we shouldn't be with them in their time of need."

"Sharon, I . . ."

"You disgust me!"

Eric got up and hurried up the stairs to the concession stand. "Two beers, please." He paid for his drinks and made his way to the stairwell, quickly drinking one of the beers in just a couple of swallows as he walked. The cold crisp liquid calmed him and stoked his confidence. He knew this was the real reason he couldn't go to the hospital in Detroit with Sharon. He couldn't be without a drink for very long anymore. Being around Sharon, Mark and Erin, he wouldn't be able to drink as much as he needed to. They would be all over him, nagging him about it. He didn't want that. He had enough problems without his family getting on his case.

While he took another long drink of his beer, he heard the gun go off for another race. He took a few steps down the stairs and realized it was his daughter's event. He quickly made his way back to his seat next to Sharon, seemingly racing the athletes as he did, wondering if he would get to his chair before the race was over. He found the row and sat down next to Sharon, just as the first runner broke the tape. People in the row in front of Eric and Sharon stood and cheered, blocking the couple's view.

"Where's Bridget? Did she win, Eric?"

"Uh, I don't know," he said, as he stood to look over the group in front of them.

Not getting an answer, Sharon jumped up on the bench to get a better view. She saw Bridget bent over with a few of the other runners, as they all tried to catch their breath just past the finish line.

"Did she win?" Sharon asked Eric again.

"I don't know."

"She had to win to get that scholarship, Eric. She just had to."

Moments later the results appeared on the scoreboard at the far end of the arena. Bridget Doyle had finished in third place.

Sharon looked at the scoreboard in disbelief. Her daughter's dream of earning an athletic scholarship had disappeared. The implications, she knew, were huge. This race was one she had been focusing on all season long. This was to be the day when all of her hard work would bear fruit in the form of a championship that would unlock the door to an otherwise unattainable education.

Tears blurred her vision as Sharon watched Bridget walk from the track to the tunnel leading to the locker rooms. Normally, Bridget would jog off the track, waving wildly to her parents in the stands.

On this day, she shuffled off, never even raising her head to acknowledge her parents' presence.

"I'm going down there; she needs her family. I know she must be crushed. Are you coming?"

"Yeah, I'll be there in a minute."

Sharon looked at her husband, a drink in his hand, and just shook her head. She picked her way through the crowd toward the dressing area, not even wondering if Eric was following.

Eric walked in the opposite direction up the stairs. "Two beers, please."

Today would be a bellwether day for the family.

~~~~~~~~~~

Monday morning. Eric awoke in the recliner in the family room and tried to recall Saturday and Sunday but couldn't remember very much of either day. He recalled the worst parts—his argument with Sharon about his drinking and her leaving in a huff to join Mark and Erin at Children's Hospital in Detroit. He also remembered trying to console Bridget about her loss at the track meet. The conversation had gone nowhere and ended up with Bridget locking herself in her bedroom. After that, Eric took a bottle of whiskey from the kitchen cabinet and settled in for the day, oblivious to time and movement. He neither saw nor heard Sharon and Bridget.

He pushed the chair handle forward and brought himself to an upright position in the recliner. Stars danced before his eyes as he felt his head pounding like a base drum. On the table next to him sat an empty bottle. *Didn't think I finished that off.* A strong coffee aroma propelled him from his chair toward the kitchen. *Sharon must be making breakfast.*

His first few steps were a bit unsteady. Nevertheless, he dragged himself into the kitchen and found his wife was not there, nor was the newspaper that normally laid wide open on the table. *Hmm . . .* he took a cup from the cabinet, poured himself some coffee, and walked to the living room. As he took a sip, he flinched as the hot brew stung his lips, but the strong caffeine perked him up. Eric looked out the window and saw a light dusting of snow covering the driveway. He spotted the newspaper still lying on the ground in the plastic sleeve. And he saw one other thing—tire tracks. *Crap, Sharon must be headed to Detroit again.*

Walking back to the kitchen he encountered Bridget as she came down the stairs with her school backpack. "Mornin', Kitten," Eric offered. Bridget continued to walk past her father, not even acknowledging his greeting.

"Hey, I said good morning. Didn't you hear me?"

The girl continued to ignore him and proceeded to the kitchen to grab a travel mug. She filled it with coffee and then walked to the kitchen door as her classmate's car pulled into the driveway.

"Dammit, Bridget, what's wrong with you? Why aren't you answering me?"

She pulled open the door and hesitated, turning toward her father. "What's wrong with me? What's wrong with you? You don't give a damn about any of us . . . Mom, me, little Brian. All you care about is yourself and your damn drinking!"

"Hey, wait a minute. I'm your father; don't talk to me like that."

"My father? You're not my father. My father loves me. He cares for me. He protects me. You're a stranger who looks like my father."

"Bridge . . ."

"I hate you!"

Those were the last words Eric heard as she slammed the door. His head still pounding, he stared at the door not believing what had just transpired. He brought his cup up to his mouth to take a drink and stopped, went over to the kitchen cabinet and grabbed another bottle of whiskey. Standing over the sink, he poured out the coffee, and refilled his mug with a generous helping of the dark brown liquid. He took a long drink.

As he stared out the window over the kitchen sink, a bird landed momentarily on the sill, walked several paces back and forth, and then took flight. He pondered the bird's actions and knew exactly what he needed to do.

18

I sustain myself with the love of family.
   —**Maya Angelou**

"Where's dad?"
"He's home; he has to work today."
Mark looked at his mother and rubbed his forehead. He could sense she was depressed and worried about her husband. She was naturally concerned about her only grandson's health, but how much more could she bear? His Dad's behavior was clearly pushing her to the brink. Yesterday, when Mark and his mother went to the hospital cafeteria for some coffee, Sharon broke down as she related what had happened at the track meet. She told her son about his sister Bridget's performance at the race, and about the weeks leading up to the event—how Bridget had grown weaker rather than stronger by not eating as she should. Compounding matters was Eric's drinking problem, brought on by the shooting death of his partner's only son, Gene.

"Mom, I don't know what to say," Mark told her, as he ran both hands through his hair. "Dad's problems are serious, I know, but right now Erin and I have to stay focused on our son. The doctors haven't given us any guarantee we're going to definitely beat the leukemia. As much as I love you both, I have to focus all of my energy on Brian. He needs me, and I intend to be here for as long as it takes." That time alone with her son was a double-edged sword—she knew Mark was totally committed to doing everything possible for Brian. That was definitely what had to happen. However, she also knew the task would consume him. She could not depend on him for any support in her struggle with Eric.

Sharon stood from her chair in the hospital room and went over to where Mark and Erin were standing beside their son's bed. Wrapping her arms around both of them, she held them tightly. "Mark, I know this is exactly where you need to be, with your wife and baby." She kissed them both and then let go. "I'm going to the cafeteria for a cup of coffee, and I need to send a text to Bridget. I want to make sure she got off to school okay."

"Alright, Mom."

She went to the elevator and took it down to the basement level, bought a cup of coffee, and then found a table in the corner of the dining room. She retrieved her phone from her purse, pulled up Bridget's number, and sent a text message:

brian still same, mark and erin say hi

She hit the send button and was about to put the phone away when she had a thought. She began to type a second message:

did u see dad this morning

Sharon sent the second message on its way and took a sip of her coffee. There were only a few people in the cafeteria, adding to the feeling of loneliness that had overtaken her in the last couple of weeks. She felt there was no one she could talk to anymore, no one she could share her problems with. Her husband and best friend was so lost in his own problems that he was clueless about everything else. Now Mark had his own crisis to deal with.

Bridget was clearly suffering from the family turmoil as well. She had isolated herself from her parents and was reluctant to discuss her feelings. The mother-daughter talks they frequently shared were now almost non-existent. It was plain to see Bridget was in crisis and was choosing her own coping mechanism—not eating—to deal with her overwhelming problems. With the poor outcome of the biggest race of the season fresh in her mind, Sharon worried that her daughter's psyche would only get worse before it got better. Not being able to share her problems with her father only caused the girl more anxiety.

Her phone vibrated on the table. Sharon picked it up and saw she had a new text message. It was from Bridget:

i don't have a father

As she read the words on her phone, her body began to shudder and tears streamed from her eyes. *I'm losing them . . . God help us.* She covered her face with her hands and wept silently.

THE YEAR WITHOUT CHRISTMAS

~~~~~~~~~~

Chief Williams walked into his office at headquarters, having just had lunch with one of the town council members.

"Chief, you had a call from the EAP therapist," his secretary advised, tearing a sheet from her telephone message pad. "She would like you to call her at your earliest convenience."

"Thanks," he replied, and took the paper from her. He closed the door to his office and sat at his desk. Signing into his computer, he made sure there was nothing that needed his immediate attention, and then picked up the phone and dialed the number on the message form.

"Hello, this is Dr. Lake, how may I help you?"

"Hi, Doctor, this is Chief Williams returning your call."

"Ah, yes, Chief Williams. Sir, I wanted to ask if you had Officer Doyle on any type of duty that would have caused him to miss his appointment with me this morning."

The chief sighed and leaned back in his chair. "No, Doctor, there's nothing that should have precluded him from being there. He's on administrative duty here at headquarters."

"Okay, Chief. Officer Doyle did not show up, nor did he call and say he wouldn't be able to meet with me."

"I'm sorry to hear that, Ma'am. I will find out what happened and get back with you."

"I understand. I wouldn't be concerned were it not for the fact that your officer's PTSD is in the early stages. This disorder is known to progress very quickly if left untreated. It manifests itself in any number of other undesirable behaviors, one of which I suspect Officer Doyle suffers from presently."

"What would that be?

"Alcoholism."

"I see," the chief responded. "Doctor, I'm sorry we wasted your valuable time. I will have Officer Doyle contact you to reschedule. I appreciate your understanding in this matter."

"You're welcome, Chief. I hope we are able to treat him in time. Any delay will be critical in his potential recovery."

The chief leaned forward. "Thank you," he said, and hung up the phone. Pressing the intercom button, he signaled his secretary to come into his office.

"Yes, Chief?"

"Officer Doyle was a no-show this morning for his counseling session. He's supposed to be working in the building at Personnel. Please find him and tell him to report to my office immediately."

"Yes, Sir."

Ten minutes later the chief's secretary knocked on his door.

"Come in."

"Chief, the supervisor in Personnel said Officer Doyle has not reported for work, and has not called in sick."

"Okay. Please get him on the phone and transfer the call."

"Yes, Sir."

Moments later, the secretary's voice came over the intercom. "Chief, there's no answer at Officer Doyle's residence or his cell phone."

"Thank you."

Getting up from his chair, the chief walked over to the window and admired the beautiful winter vista. *What's going on with Doyle, and what are my options? He's a good cop, but he's turning into a liability for everyone involved—including his family. It's time to make a decision.*

19

*Alcohol is the anesthesia by which
we endure the operation of life.*
　—**George Bernard Shaw**

The first ring seemed distant. Eric thought he was dreaming until he felt the phone vibrating. By the time he changed position on the couch and was able to get the cell phone from his pocket, the ringing had stopped. He cleared his throat, feeling the dryness; it was rough and felt like sandpaper. Moments later the house phone in the kitchen began to ring.

Swinging his legs off the couch, he set both feet on the floor and glanced at the clock on the cable box beneath the TV—1:15 pm. *Crap, I missed work.* He realized both calls must be from the police department. Seconds later the answering machine kicked in: "Officer Doyle, this is Chief Williams' office. The chief would like you to contact him immediately."

"Damn!" Eric got up and went into the kitchen. He needed something cool to drink to soothe the pain in his throat. Opening the refrigerator, he peered inside and saw a gallon of milk and a container of orange juice. On the shelf below, he spotted a six-pack of beer and grabbed a can from it. Phht. The sound of the can opening soothed him, and as he took a long swig, the cold liquid coated his throat and the fresh infusion of alcohol bolstered his bravado. *Screw the chief. I'm no pencil pusher—I'm a cop.* In one gulp, he finished the contents of the can and grabbed another from the fridge. *I didn't become a cop to file reports in headquarters.*

Eric walked around the house as he worked on the second can of beer. Thinking of how he was going to explain his absence to the chief, he quickly remembered one other important item—his appointment with the therapist. "Aw, hell, I'm in big trouble," he said aloud.

It was almost time for Bridget to get home from school. There were no more practices; the track season was over. He didn't want to be there when she walked through the door. He couldn't face her, particularly not after she had told him this morning she hated him. If she saw him drinking, it would only make matters worse between them.

Eric finished his beer and tossed it in the kitchen trashcan, grabbed his jacket and took his keys off the counter. He hit the remote for the garage door. His truck was parked by itself in the garage. No telling when Sharon would return home. He wasn't even sure where she was, but he assumed she was in Detroit, at the hospital. *I should call . . . no, it would only start another fight.*

The bright sunlight had warmed the temperature, and the light snow cover was beginning to disappear. But the reflection off the remaining snow had a blinding effect on Eric. As he walked to the truck, he misjudged the edge of the garage and walked into the frame, striking his head. "Ow!" He bounced off the garage doorframe and got into his vehicle, focused on making his way to Christy's Tap. As he backed out onto the street, he saw Bridget pull up in her friend's car. The vehicle waited to pull into the driveway while Eric backed out. He didn't know if he should say anything or not, so he simply waved and allowed the car to pull in. Bridget didn't acknowledge his gesture, and the car with the two girls drove to the end of the driveway.

"What's up girlfriend? You didn't even wave to your dad."

"Yeah, I know," she replied. "Listen, I don't want to talk about it. I'm kinda bummed right now. Thanks for the ride; see you in the morning?"

"Sure; bye."

Eric pulled away en route to the bar. *I'm a nobody . . . a damn file clerk. My wife and kids hate me, and my chief thinks I'm nuts.* A single tear escaped from his eye. When Eric went to wipe it away, he found his hand had blood on it. He dropped the sun visor down and looked in the mirror. His forehead was bleeding. *Crap.* Grabbing a tissue from the glove box, he pressed it to the cut as he drove.

~~~~~~~~~~

It was close to ten o'clock when Sharon got home. She pulled into the garage and saw that Eric's truck wasn't there. She had almost expected it wouldn't be. At around six o'clock, while she was still at the hospital, she had received a call from the Chief, asking her if she knew her husband's whereabouts.

"Have you talked to him today?" the chief inquired.

"No, Sir. I left early to drive to Children's Hospital in Detroit to be with my grandson."

"Oh? Uh, Mrs. Doyle, I don't mean to pry, but is your grandson okay? I mean, I hate to bother you at a time like this."

The chief's concern unsettled Sharon. She found herself beginning to weaken to the point of wanting to cry. The man's sincerity and compassion was something she longed to have back in her life, something she used to get from Eric. She left Brian's hospital room and went out into the hall.

"Mrs. Doyle, are you there?"

"Yes . . . I'm here. I haven't spoken with my husband today."

"Okay, Ma'am. I don't mean to trouble you, but Eric failed to report to work today and he also missed his appointment with the EAP therapist. I thought you might know why."

"Therapist? I know I asked him to see one, but I didn't know he had actually done it." Sharon paced absent-mindedly back and forth, wondering why Eric hadn't shared this with her. "What did the therapist say, Chief?"

Silence.

"Chief?"

"Ma'am, Eric's condition is supposed to be confidential; I'm not at liberty to discuss it."

"What? Confidential! I'm his wife, I need to know what his problems are so I can take care of him." Sharon stopped pacing and leaned against the wall. A nurse walking past heard Sharon raise her voice.

"Shhh. Keep your voice down, there are sick children here."

Embarrassed, Sharon continued with her conversation. "Chief, you don't know what it's been like for us since the shooting. Eric's not the same man—he's apathetic and inattentive. He's been drinking heavily, not sleeping . . . our life has been turned upside down."

"I'm sorry to hear that, Mrs. Doyle. Listen, I'm going to break the rules this one time because of all that's involved. Eric has PTSD. He's been unable to cope with what happened the night of the shooting incident. I put him on limited duty at headquarters with orders to undergo therapy. I won't lie to you—he's in a bad way. He couldn't even qualify at the range the other day; couldn't bring himself to fire his weapon."

Hearing about her husband from the chief, and being at the hospital with her sick grandson smothered her. She felt as if the weight of the world was on her shoulders. She had no idea how to fix any of her problems, nor did she know where to turn for advice.

"Mrs. Doyle, are you still there?"

Sharon walked to the end of the hall and looked out over the city of Detroit. From the fifth floor of the hospital, she saw that the few streetlights that still burned illuminated skeletons of a once vibrant city. Vacant blocks marked areas where poverty and drugs had won the war between good and evil. Factories stood abandoned, their windows shattered, their contents plundered. It was a cold, stark scene, one that mirrored Sharon's soul.

"Mrs. Doyle?"

"I'm here, Chief. I'm here."

~~~~~~~~~~

Walking from the garage to the back door, Sharon unlocked it and walked inside to a dark house. She surveyed the kitchen—a couple of coffee cups in the sink, but no other dishes. An almost empty bottle of whiskey stood alone on the counter.

Was Bridget home?

She threw open the refrigerator and saw that the casserole she had prepared before she left this morning was still sitting there. Making her way to the family room, she turned on the lamp and saw an empty whiskey bottle on the table. She picked it up and carried it to the kitchen trashcan, the weight of the bottle in her hand almost too much to bear. The bottles had become a hateful symbol for all that was wrong in her life.

Climbing the stairs, she went to her daughter's room. Knocking gently, she let herself in. "Bridge?"

Her daughter lay in bed, the only light in the room coming from the TV—no sound. "Honey?"

Sharon sat on the edge of the bed. Her daughter's back was to her, so she gently took hold of Bridget's arm and rolled the girl toward her. She saw Bridget had been crying, her face was red, as were her eyes.

"Bridge, are you okay, Sweetheart?"

The young girl broke down. Sitting up, she hugged her mother. "Mom, everything is going wrong. Dad hates us, Brian is going to die and I'm a complete failure."

Seeing her daughter upset like this broke her heart. Sharon hugged and rocked her little girl like she had when Bridget was a youngster. "Sweetheart, listen. Your father doesn't hate us; he's sick. He's suffering from Post Traumatic Stress Syndrome, but he'll get better. He's seeing a therapist."

"He is? That's good, isn't it, that he's getting help?"

"Yes, Honey, it is." Sharon didn't have the heart to tell her that her father had missed his session today, but she needed to reassure her daughter that things would improve. "Have you seen your father today?"

Bridget grabbed a tissue from the nightstand and dried her eyes. "I saw him for a minute this morning, but it wasn't good."

"What do you mean?"

"Well, he fell asleep drunk in the recliner last night. Mom, I got so mad at him. I can't even talk with him about anything. Anyway, he was just waking up as I was leaving for school and . . . "

"What, Bridge?"

"Mom, I told him I hated him."

Her daughter hugged her mother as she broke down and cried. Sharon felt the girl's newly frail frame shudder as the girl cried tears of despair. Despite the situation, Sharon felt a sense of accomplishment—she was mothering her little girl. Just holding the child brought comfort, this kind of close contact with a loved one had been missing for far too long.

"It's going to be okay, Bridge. Your Dad and Brian will both get better. And, by the way, you are not a failure, young lady. You still have plenty of college options, and you and I are going to explore them together."

Bridget let go of her mother and wiped the tears. "Thanks, Mom. I love you. I hope you're right."

"I love you too. Goodnight, Sweetheart." Sharon got up and closed the door behind her. *I hope I'm right, too, Bridge.*

20

Fear is the parent of cruelty.
—**James Anthony Froude**

Sharon had abandoned the practice of waiting up for her husband to come home. With the progression of his drinking, it was an exercise in futility that more often than not did more harm than good. She awoke early this morning, having barely slept. Her conversations yesterday with the police chief and Bridget caused her to toss and turn all night. She worried about her family, and wondered why this calamity had befallen them. Their family life seemed so comfortable, almost idyllic. What had she done to shatter that once beautiful existence?

Her Catholic faith had always been sound. She attended Mass on Sundays and holy days, went to confession on a regular basis and volunteered at various charitable events throughout the year. Why would God punish her like this? She wrestled with the question all night, but found no suitable answer.

Sharon got up, rinsed her face and combed her hair. Her plan was to fix breakfast for Eric and Bridget. Hopefully, they would all sit down together like they used to before the shooting. She knew she had to bring some sense of normalcy back to her family. After breakfast, she would drive back to Detroit to be with Mark, Erin and Brian.

When she reached the bottom of the stairs, she saw Eric sleeping on the couch, an empty beer can sitting on the coffee table. She went over to him and shook him. "Eric, Eric, time to get up."

"Huh, who . . . what?" Eric opened his eyes, blinking them. "Sharon? Uh, what time is it?"

"It's time for you to get up, take a shower and go to work. The Chief has been looking for you."

Eric sat up. "What, the Chief? What do you mean?"

Sharon looked at her husband. He had a cut on his forehead and blood on his shirt. "Eric, you're hurt, what happened?"

"Uh, I slipped on the snow yesterday. It's nothing to worry about."

"Let me clean it up for you and put a band aid on it."

"No, Sharon, forget it. I'm fine. So why did you call the Chief on me?"

"I didn't call him, he called me at the hospital yesterday and told me you didn't go to work. He said you also missed your appointment with the EAP counselor. Eric, why didn't you tell me you started therapy?"

His head ached, and he closed his eyes as the pain pounded in his head. *The chief called her? Damn.* Embarrassed about his behavior, Eric tried to change the course of the discussion. "Listen, the chief has no business calling you about this matter and prying into my private life. I'm going to take care of it today, don't worry."

Sharon knew she was risking angering her husband. When Eric became angry, all communication ceased. "Honey, he called only because he was worried. He was unable to contact you, that's why he called me. He wasn't prying."

"Yeah, right." Eric spotted the beer can on the table and picked it up. *Empty.* He set it back down.

Sharon promptly picked the can up. "Go ahead and shower, I'll fix some hot coffee and a nice breakfast for you and Bridget."

"Don't bother," he said as he got up from the couch. "Bridget hates me. I don't think she'd enjoy sitting with me at breakfast." Eric went to the fridge and grabbed a beer, popped it open and took a drink.

"Eric, please don't start drinking. You have to go to work."

"Don't lecture me, Sharon." He took another drink. "Work? Do you know what my job is?—I'm a friggin file clerk, not a cop. I sit around the office with a bunch of paper pushers and put things in alphabetical order. Pretty important, huh? Yeah . . . I need to go to work. What a joke."

Wringing her hands, Sharon looked at her husband in disbelief. She had never witnessed this kind of behavior in him before. *What happened to this man? I hardly recognize him.* "Eric, will you at least call the counselor and set up an appointment?"

He brought the can to his lips and took a long drink. "All that counselor wants to do is build a case so the department can fire me.

You don't think I know what's going on here? They're all doing their best to get rid of me."

"Who, Eric?"

"It's pretty plain to see, isn't it? The chief, the shrink and probably Al. Yeah, Al, he wants revenge—wants me to pay for what happened to his son. Like I shot Gene on purpose. Al probably wishes I was dead, probably wouldn't mind killing me himself."

Sharon saw her husband become more agitated. She nervously brought her hands to her throat, uncertain about what to do next. "Eric, stop it, that's crazy and you know it."

"Crazy? I see they have you onboard too, thinking I'm nuts. Well I have news for all of you—I'm not nuts. I see through the whole damn scheme!" Eric finished his beer, crumpled the can and threw it at the wall, just as Bridget walked into the kitchen.

"Dad . . . ?"

"Crap." Eric grabbed his coat and car keys and stomped out the door.

A few seconds later, they saw Eric's truck back out of the driveway. Bridget rushed over to her mother and held on to her like a little child who has seen something frightening.

"Mom, please, I'm scared. What's wrong with Dad? Why is he acting like this?"

As she stroked her daughter's hair, she tried to come up with an answer that would give them both comfort. *I wish I knew . . .*

~~~~~~~~~~

As he drove toward the bar, Eric thought about his situation. *How had things gone downhill so quickly, and why? Can't anyone understand . . . it was an accident . . . I didn't mean to kill him!* He soon arrived at Christy's Tap and parked in the rear. Checking the time on the dashboard clock, he saw it was only six-thirty, too early. Christy's didn't open until seven. Eric slid the seat backward, reclined the back and stretched out his legs. *I'll just take a nap until it opens.*

Two hours later, Officer Joe Gandurski was on patrol in the area of Main Street. He spotted what looked to be Eric Doyle's truck parked in the lot at Christy's. The motor was running. Gandurski could see the exhaust fumes, but the cop didn't see any occupant. As he pulled slowly into the lot and positioned his vehicle behind the

THE YEAR WITHOUT CHRISTMAS

truck, he ran the license plate to ensure it was his fellow officer's vehicle. Seconds later, his computer terminal confirmed the registration.

Gandurski didn't think his colleague was foolish enough to leave his vehicle unattended, but given all that had occurred with the man lately, he thought it might be possible. Granted, the weather was cold, but leaving a vehicle with the motor running was an open invitation to auto thieves. Many of the stolen vehicles in Websterville during the winter months were attributable to this irresponsible practice. The cop got out of his squad car and headed toward the truck. He intended to take the keys, lock the truck and then drive off, teaching Eric a valuable lesson.

As the officer approached the driver's side door and looked inside, he spotted Eric, asleep. *Uh oh, he must have been drinking last night and passed out in his truck.* "Eric . . . Eric," Gandurski said, as he opened the door and shook the man. "C'mon, wake up. Time to go home."

Still in a fog from drinking all day yesterday, the only thing Eric saw was a figure and then he felt someone's hands on his body. *This guy's trying to rob me!* Eric instinctively went for his gun, but the cop saw what was happening. He grabbed Eric's arm, yanked him out of the truck and threw him on the ground. Putting Eric in an arm bar, he held him down and shouted, "Police! Don't move!"

Stunned, and his shoulder stinging from the pressure of the arm bar being applied by Gandurski, Eric submitted. "Hey, what's going on? What the hell are you doing?"

The cop remained firm. "Stay right there, Doyle." Gandurski did a quick search of Eric, looking for any weapons. He found none. Satisfied that Eric wouldn't do anything that might harm him, Gandurski let go of Eric and helped him to his feet.

"What the hell's gotten into you, Doyle? I could've killed you when you went for your gun. What were you thinking?"

Realizing the would-be robber was one of his colleagues, Eric brushed the snow off his jacket and pants. "Hey, I'm sorry. I thought you were somebody trying to rob me. Besides, I don't even have a gun. The chief took it."

The officer stared. "Trying to rob you? I'm in uniform—are you so drunk you can't see that?"

"No, I . . . you see. . . I mean, yeah . . . well, I was sleeping." Eric stammered as he tried to explain the unexplainable. "I know it looked like I was going for my gun, but . . . Listen, I'm not drunk."

"C'mon, Doyle, I can smell the booze on you. If you want to tell stories, I'll just arrest you for DWI."

"DWI? You're crazy. I haven't been drinking; the bar's not even open, and I wasn't driving."

"It's nine o'clock, the bar's been open a couple of hours, and you and I both know you don't have to be driving. As long as the vehicle is running and you're behind the wheel, you can be charged."

"I wasn't drinking; I was sleeping," Erick shot back.

"Look, I'm not gonna argue with you." Gandurski grabbed the radio mic and requested a supervisor. "Get back in your truck, the lieutenant's on his way over here. He can decide what to do with you."

Minutes later, the day shift commander arrived. Eric watched in his rear view mirror as Gandurski got into the supervisor's car. The pair had a conversation for several minutes before the lieutenant got out and walked up to Eric's truck.

Eric rolled down his window. "Hi, Lew. Sorry about the misunderstanding."

"Misunderstanding, huh?" The man gave Eric a stern look, furrowed his brow, and continued. "I'll make this very clear, Officer Doyle. I'm reluctant to do this, but I'm going to take a leap of faith and give you a chance. You have two choices: you can either lock your truck and hand the keys over to me for safekeeping, or you can be arrested for drunk driving. You decide."

Eric looked straight ahead, seeing nothing except his life continuing to spiral downward. He had reached a point he never could have imagined: sitting in the parking lot of a bar, threatened with arrest by his colleagues. "Okay, Lew."

Eric rolled up the window, turned off the engine and got out of his truck. He handed the keys to the supervisor.

"You made the right decision, Doyle. Get in my car, I'll take you home."

"Thanks, but I don't need a ride." Shoulders sagging, Eric turned and headed toward the back door of the bar.

The lieutenant walked back to Gandurski's car. "I've got a bad feeling about this. I hope it doesn't come back to bite us in the butt."

21

There are wounds that never show on the body that are deeper and more hurtful than anything that bleeds.
—**Laurell K. Hamilton**

Sharon and Bridget clung tightly to each other as they watched Eric's truck depart. The mother and daughter were shaken by what they'd just witnessed. Bridget kept her head buried in her mother's neck, something she did as a baby whenever she was frightened. Sharon tried not to cry, but tears rolled down her cheeks and into her child's hair. She wept for Eric, a good husband, good father . . . and now a good grandfather, whose life had suddenly begun to fall apart. She cried for her daughter, distressed that her little girl had to see her father in the throes of alcoholism. And she cried because she felt a profound sadness, knowing her husband and best friend was in trouble and she was powerless to do anything about it.

"Mom?" Bridget asked, finally letting go of Sharon. "I'm afraid for Dad. I've never seen him like this; he's always been someone I've looked up to, a role model for me. He's always been so strong."

Sharon felt weak, probably from the stress of everything that was happening. She sat down at the kitchen table; Bridget did the same. Aware she could no longer shield her daughter from the reality of what was happening in their family, Sharon faced Bridget and told her everything that had happened since the shooting. When she finished, Bridget shook her head.

"I had no idea Dad was having such problems. I mean, I obviously knew about the shooting and all, but I didn't know he wasn't working the street and that he had his gun taken by the department."

"I think that's what bothers him as much as the shooting itself," Sharon replied. "Your father has always prided himself on being the tough cop. He never shied away from anything or anyone on the street. When they put him on administrative duty, he felt he was being punished unjustly, didn't even feel like a cop anymore."

"Is that when he started drinking?"

Sharon sat at the table with her daughter as she explained. "No, it started right away. The day after he shot Gene he started drinking wine. Heavily. He used to have a glass, maybe two, every so often. But after the shooting, I began to notice the empty bottles in the trash."

"Me too, Mom. I was wondering about that."

Sharon nodded. "Yeah, then the wine apparently wasn't enough for him. He started going to the bar downtown and staying until it closed. It seemed he was intent on trying to escape his troubles by staying drunk. I begged him to stop, but he wouldn't listen."

Sharon teared up. "I feel helpless. I love him so much; it hurts to watch him slip deeper and deeper into depression."

Bridget got up from her chair and hugged her mother. "Mom, it's okay. I know you—you would never let anything bad happen to Dad." She kissed her Mom on the cheek. "But didn't you say he was going to therapy?"

Sharon grabbed a napkin from the holder on the table and wiped her eyes. "Apparently he went to one session. They diagnosed him with Post Traumatic Stress Disorder and scheduled him for more visits, but your Dad never showed up."

"I know about PTSD, we studied it in school—it's bad."

"You're right. I worry that your father will get worse if he doesn't follow through with treatment."

Bridget sighed and looked at her mother. "So what can we do?"

Wiping her tears, Sharon could only answer, "At this point, pray."

~~~~~~~~~~

Eric walked through the back door of Christy's Tap. His jaw set tight, he was agitated by what had happened in the parking lot. Gandurski yanking him out of his truck was the ultimate insult. *By now, the whole damn department has probably heard about it.* He took a seat at the bar and ordered a shot, finishing it quickly. It stung as it flowed down his throat, but the rush from the alcohol was as welcome as a warm jacket on a winter day. "Gimme another," he announced, putting a stack of bills on the bar. Having just cashed his paycheck yesterday, money was about the only thing he didn't have to worry about.

Two drinks later, he sat with his head in his hands convinced his life, as he knew it, was over. He thought about Sharon and Bridget, the fear in their eyes as he threw the beer can at the wall and stormed out of the house. *I'll never be able to face them again. And Brian . . . the little guy is battling leukemia and I'm not able to help him. Some grandpa I turned out to be.*

A stranger walked in the front door and sat two stools away from Eric. "Mornin'. Let me have an Irish coffee, and give my friend there another drink.

Minutes later the bartender placed another shot in front of Eric, and gave the man his coffee drink.

Eric grabbed the shot glass, looked over at the man, and raised his glass. "Thanks."

"My pleasure," said the stranger. He leaned over and extended his hand to Eric. "My name's Jim Salens. Yours?"

"Eric."

The stranger took a drink of the Irish coffee. "I'm on my way home to Chicago. Just finished a very nice real estate deal here on the lakefront—a 25 unit high-end condominium complex. We break ground this spring. Thought I'd stop for a quick celebratory drink before I hit the road."

There was something about the man that made Eric comfortable, maybe his upbeat attitude, his generosity, or just the fact that he treated Eric kindly—something which had been missing lately in his life. "Well, congratulations to you, my friend, I'm glad something good has happened to somebody in this town."

"Thank you, sir. I think Websterville is a well-kept secret, in terms of real estate. The potential for future development here is through the roof."

No potential for me; no future.

"Sounds like you're kind of down on your luck," Jim said. "What do you do for a livin'?"

"Uh, I'm kind of between jobs right now."

The man took another drink. "Yeah, I hear that. Jobs are scarce, especially in small towns. Tell you what, there's plenty of jobs in Chicago. Big city—all kinds of opportunity. If you want to catch a ride with me, we can be there in about four or five hours."

Eric quickly ran the man's offer through his mind. *Why not? There's nothing here but trouble ahead for me. My family hates me; they're better off without me. Crap, I don't even have my truck. I'm probably going to lose my job. . .* "When are you planning on leaving?"

"Right now, my car's out front."

Eric grabbed his money off the bar, put his money clip around the bills and stuffed the cash into his jeans. "Let's go. Chicago can't be any worse than here."

A minute later Eric and the stranger headed down Main Street toward the freeway that would take them to Chicago.

~~~~~~~~~~

Eric's supervising lieutenant sat in the chief's office. For the past half hour, the two cops had been discussing what to do about their officer who seemed headed down a disastrous path. "I'd like to see him put on medical leave while this PTSD issue is resolved," the chief said.

"Yeah, I think that's probably the right course of action. I tell you, I didn't recognize Doyle this morning. The man in that truck was not the man I know."

"I'm sure. Speaking of the truck—take somebody with you and go get it. Drive it to Doyle's house and give the keys to his wife."

"Okay, Chief."

The lieutenant stood. "And, Lew, if Doyle is there, don't let on about the whole medical leave thing. It's liable to set him off."

"Yes, Sir." Twenty minutes later, the lieutenant was ringing the door bell at Eric's house.

Sharon sat in the family room, nursing her umpteenth cup of coffee. The incident with Eric this morning had left her too shaken to drive to Detroit, and too upset to eat. Her stomach roiled as if she was on the deck of a boat in turbulent waters. She saw Eric's truck pull into the drive and park. *That's strange. I wonder why he didn't pull into the garage? Well, at least he's home.*

Moments later, Sharon heard the doorbell ring. *Now why would he ring the bell? He must be drunk.* She had been thinking and praying all day about what tact to take with her husband. *Should she be firm, put her foot down and demand he change his ways? Or, should she comfort him and offer to do whatever it takes to get "them" through this crisis. She opted for the latter.*

Walking to the door, she opened it quickly. "Eric . . .? Oh, excuse me, Lieutenant," she said, seeing the man in uniform. "I thought you were my husband. I saw the truck and . . ."

"No, sorry, Ma'am. Is your husband home?"

"Uh, no."

"Do you know where he is?"

Sharon became anxious, wondering what was going on. Her heart raced, while horrible thoughts about her husband crossed her mind. "I don't know where he is. Do you?"

"No, Mrs. Doyle, I don't. I just came by to bring your husband's vehicle home."

"Why?"

"Well, this morning, one of my officers found Eric asleep behind the wheel. We woke him up to make sure everything was okay and he became a bit uncooperative."

As she listened to the man explain about her husband, any hope she had for the problem being resolved quickly faded. "Where was he parked, Lieutenant?"

"Christy's Tap on Main Street."

Sharon nodded. "I see."

"Anyway, it appeared he had been drinking, so I took his keys from him so he couldn't drive his truck and possibly injure himself or others." The officer handed the keys to Sharon. "When I got in the truck to drive it over here, I found these, they must have fallen out of his pockets and landed in between the seats while he was sleeping." He handed Sharon Eric's wallet and cell phone.

"Oh my. Uh, thank you, Sir."

"Listen, Mrs. Doyle, this is as difficult for me as it is for you. Your husband is a good cop, but he's going through a helluva rough patch right now. The Department is willing to help him get through this, and all it takes is for Eric to cooperate. Please, have your husband call Chief Williams when he gets home."

Standing at the door, her hands filled with her husband's belongings, Sharon felt like the officer had just notified her of Eric's death.

The lieutenant took a step backward. "Sorry to have to bother you like this, Ma'am. I just hope your husband comes home before we have to start looking for him. Good night."

Sharon closed the door with her hip, leaned back against it, and slid to the floor. Clutching Eric's wallet while she sat on the cold hard tile, she had a terrible sense that their nightmare was now only just beginning.

~~~~~~~~~~

"Where are we?" Eric asked as he looked out the window of the stranger's car.

"The Windy City, Chi-town, the city that works, if you believe what the politicians say."

Eric sat up straight and stretched his legs. "We got here quick."

The man looked over at his passenger. "Probably seems that way to you; you slept the whole way. Had to turn up the radio to drown out your snoring."

"Sorry."

"Yeah, well, it doesn't matter. We'll be downtown in fifteen minutes and you can explore the big city."

Eric absorbed what the man said. The thought of leaving Websterville seemed like a good idea at the time, but now he wasn't so sure. "So, where are you planning on going? Do you live downtown?"

"Nah, I'm in a neighborhood a little north known as Lincoln Park. Got a great condo just off Halsted Street." The man answered, as he pushed the vehicle past the slower traffic. "Where do you want me to drop you?"

Drop me? How the hell do I know? "Uh, I don't know. I've never been to Chicago."

"Hmm, well . . . tell you what. I'll let you off at the McDonald's on Michigan Avenue near the Water Tower. Great area. Scene of the Chicago Fire that killed a few hundred people back in 1871. That building is about the only thing that didn't burn. Lots of history there—you'll love it."

Eric felt his heart begin to race; beads of sweat appeared on his forehead. He was beginning to regret his decision to leave Websterville, but he didn't want the man to see he was anxious about being dropped off. "Okay, I guess that's about as good a place as any."

"Yeah, great area. Walk a few blocks north and go to Water Tower

Place—big shopping mall—high end stores and plenty of gorgeous women."

Ten minutes later, Eric and the man were crossing over the Chicago River in front of the Wrigley Building. Eric was spellbound. He'd seen photos and movies of Chicago, but seeing the town in person was awesome and sort of intimidating. It was early afternoon and Eric's stomach began to growl as the man's car pulled to the curb in front of the restaurant.

"Well, here we are, my friend. Enjoy your stay. I hope you land a job and make tons of money."

Eric reached out and shook the man's hand. "Thanks, I appreciate the ride."

"Glad to help. Good luck."

Eric closed the car door and the vehicle pulled away, leaving him alone at the curb. He turned around and saw the arches then headed inside. As he approached the counter, he detoured to the restroom. It had been a long ride and he needed a break. Finishing up, he went to the sink to wash his hands, after which he took a good look at himself in the mirror. Bloodshot eyes and a two-day-old beard made him look like he had aged ten years. His stomach reminded him he was hungry, so he exited the men's room and ordered a hamburger and coffee.

A few bites of the burger and a sip of the coffee were all he could take. He needed something else, something he couldn't get here. Getting up from the table, he carried his tray to the trash. "Hey, Man, you ain't tossin' that," said a man wearing two WW II overcoats, a floppy hat and earmuffs. "I'll take it." The man grabbed the tray from Eric's hands, spilling the coffee in the process.

"Damn, now look what you did, fool!"

Startled, Eric shot back, "You're the one who grabbed it."

The man shoved Eric just as two Chicago police officers walked in, about to take their lunch break. "Hey, you two, knock it off," said one of the cops, as each of them separated the would-be combatants. "What's going on here?"

The man appeared to be homeless and instantly accused Eric of instigating the disturbance. "He spilled my coffee for no reason. Man, I want him arrested."

The older of the two cops looked at Eric. "That true?"

"Of course not, I was about to throw my trash away when this guy came up and grabbed the tray, spilling the coffee."

"You a liar!" The man shouted.

"Shut up, Wilson."

"You know this guy?" Eric asked the cop.

"Yeah, he's a regular; always bothering people for food and money. Sleeps on the street, most times by the Radio Shack store during the winter because the manager gives him a cup of coffee when he opens the store every morning. Do you work nearby?"

"No, I'm just visiting."

"Got any I.D.?"

"Sure," Eric replied, reaching into his jacket pocket for his wallet. His heart sank, as he was unable to find it where he normally kept it. He searched every pocket in his coat and jeans. His money clip was where he'd put it, but his wallet was missing. "Officer, I must have misplaced my wallet. Listen, I just got in town a half hour ago. I hitched a ride from a guy . . . uh, Jim was his name . . . maybe Jim Salent or Salens, something like that. He's in real estate."

"Okay, no big deal. If you're new here, just watch yourself around the homeless. Some of them can get aggressive at times and will take advantage of you. If you want to make a report on your wallet, head over to the 18th District on Larrabee Street. The desk sergeant will fill one out so you can get replacement IDs."

"Thanks, Officer." Eric wasn't about to reveal his plight to a fellow officer, and quickly walked out of the restaurant, making his way to the first intersection. Looking down each street, he spotted what he was looking for about a block away: Lucky's Lounge. Several minutes later, a bottle of beer in hand, Eric felt his anxiety dissipating.

22

The activity of worrying keeps you immobilized.
   —Wayne Dyer

Tossing and turning most of the night, Sharon decided it was useless to stay in bed. There was no way she would be able to sleep. Eric had not come home. A first. Even when he was working the midnight shift, he always came home right after work. That is, until "the shooting." That was the beginning, when she began to lose her soul mate to another lover—alcohol.

She climbed out of bed, put on a robe and walked over to the bedroom window. A light cover of snow sparkled in the glow of the streetlights. Such a beautiful sight to behold—virgin snow—no tire tracks or footprints to mar the surreal image. The Currier & Ives-like scene would remain this way for at least another hour or so, not many people are up at 4:30 in the morning. Only those who are ill or anxious.

Sharon was both. Her head throbbed, and the pain made it feel like her eyes were being pushed out of their sockets. The night had not been kind to her; it took an eternity for the clock to advance one minute. After staring at the red numerals for hours, she had suffered enough. She took one more look out the window. As much as she wanted to see her husband's footprints coming toward their home, it was not to be.

Walking by her daughter's room, she peeked inside the cracked door. Bridget was still asleep. The past weeks had been particularly hard on the girl. Her father's slow decline had a huge impact on Bridget. The two had been close, they shared a tight bond. After all, she was still the baby of the family. Her dad had spoiled and protected her, and Bridget knew it. She took full advantage of her exalted status every chance she could. The symbiosis was touching to observe, the love and respect they showed each other did not go unnoticed by Bridget's girlfriends. They envied what Bridget shared with her father. Even Bridget's brother, Mark, seemed a bit jealous, making an occasional remark about how Bridget could do no wrong while Dad was around.

While she crept softly down the stairs to the kitchen, she passed the empty space where Eric had accidently knocked a photo off the wall after coming home drunk. *I shouldn't have yelled at him.* They had yet to replace the frame; the picture was of Sharon and Eric holding their newborn grandson, Brian. *Oh, Lord, please heal our little boy.* Just thinking of Brian in the Detroit hospital caused her to tear up. *And now Eric, missing . . . ?*

She turned on the coffee pot and began to make a few cups for herself. *Can't sleep anyway, caffeine will hopefully soothe my nerves.* While the coffee began to brew, she sat at the kitchen table staring out the window, trying to get a grip on all that was going on around her. A seriously ill grandchild, a damaged marriage, a husband at the lowest point in his life, and a daughter whose mental health and self confidence was suffering. *How? Why?*

Sharon folded her arms on the table in front of her and laid her head down. A profound sense of loneliness enveloped her like a cocoon, rendering her helpless. Alone. She cried, soft sobs producing tears that emanated deep within her soul. *I need help, God. Please, don't abandon me. Tell me what to do.*

"Mom?"

The mother looked up, and through her tears she saw her daughter.

"Mom, what's wrong? Why are you up, and why are you crying?" The girl walked over to where her mother sat.

"Oh, Bridget."

The girl bent over and hugged her mother. "Mom, you're scaring me; what's wrong? Is it Dad? Where is he?"

She held her little girl and tried to wipe her own tears at the same time. Sharon was torn between letting her daughter comfort her, and trying to be strong and not allowing the girl to see how scared she was. "Bridge, I don't know where your father is. He didn't come home." She went on to explain about the police finding Eric's wallet

THE YEAR WITHOUT CHRISTMAS

and cell phone in his truck.

Dropping to one knee, Bridget let go of her mom, but Sharon took one of her daughter's hands in her own. "So what do we do?" The girl asked. "We can't even try to call him. Mom, I'm really scared, should we contact the police?"

"I'm not sure, honey. I think we need to give it another day at least. If he's not home by tonight, I'll call the Chief."

Sharon saw her daughter's eyes begin to moisten. "I know this is a lot for you to handle, sweetheart, but we'll get through it." She grabbed the girl, pulled her head to her bosom, and began stroking the girl's hair. "I'm going to drive to the hospital in Detroit today to be with Mark, Erin and Brian. Your brother needs me, and I need him, especially now. Can you get to school on your own?"

"I don't want to go to school today, Mom. I can't possibly concentrate on anything. Can I stay home? Please?"

"I guess so. Besides, it will be good for you to be here in case your father shows up. You can call me if he does."

Although mother and daughter now had plans for the day, they nevertheless felt nothing would distract them from worrying about Eric. *Where was he?*

~~~~~~~~~~

The noise roused him from his drunken stupor. Eric opened his eyes and looked at a graying, cracked plaster ceiling with a damaged light fixture above him that threatened to drop at any minute. The fixture had two bulbs, one missing, the other lit. He blinked his eyes a few times, trying to clear his vision, but also wondering where he was. He knew he wasn't home. Daylight streamed through smoke stained sheers, mockingly serving as curtains across the motel window. Throwing the blanket off, Eric realized he was fully dressed, including his shoes.

He sat up and hung his feet over the edge of the bed. A familiar pain vibrated in his forehead, and as he tried to rub it away, he heard it again. The noise. *What the . . .?* Eric stood and walked over to the window and pulled the decrepit yellow-tinged curtains aside. He saw a huge metal structure looming overhead, one that ran the length of the entire street and then curved off in another direction at the next intersection. A few minutes later, he heard and saw one of the elevated commuter trains passing by, making a screeching, grinding groan as it slowed to make the turn on the Lego-like train tracks.

Satisfied he knew the source of the awful sound, Eric tried to regain his bearings. *Where am I?* He looked around the tiny room, which consisted of a double bed, a nightstand and lamp, a portable TV and a tiny alcove containing a sink. Adjacent to the sink was a room barely large enough to accommodate a tub and toilet.

He spotted a notice on the back of the door to his room; he walked over, read the information card and discovered he was staying at The Destination Motel on Wells Street. Scratching his head, he tried to recall how he had ended up in the bare bones flophouse, but was unable to find an answer. He did recall drinking at Lucky's Lounge where he'd met two guys who said they worked for the city as garbage men. They had just finished their shift and stopped for a drink after work. *Maybe they gave me a ride?*

It didn't matter. Eric needed to find out where he was. About to open the door, he quickly thought about something. Money. Did he still have his cash? He instantly went into his pocket and felt the money clip. Breathing a sigh of relief, he took the bills from the clip and counted them—three hundred and seventeen dollars. He recalled that when he cashed his check in Michigan a couple of days ago, he kept five hundred cash. *How had he spent almost two hundred dollars?*

Eric turned the doorknob and walked out of the motel room into a gray landscape, dotted with piles of slushy snow lining the sidewalk like parade watchers. A light yet chilly wind caused his vaporized breath to lead the way as he walked down the street, trying to determine what part of the city he was in. Stopping at the first intersection he came to, Eric looked around. He saw the tall buildings of the downtown area off to his left, and what looked to be a park-like area and the lake off to the far right. As much as he needed to discover where things were in this town, his first priority was coffee and food.

Looking down the block he saw someone leave a store front with a Styrofoam cup in hand. *That's where I need to be.* It took only a minute to reach what turned out to be a place simply named Sophie's. Eric took a seat at the counter. The establishment had a vintage look and feel. Counter tops were Formica, and the red-topped swivel stools attached to the floor spun a full 360 degrees.

Most of the tile surrounding the seats had worn through to the floorboards, reflecting years of customers. Ralph's Classic Diner, the only old-time eatery still open in Websterville, immediately came to Eric's mind.

A large woman, with thinning graying hair, turned from the skillet she was focused on and called out to Eric. "Coffee?"

"Yes, Ma'am."

She grabbed a white mug off the rack on the wall above her head and filled the cup to the brim. Without spilling a drop, she set the mug in front of Eric, and then went back to her skillet. "Cream and sugar's right in front of ya, Darlin'. You gonna eat or just stay warm for a bit?"

"I'll do both."

"Fine. Ain't got no menus here. You just tell Sophie what you want and I'll get close to it as I can." The woman emptied what she had been cooking onto a plate and set it in front of a scraggily looking man seated at one of three booths along the wall. "Here ya go, Harold. Now you make sure you eat every last bite, else ways I ain't feedin' you no more free food."

Eric took a look at the plate in front of the man in the booth. "Sophie, I'll have what Harold's having."

"Good choice, Darlin', good choice." The woman broke two eggs in a bowl, beat them, and then dropped a spoonful of butter on the grill before she poured the eggs on top. She added three strips of bacon next to the bubbling mixture before dropping two pieces of bread in the old, two-slice toaster.

"You new here, ain't ya?"

He grabbed the coffee mug and took sip of the steaming brew. "Yeah, just got here yesterday."

"Thought so. You got that look—like you don't know where you at. But you don't look too shabby; hope you got money to pay your bill."

"Yeah, I can pay."

The woman flipped over the bacon, continued to scramble the eggs with one hand and then removed the toast from the toaster. "Good. I get folks like Harold in here, don't have no money, but I ain't got the heart to turn 'em away. Momma taught me years ago, she said, "Sophie, the good Lord done give you a lot. Long as he keep givin' to you, you got to share whatever you got."

"Your momma was a wise woman," Eric said, as he looked over at Harold. The man was in his own world, and didn't seem to know or care that Eric and the woman were talking about him.

"Harold don't got no home. Lives on the street like lots o' other folks. Times is tough, ain't no jobs like they used to be. So when I get folks down on their luck like Harold, I take care of 'em."

Sophie buttered the two slices of toast, set them on the plate with the eggs and bacon, and then brought them to Eric. "Here ya go, Darlin."

"Thanks, you're a good woman." He took a bite of the eggs and bacon, and said, "And a good cook."

"Thanks. So what you gonna do here in Chicawga? You fixin' to look for work?"

"I don't know." Eric replied between mouthfuls of food. He was beginning to feel good again with the coffee and food.

"Well, winter's here now, and it's only gonna get worse. Don't know if you runnin' from the law or some other kinda trouble, but you better have some kinda plan, else ways you gonna wind up like Harold—livin' on the street. You don't want none o' that."

Finishing another strip of bacon, Eric glanced over at Harold." Yeah, you're right. I don't want none of that."

23

The strength of a family, like the strength of an army, is in its loyalty to each other.
—**Mario Puzo**

"Mom, is that you?" Bridget called out from the next room.

"Yes, Bridge." Sharon locked the side door to the kitchen, looked through the window and pushed the garage door remote, staring as Eric's truck disappeared while the door slowly closed. Yesterday she took his truck to the car wash and had it cleaned inside and out, thinking that he'd be surprised when he came home and found it clean and shiny. *When he came home.*

It had been a week since she'd seen her husband. Despite her daily trips around town, driving slowly and methodically up and down the business district looking for him, there was still no sign of Eric. What made matters worse, was driving down Main Street with its Christmas lights and stores brimming with presents.

As Sharon hung her coat and keys near the door, Bridget walked in. "Anything?"

The question, and its answer, "No," was quickly becoming routine.

"Have you eaten yet?"

"Yeah, Grandpa was here and made spaghetti, but the sauce was from a jar. Not nearly as good as yours, Mom."

Walking to the refrigerator, Sharon opened the door. "Did you save any for me?" She asked as she rummaged through the contents.

"There's a bunch left. You know Grandpa, he thinks he's cooking for an army."

Sharon pulled out the covered dish, put a helping in a bowl, placed the bowl in the microwave and started warming it up. "So what did you do today? How was school?"

Bridget sat at the kitchen table while her mother prepared her meal. "Actually, I left school a little early. Kids were peppering me with questions about the article in the paper this morning about Dad."

"What? What article?"

Bridget grabbed the paper lying on the table, opened it to the section with the story, and handed it to her mother. "It's not much, just about Dad being missing and all, but my friends wanted to talk about it all day. I got tired of it and called Grampa to pick me up."

Sharon read the one-paragraph article:

Police advised that one of their officers, Eric Doyle, has been reported missing by his family. Foul play is not suspected at this time. Just before Thanksgiving, Officer Doyle was involved in a fatal shooting in which his partner's son, Gene Giordano, was killed during a break-in. The shooting was ruled justifiable homicide. According to Websterville Police, Officer Doyle has been on administrative leave. They declined to comment any further. Anyone with information regarding the police officer's whereabouts should contact the police department immediately.

"Great," Sharon sighed. She heard the microwave buzz and got up to retrieve her supper.

"I know. Gramps was ticked off after he read it. I overheard him on his phone arguing with the police department. I'm pretty sure it was the Chief he was talking to. Anyway, he called them a bunch of amateurs who couldn't find a two-headed dog in a room full of cats. He was so mad he was turning red."

"That's not good. His blood pressure's always been high." *That's all I need is for Eric's dad to have a stroke.*

She placed her bowl of spaghetti on the table and began to eat.

"Did you go to Mark's house today? How's Brian doing?"

Sharon swallowed a forkful of pasta and looked at her daughter. "He's sick from the chemo but at least he's home for a while. I think Mark and Erin are totally wiped out from being at the hospital every day. Hopefully, being home will bring back some sense of normalcy in their lives. And I sure won't miss driving to and from Detroit each day."

"Mom?"

"What, sweetheart?"

"Tomorrow is Saturday, and I know you said we were going to put up the Christmas tree and decorate the house, but . . ."

The woman laid her fork on the table and stared into her bowl of food.

"Mom?"

"Listen, Honey. I'm not in the Christmas spirit anymore than you are, but I've thought about this and I think we need to do things like we've always done. That includes decorating our house for Christmas."

"But Dad's not here! How are things normal, and what is there to celebrate?"

"You're right. Your father isn't here at this moment, but I know he will be. I just don't know when that will happen, but when it does we will celebrate Christmas as usual—whether that's in a few days, or in a few months—we'll be ready to celebrate."

Her appetite gone, Sharon got up and dumped the rest of her meal in the trash. *I'll wait for Christmas, Eric. I'll wait for you."*

~~~~~~~~~~

"Stop, or I'll shoot!" Eric pointed his weapon at the man. It was dark, and a strange cloud enveloped everything, making it difficult to see clearly. As Eric began to take up the slack on the trigger of his gun, his partner, Gene Giordano, came into view.

"Noooo . . .!" Giordano shouted and pointed his own weapon at Eric. From the corner of his eye, Eric watched as the suspect was no longer a man, but rather a young boy whom Eric recognized as Giordano's son, Gene. His partner's gun exploded, the muzzle flash blinding Eric and the report of the shot sending a deafening roar toward him.

Sweating, and breathing rapidly, Eric sat up in bed. *Oh, God.* He looked around, and for a moment he had no idea where he was. Then he heard the noise of the El train outside the front door of the cheap motel where he had been staying. He lay back down, controlling his breathing and getting his bearings. The dream, which had begun just a couple of days after the shooting, haunted him. He hadn't told anyone about it, neither Sharon nor the counselor. The dream always ended the same way: his old partner trying to prevent Eric from shooting the suspect, who always turned out to be Gene's son. Only in the dream, little Geno had regressed back to grade-school-age.

Terrifying.

Eric checked his watch. Six o'clock. He threw his legs over the side of the bed and saw an almost empty bottle of wine on the nightstand. With his money running short, he could no longer afford to sit in a bar and drink all day. Buying wine by the bottle was his new strategy. It allowed him to stay warm and drink in his room. The only problem was that even his motel room, as shabby and dirty as it was, cost money. He checked his money clip and counted the bills—almost two hundred dollars left.

The bottle of wine beckoned. He grabbed it and finished the remainder in one swallow, and then walked over to the window. The first signs of life began to emerge on the street. Two distinct groups of people moved about, each tolerant of the other while navigating the city sidewalks. The workers rushed forward, heads down and bundled against the cold Chicago wind, as they headed off to work.

The homeless began their daily ritual of scavenging through trash put out at the curb by shop owners and apartment dwellers. It was a sketch acted out daily with the same characters and same ending. The only variation to this daily saga was whether the homeless were able to get to the trash before the Department of Sanitation garbage trucks could scoop up the potential treasures of discarded food and aluminum cans. The cans were cashed in later at the recycler, thus providing much-needed funds for the daily dose of alcohol and maybe a bit of food.

Eric turned from the window. He had a decision to make. He had to decide how he was going to survive the winter. His money would only last a week or two at most, particularly, if he continued to stay at the motel. And while he wasn't eating three meals per day, he was spending money on alcohol.

Furthermore, how would he tend to his own hygiene? He hadn't shaved since he left home, and had only showered once. The only clothes he had were the ones he was wearing. His toiletries consisted of a cheap tooth brush and a bar of soap he'd purchased at the local drug store. If he gave up his motel room, where would he stay and how would he take care of himself?

He pulled on his pants and shoes, put on his coat, and stepped out into the single digit air. *Hat and gloves, today.* He'd find a resale shop and get what he needed to stay warm. In the meantime, he headed toward Sophie's. Eric had a feeling that if it he ran out of money, Harold, the homeless guy might have some idea about what to do.

24

Love is staying up all night with a sick child...
—David Frost

"Where's Papa? I want Papa."

"I know you do, Son, but Papa's at work." Four-year-old Brian was agitated. The chemo treatments and medication for his leukemia made sleep difficult for the little boy. He was often fatigued and restless. The flu-like symptoms that initially caused Mark and Erin to investigate his illness persisted. The constant runny nose and chills were not only uncomfortable, but aggravating to Brian as well.

"Why can't we go see Papa?"

"Sweetheart, we can go visit Nana and Bridget today," answered Erin, "but Papa won't be there."

"I want Papa," the boy persisted and began to sob.

Erin scooped the little guy up in her arms and sat on the couch, cradling and soothing him as she'd done since Brian was an infant. "I know, Baby, I know." As she sang the boy's favorite lullaby, Hush, Little Baby, she tried to control her own tears. *Where was her father-in-law? Didn't he realize they needed him now more than ever?* Brian and Eric had developed a special bond. It was not unusual for the proud grandparents to suggest they babysit so Mark and Erin could go shopping or out for dinner. They enjoyed caring for their only grandchild, and Eric had even turned his office into a bedroom/toy room for his little "Bri-Bri."

Minutes later, Mark joined his wife on the couch as their son napped in his mother's arms. "Thank God he's asleep."

Erin nodded. "These long nights are wearing me out, Mark. I don't know how much more I can take. If he doesn't start sleeping through the night soon, I'm going to be a wreck."

Mark stroked his wife's hair. "I know, Honey. I'm as worn out as you are. As much as I hate to, I think I'm going to ask the doctor for something we can give Brian to help him sleep."

"I don't know, Mark. I don't want to give him any more medication than we have to, but the two of us are becoming like zombies. I think it would help matters if we knew what was going on with your father."

Sighing, Mark stood up and walked to the window. "I know he's out there somewhere, and I know he must need help. Dad's always been there for us, Baby, particularly for Brian. This isn't like him at all, not to be helping us in our time of need."

He turned and walked back to where his wife and son were sitting. "Mom is trying to stay strong through it all, but I know that Brian's illness and Dad's disappearance are taking their toll on her. Bridget told me that Mom drives around town every day looking for him." As he spoke, his eyes filled with tears. "I don't want anything to happen to her, but I don't know what to do. The stress can't be good for her."

Now it was her turn to reassure her husband. Erin patted the cushion next to her, signaling for Mark to sit down. When he did, she pulled his face close with her free hand and kissed him. "Sweetheart, this is a tough time for us, but I know in my heart that we're going to be okay. Brian's going to be okay. As far as your Dad is concerned, I know one thing is certain. No matter what demons he's facing, and regardless of where he is, he will come back to us. He loves us; he loves your Mom. It may take a while, but Dad will eventually return. In the meantime we just have to continue to trust that God will protect him and get him through this storm."

He held his wife's hand. "I hope you're right."

~~~~~~~~~~

Sharon knocked on the door of the suite the Chief had directed her to and let herself in. After she entered the office, a woman greeted her. "Hi, I'm Dr. Sally Lake," she said, extending her hand." You must be Mrs. Doyle."

The two women shook hands. "Please, sit down." The woman directed Sharon to one of several chairs arranged around a coffee table. "I have coffee or tea, whichever you'd prefer."

"Coffee, please." Sharon removed her coat and took a seat.

"Cream and sugar?"

"Just black, thank you."

The therapist set the coffee on the table in front of where Sharon was seated, and then poured a cup of tea for herself. Choosing a chair to the side of Sharon, Dr. Lake sat down and sipped her drink. "I'm so glad you accepted the Chief's offer. In cases like your husband's shooting, we recognize that the event is not only traumatic to the officer involved, but to his family as well."

Sharon nodded, and picked up her coffee.

"The Websterville Police Department, under Chief Williams' leadership, is on the cutting edge of treating officers involved in critical incidents. The department's Employee Assistance Program is one that we as practioners think is key in healing individuals who have undergone emotional upheaval. Your husband, Eric, is in dire need of this type of therapy."

Placing her coffee back on the table, Sharon responded. "I know that, Doctor. I knew he needed help soon after he was involved in that shooting. I only wish he would not have been so stubborn." Sharon paused and looked down at the floor. "My husband has always prided himself on being strong—someone who can handle anything thrown his way. He would be the last person to ask for help."

Dr. Lake smiled. "I know. I sensed as much as soon as I met Eric. He's a proud man, but emotionally, he's not as strong as he thinks he is. After my evaluation at our first and only meeting, in fact, even before he completed the questionnaire, I knew he was suffering from PTSD."

"You did?"

"Yes. Eric looked agitated when he walked in. To say he was reluctant to visit with me would be an understatement. He certainly wasn't very happy when I asked him to fill out a questionnaire associated with the Clinician Administered PTSD Scale."

Sharon sat back in her chair. "What's that?"

"We call it CAPS for short. It's a standard measuring device used to determine if someone is suffering from PTSD, and how intense the symptoms are. It also asks about other symptoms that commonly occur with PTSD. After a brief interview, the patient is asked to fill out a PTSD checklist, kind of a self-reporting tool. The list is then scored, that number gives the therapist a number by which we measure the amount of stress the person has."

"And my husband's score?"

"Without revealing the number, I will tell you that Eric is suffering from a high degree of stress as a result of the incident."

Sitting quietly, Sharon nursed her coffee. *No big surprise here. I could have told you Eric was stressed out without any fancy test.*

Breaking the silence, Dr. Lake began. "Anyway, the reason the Chief contacted you is because PTSD affects the family in many ways. Moreover, even though I'm not treating Eric, the department's program covers the treatment of the family. Participation is entirely voluntary. If you'd like our help, and I hope you'll say you do, I'd like to begin working with both you and your daughter."

As she recalled her own depression, and that of Bridget's as well, she knew it was critical they get any help available to them. She was at a point where she knew if she continued down the same road, one that had her up half the night worrying, she would be a mess when Eric finally came home. More importantly, she'd be of no help to Mark, Erin and Brian, who needed her now.

"I think I'd like to try it, but let me ask my daughter how she feels about it."

"Good, I think you're making the right decision. Do you sense that your daughter, is having problems?"

Nodding, Sharon answered. "Yes, maybe more so than I am."

"Okay. That's not unusual, but treatment needs to commence immediately to avoid future problems."

Sharon sat forward. "Like what?"

"Things such as depression, anger, guilt, even health problems. Family members may begin to drink excessively or use drugs as they try to cope with the new family paradigm."

Thinking about her daughter's decreased eating and increased running, Sharon asked, "What about exercise, I mean, like excessive exercise, running morning and night, and then only eating enough to get by?"

"Is that what Bridget's been doing?"

"Yes. She's out the door early in the morning, and then out again at night. Most days she runs for at least an hour or more each time she exercises. Plus, she's hardly eating anything."

Dr. Lake picked up her appointment book and paged through it to the following week. "I have an appointment available Friday of next week. Can you bring Bridget in after school?"

"I'll talk with her and see if she's willing to come for treatment."

"Great. Now, in the time we have left today let's talk about your relationship with your husband."

~~~~~~~~~~

The hour was up and Sharon walked to her car in the parking lot and got inside. She started the engine. While it warmed up and the heater took the chill out of the air, she wondered if talking about Eric being missing was worthwhile or not. Would the sessions with the therapist help or hurt? While there was no question Eric was constantly on her mind, was it a waste of time to talk to a stranger about her feelings?

She was hurt. Who wouldn't be? She cried herself to sleep at night. She was angry and depressed and . . . and . . . she just wanted Eric to come home. *Why Eric, why?* She banged her hands on the steering wheel, and then grabbed it as tight as she could, trying to rid herself of the frustration building inside of her.

Finally, moments later, Sharon put the car in gear and headed toward home. Before she turned down her street, she changed her mind and did what she'd been doing since Eric left. She systematically began searching the streets for her husband. *Where are you Eric?*

25

People who are homeless are not social inadequates. They are people without homes.
—**Sheila McKechnie**

Eric's head hurt. Waking up this morning, he saw two empty wine bottles in his room. He remembered drinking one bottle, but not the other. Right now he needed something, probably coffee. He looked out the window of his motel room. *Snow. Damn.*

He dragged himself over to the bathroom sink, ran some water and rinsed his face. Looking in the mirror, he was surprised to see his ever-burgeoning beard had streaks of gray in it. He looked haggard, unhealthy, the product of weeks of heavy drinking and poor nutrition. If he was surprised at his appearance, he imagined his family and friends would be shocked.

Family. Eric leaned on his hands at the bathroom sink and hung his head in despair. *I love them so much, but I can't bear for them to see me like this. It's better this way.* He pulled on his clothes and walked out into the snow. As the white flakes fell gently on his face, he remembered winters in Websterville. *Bri-Bri . . .* His little grandson had taken to calling his Papa whenever snow began to fall. "Papa, can we go bogginin?" The little guy couldn't pronounce the word—toboggan, but he loved it when Eric took him down the big hill near their house. *Oh, God, please heal him.*

As Eric walked past the motel office, the clerk was sweeping snow away from the office door. "Hey," he called to Eric, "You stayin' another week? Money's due today."

"Uh, I'll be back in a bit and talk with you then."

Crap. With less than $200 left in his pocket, Eric needed to make a decision about where he was going to spend his nights. He pulled the hat and gloves he had bought yesterday at the thrift shop from his coat pocket and headed toward Sophie's. Maybe Harold will have some ideas.

~~~~~~~~~~

"Mrs. Doyle, I promise you we're doing all we can to locate your husband. We want to find him as much as you do."

Sharon chewed on her thumbnail while she listened to the police chief.

"We have missing person bulletins distributed state-wide, and we've contacted the FBI as well."

"What about the bar?"Sharon asked. "What did the bartender say about the guy Eric was drinking with?"

"There's nothing new there. The man came in for one drink, struck up a conversation with your husband, and they both left shortly thereafter."

Sharon walked over by the window and looked out at the front window. A beautiful snowfall had left the front yard covered in a sparkling down blanket. Eric would normally be out shoveling the front walk right now. Instead, he was missing. Gone.

"You mean to tell me that's it, there's nothing else—no car or license plate—nothing?"

"Mrs. Doyle, please. I personally spoke with the bartender. Other than a physical description of the man, which I've also included in the missing person bulletin as a person of interest, the bartender has no other information. He didn't follow them out of the bar. Why would he?"

Shaking her head, Sharon knew the chief was right but she was frustrated over the lack of information. It seemed she was doing more with her daily searches than the police.

"Mrs. Doyle, the reason I called is . . . and I know this is unpleasant, but I have to tell you anyway, technically, Eric's status is absent without leave. Being AWOL presents a problem in that the city can't justify paying Eric's salary when he's not officially working."

The impact of what the chief had just told her struck her like a Mack truck. She wasn't expecting a complication like this, one that would change the family dynamic more than it had already changed.

"What are you saying, Chief?"

"Just that the city attorney informed me yesterday that unless Eric returns to duty by the end of December, the city is no longer obligated to pay him a salary."

Oh my god, how will we live? A million thoughts raced through Sharon's mind at once, making her dizzy. She sat down on the sofa near the window. *The house payment and other bills . . . what will I do?*

"Mrs. Doyle? Mrs. Doyle, are you there?"

"Uh, yes, I'm here. Chief, this can't be right. Eric's missing, it's not his fault. It's all because of the shooting. Chief, he's sick, he doesn't know what he's doing. He's . . ." Sharon began shaking, and tears flowed, filled with fear and uncertainty, moistening her blouse as she sat listening to words that were about to change her life.

"I'm sorry, Mrs. Doyle. It's out of my hands."

Sharon closed the phone and held it to her breast. She shut her eyes, as if to block out the enormity of what the police chief had just told her. *How would they survive? What would she do?*

Awash in despair, she heard a voice.

"Mom? What is it? What's wrong?"

Oh, God . . .

~~~~~~~~~~

Eric stepped inside Sophie's and kicked the snow off his shoes, pulled off his hat and gloves, and made his way to the counter. Sophie was her usual self, cooking orders for a handful of customers and giving each of them advice on how to live their lives. She set an order of eggs in front of a portly, retired type a couple seats away from where Eric sat. "Here you go, Sunshine, sunny side up and white toast."

"Thanks, Sophie." The man kept his head down and immediately grabbed a slice of toast and began dabbing it into the egg yolk."

The woman looked over at Eric. "You back . . . good. Didn't think you was gonna stay 'round here. Black coffee, right?"

Eric nodded.

"You had old Harold's breakfast last time. You want that again?"

His stomach was churning and his head ached. "Nah. I think I'll just have some toast."

"Okay, Darlin'." Sophie grabbed two slices from the open loaf on the shelf above the toaster and popped them in.

Eric noticed that Harold was missing this morning. "Uh, Sophie?"

"What you need? Toast is almost ready."

"Was Harold here today?"

"No, not today. Won't be here for a few more days. He come in maybe once a week, 'specially when he really hungry. Harold's a good man, don't take advantage of my kindness."

A few moments later, Eric watched as Sophie dipped a spreader into a tub of butter, just as Eric's bread popped up in the toaster. She slathered both pieces with a greasy glob, set the toast on a plate, and set it in front of Eric. "That gonna do you good, get rid o' that bangin' in your head." *She knows me.*

Picking up a piece of the warm food, Eric nodded and took a bite. "You a mind reader, Sophie?"

"No, Darlin', but I been feedin' your kind all my life. I know you don't even feel like eatin', but know you got to, else wise that booze gonna eat you up inside."

Your kind . . . He took a couple of bites and finished half his coffee. Feeling a little better, his headache slowly subsiding, he wanted to find out if Sophie knew where Harold was. "Hey, Sophie," he called out to her as she began to collect some dirty dishes. "Where can I find Harold?"

"Harold? That's easy. You take a lef out the door and walk a couple o' blocks to where the El train start to turn. Make a right and go to the first vacant lot—that's Harold."

Eric frowned. "Harold lives in a vacant lot?"

"He hang there most times. Got him some brothers hangs wid him. Winter time and all, they be standing around a trash can tryin' to stay warm."

"Okay. Thanks, Sophie. What do I owe you?"

"I know you gotta be runnin' low, but if you got two bucks we square."

He left two singles on the counter and put his coat and gloves back on. As he headed toward the door, he waved. "See you later."

Sophie smiled a big smile. " I hope you will, Darlin', I hope you will."

26

It is in the shelter of each other that the people live.
—**Irish proverb**

Eric saw a group of men standing near a barrel. Sparks flew like fireworks as one of the men used a long stick to stir and adjust the contents, making them easier for the fire to digest, and thus providing more heat. He spotted Harold, a diminutive man compared to the other three, and approached him. As Eric neared them, he felt the fire's welcoming warmth, and hoped someone invading the men's territory wouldn't threaten the group of strangers.

"Harold," Eric called out to the man. "Sophie said you'd be here."

Harold pulled back the hood on his jacket and looked closely at Eric. "Can't say I know you. How do you know me, and more importantly, what do you want?"

"Uh . . . " Eric was somewhat surprised by the man's articulate reply. The last time he saw Harold, the homeless man sat in a booth in Sophie's Restaurant, staring transfixed at the wall. "I don't really know you, I mean, we haven't actually met. I saw you one morning at Sophie's; she told me your name."

"Okay, that explains how you know my name. Now, what do you want?"

"Well, I guess I don't really know what I want, Harold. To tell you the truth, I guess I'm trying to find out how folks like you survive day-to-day on the streets."

"Are you some kind of social worker or reporter?" Harold asked, as he stepped closer to the fire and held his hands out, palms facing the warmth. "If you are, I'm not interested in what you may be selling." The three other men stood mute, content to allow Harold to be their spokesman.

"No, nothing like that. I'm . . . actually . . . well, I guess I'm in the same boat as all of you."

"What boat would that be, Mister, whoever you are?"

"Oh, sorry, my name's Eric. I guess I'm homeless."

The man who had earlier stirred the fire spoke up. "Man, you runnin' a game on us? You look too new to me."

"New?" Eric tried to explain. "I guess I'm new, I mean, I haven't been homeless but for a few days or so. I ran low on money, so I can't stay at the motel any longer. That's why I wanted to talk with you, Harold, to get an idea of how to survive on the streets."

Harold rubbed his hands together and then put them back in his pants pockets. "There is no manual on how to survive this kind of life, Eric, so if that's what you're looking for, you're out of luck. I don't know anyone who chooses to be homeless. Those of us who are in this situation, are here because life dealt us a hand we couldn't win."

"Makes sense." Eric moved closer to the fire and mimicked how the others stood in relation to the barrel. He quickly discovered why they all faced him—the wind was blowing in Eric's face, making it feel colder than it actually was. They had their backs to the wind, saving the effect of the bitter chill on exposed skin. "I guess I qualify, if being dealt a losing hand is the sole criterion."

The group eyed him suspiciously. "You don't talk like you're beaten down," Harold interjected. "You sound educated, and your clothing tells me you're probably upper middle class."

Eric laughed. "That's funny. I was thinking the same about you just now. You sound well educated. You're not the typical homeless person."

"Typical? Is there a certain trait or traits that allow you to identify the homeless?" Harold sounded agitated, his voice rising.

"No, don't get me wrong. I guess when I think about homeless people I picture them dressed in rags and layers of clothing, unkempt, and maybe pushing a shopping cart with all their belongings."

The fire-stirrer spoke up. "Look over there," he said, pointing to a shopping cart parked in an alcove of the building next to the vacant lot. "That's mine."

Harold unzipped his jacket to reveal another jacket underneath. He pointed to himself and said, "The layered look." Bending over, he picked up a couple of pieces of cardboard, folded them up, and then tossed them in the fire. In seconds, the group was rewarded with more heat. "You have a lot to learn about living on the street, Eric. You're not from here, are you?"

Eric hesitated. He didn't want anyone to know who he really was or where he was from. "No."

"But you're from the Midwest, I can tell from your accent."

"Accent?"

"Yes, Midwesterners pronounce their consonants very hard, and most Midwesterners don't realize they have an accent until they travel to the Deep South or East Coast. If I had to guess, I'd say you are from Michigan. The accent there is a bit softer than here in Chicago."

Eric was stunned. The man seemed psychic. "I'm sorry, Harold, but you seem too well educated to be homeless."

"He's a teacher," said the fire-stirrer, as he resumed his barrel duties. "We call 'im professor."

"Was a teacher, Jackson." Harold quickly added.

"Yeah, he was." Jackson took his stick out of the barrel and set it down by his feet. "Professor taught right here at the university. He's a smart man."

Eric shook his head in disbelief.

A ray of light broke through the gray cloud cover and bathed the empty lot in sunshine. Harold turned his face upward toward the sun. "Take advantage of the warmth of the sun whenever you can, my friend. Chicago winters are cold and bleak, sunlight is an infrequent but welcome guest."

"Harold, er, Professor, can I hang out with all of you today?"

Harold laughed, which caused the others to join in. "Yeah, sure, I don't have anything on my calendar today," he said, sarcastically. "Besides, I think you need a reality check if you're going to make it alive through the winter. But before we waste any more daylight, we need to get a fresh supply of materials for the fire." He looked at the others. "See you back here in a bit. Eric, you come with me. Lesson number one: never wait till you're cold before you go looking for things to burn."

~~~~~~~~~~

Al Giordano looked up from cooking the pasta as his wife, Sandy, came in through the garage door. "Hi."

Sandy flipped off her boots and set them in the tray beside the door, allowing the snow to melt in to the tray. "Weatherman said we're supposed to get four to six inches tonight. Glad I don't have any catering jobs to deliver in the morning."

"Yeah," he replied as he turned off the burner and let the pasta sit as he focused on the final touches to the sauce. "I took tomorrow off."

"You did? Why, what's up?"

"Nothing in particular, the morning will probably see a slew of accidents as people hurry to work and school. I'm just not in the mood to write reports most of the day. Besides, I wanted to finish sanding and refinishing that chest of drawers in Geno's room."

Sandy smiled at her husband. Lately, some of the tension between the couple had begun to dissipate as they both adjusted to life without their son. At first, the boy's death seemed to signal the death of their marriage as well. Gene and Sandy could barely share the same space without getting into an argument. Later, a period of silence marked their existence, neither caring to talk with the other. Somehow, at least on Sandy's part, things began to get better. Not exactly like they were before the shooting, but at least they were talking and interacting.

She moved closer to where her husband was stirring the sauce and kissed him on the cheek. Rubbing his back, she breathed in the aroma of the garlic and tomatoes coming from the pot. "Mmm, smells great. Thanks for fixing dinner."

He didn't look at her, but shrugged his shoulders instead. "Hey, we gotta eat. Would you cut up some bread and mix the garlic butter?"

"Sure."

As the couple went about their food preparation, Gene set the spoon aside and left the sauce to simmer. "You'll never guess what I heard today."

"What?"

"Doyle is officially a missing person. The lieutenant read a lookout message at roll call. He said a nation-wide alert has gone out, even the FBI was notified. I don't know how they can keep him on the rolls if he's AWOL. Hell, he's liable to lose his pension."

Sandy stopped what she was doing. "Oh my, that family has been through so much. I feel sorry for Sharon and Bridget."

Gene took a deep breath. "*They've* been through so much? What about *us*? Who feels sorry that we lost our boy? At least they're still a family. Hell, Doyle's probably lying in the gutter somewhere, drunk on his ass."

"C'mon, Gene, you don't mean that. Sharon's family isn't responsible for what happened. She doesn't deserve the heartache she's going through."

"What heartache? Her old man made a mistake and now they're paying for it. It is what it is—they gotta live with it."

Sandy shook her head. "Listen, Gene, that woman has problems. Believe me when I tell you, she is suffering more than we'll ever know. I was at a catering job at the computer company on Main Street last week, talking with the wife of one of the executives of the firm. I guess Sharon's son, Mark, does that company's taxes. She told me that Sharon's grandson has leukemia. Sharon must be beside herself with grief. I mean, her husband's missing and her grandchild is seriously ill. That's a heavy burden to bear."

"Yeah, well, I don't wish her any ill will, I guess. I hope the kid gets better. But, dammit, Sandy, I just can't forgive Doyle for what he did."

Sandy finished mixing the garlic and butter together and began spreading it on the pieces of French bread she had broken off the loaf. "That's too bad. I bet Eric can't forgive himself either."

27

Compassion is a two way street.
   —**Frank Capra**

Christmas week. Eric would not have known the holiday was almost upon him were it not for the city's decorations and increased traffic from shoppers and tourists. The last couple of weeks were mostly spent in a fog, as he grew accustomed to his new life, tutored by those who had worn the homeless mantle for years. The "barrel group" had quickly adopted him, particularly since Eric had money for booze. The men diligently schooled their protégé regarding where to buy the cheapest wine and liquor, products that allowed them to remain anesthetized to their situation.

Rolling out of his cardboard box, Eric winced as his back spasmed from a long night lying on the hard cement surface. The first few nights he tried sleeping on the ground, he awoke several times as he tried to get comfortable. He quickly learned the remedy—more alcohol. The problem was that his money was almost gone. He reached into his pocket and pulled out several crumpled bills. His money clip was gone—traded for a pint of cheap bourbon the week before. Straightening each of the bills, he counted them: thirteen dollars. *Crap. Now what?*

He heard the sound of the El train several blocks away, its wheels screeching in protest as they rubbed and pushed against the track while the train turned toward the Loop. Yesterday, he and the Professor walked over to State Street. Harold was schooling Eric in the fine art of pan handling. "This time of year is prime time, Eric, " the Professor told him, as they walked past light posts and storefronts heavily laden with Christmas decorations. "People come down here to see the festive decor and to shop. Their wallets *and* hearts are in the holiday spirit."

THE YEAR WITHOUT CHRISTMAS

As the two men trudged along the street teeming with visitors, Harold, a short man who could not have weighed more than 130 pounds, led the way while Eric, tall, and now lean, trailed a step behind. Eric's head swiveled as he marveled at Chicago's extravagant displays. It seemed each block they walked was better than the last. Even in his alcohol-diminished cognitive state, Eric was in awe of the length to which the city had prepared for Christmas.

"Right up there," Harold said, pointing to the next corner. "That's State and Madison, one of the busiest intersections downtown. Plenty of foot traffic, lots of compassionate folks passing by. You take one corner, I'll take another."

"Why don't we just do it together?"

"Uh-uh. People are intimidated by two homeless dudes. It's better if we separate."

"Okay."

As the pair approached the intersection, Harold pulled a plastic cup from his pocket. "Get your cup out. Folks don't like to touch us. They're more likely to put some money in the cup, rather than in your hand."

Eric did as the Professor instructed.

"Okay, here we are." Harold stopped. "I'll stay on this corner; you go across the street and work that one."

Eric nodded and started to cross the street, but stopped and asked his partner, "So, what do I say?"

"Whatever comes naturally. Just be honest. Tell them you're homeless and hungry, but don't bully anyone. If they're afraid of you, they won't give you any money. If a cop comes along and tells you to move, don't argue with him. There are plenty of places around here to pan handle."

"Okay, see you later." Eric crossed the street pressed among a crowd of shoppers, but while the others moved on, Eric stopped at the corner of the building and took out the plastic cup from his coat pocket. People moved in all directions, causing Eric to turn, dance-like, in complete circles, while he held out his cup and tried to attract attention. Most people ignored him, too busy in their pursuit of Christmas shopping. After only a few minutes, Eric tired. Maybe it was from lack of food and rest, or perhaps he was just dizzy from constantly turning. He decided the best position for him to assume was to lean against the corner of the building.

"Can you spare some change? Hi, I haven't eaten today . . . care to help?" Feeling uncomfortable at first, Eric mumbled the words to himself. But he soon discovered that no one paid him any attention. He tried a new tactic. He picked someone out of the crowd and locked eyes on the person. As the stranger approached, Eric aimed his plea directly at him or her. "Sir, I'm hungry, can you help?"

The first person who stopped was a woman. She stood next to Eric and fished around in her purse, coming out with two one-dollar bills. "Here you go. You must be freezing standing on this corner. I wish I could spare more, but I hope this helps." She placed the money in Eric's plastic cup and continued on her way. Smiling, Eric felt good about his technique and continued to use it. Two other people donated, one with a pocketful of loose change, the other with a five-dollar bill.

Across the street, the Professor was talking with a well-dressed man. As Eric watched, the stranger took out his wallet and handed some money to Harold, and then actually shook Harold's hand. *The Professor's a pro at this.*

Eric turned his attention back to his own endeavor, shaking his cup while saying, "Homeless; need help." Three young men in their twenties approached him. Eric looked at one of the men who appeared to be intoxicated. *Uh-oh.*

"Hey, you homeless piece of shit!" The man yelled as he invaded Eric's space. "You got energy to be out here beggin'? Man, you should get yourself a damn job!"

Standing six-foot-one, and weighing 235 pounds (at least before becoming homeless) Eric almost never gave ground. Nevertheless, he backed up, even though his first inclination was to grab the guy, bring him to the ground and cuff him. That was then; this is now. Besides, the Professor told him not to cause any trouble.

"Why should I give you any money, you worthless piece of crap? How much money you got there, anyway?" The man went to grab Eric's cup, but his reflexes were slowed by his alcohol consumption. Eric easily pushed his arm aside and knocked the man off balance.

"Hey, back off. I don't want any trouble." Eric warned.

Catching himself before he fell, the man continued. "Don't put your hands on me, scumbag. I'll kick your ass!" The inebriated stranger moved toward Eric, who by now had put his cup back in his jacket pocket and was preparing for a confrontation. The two men who had accompanied their friend intervened and attempted to restrain their companion, just as a police officer on foot patrol rounded the corner.

The cop quickly intervened, grabbing hold of the combative pedestrian. He locked the man's arm behind his back, forcing the surprised miscreant to get up on his toes to avoid more pressure. Shoving the-would be fighter against the wall, the cop barked: "Settle down. What's going on here?"

"That bastard tried to start a fight with me," the man shouted, while his face became one with the wall. "I want him arrested!" Although firmly planted against the building, the drunk continued to struggle against the cop's restraint. Finally, the cop had enough. Pulling out his handcuffs, he placed them on the uncooperative subject and sat the man on the ground. "Stay put." The cop radioed for a car to come by and collect the arrestee.

Any other time, Eric would have felt a kinship with this police officer, and would have helped cuff the obstinate man. Now, living a different lifestyle and wishing to remain anonymous, Eric kept silent. The cop turned to him. "You—what happened here? You causin' trouble?"

"Uh, no, Sir, I, uh . . . the guy just walked up and started yelling at me."

"That so? What were you doin', pan handling?"

Eric didn't answer. Not knowing what the cop would do if he told him the truth.

One of the other two men from the group spoke up. "Officer, this is all a misunderstanding. We're buddies," he said, pointing to the man on the ground and his other friend. "We were out to lunch, and Phil," he pointed to his friend seated on the sidewalk, "he had a bit too much to drink. We didn't mean any harm."

The cop pulled a small notebook from his jacket pocket. He looked at the two men and said, "Let me see some ID." Taking their licenses, the cop copied the information and returned the documents as a squad car pulled to the curb. "You two can go; your buddy's goin' to the drunk tank for a while to sober up. I've got better things to do than waste time on someone wantin' to beat up the homeless."

The two men turned and walked away, while the driver of the beat car helped his fellow officer load the drunk into the back seat. That done, the cop turned to Eric. "Listen, you're done here for the day. Go get your buddy across the street and move on. I don't want any more trouble. Got it?"

"Yes, Sir. Thanks." Eric crossed the street and walked up to Harold.

"What the hell were you doin' over there?" Harold asked. "Didn't I tell you not to cause any trouble?"

"I know, I know. Listen, the cop said we've got to move."

Harold put his cup in his pocket. "Damn, Eric, we had a couple more good hours here. Coulda made some decent money."

"Sorry."

"Well, it's not a total waste. As long as we're over this way, let me show you a couple of places you need to know about if you're going to survive on the street." The Professor pointed north. It's up this way; let's go."

Including his misunderstanding with the homeless man at McDonald's on his first day in Chicago, this was Eric's second encounter with the law. Hopefully it would be his last.

28

The real measure of your wealth is how much you'd be worth if you lost all your money.
—Author Unknown

"I'm sorry, Bridge," Sharon blurted out. "That was the chief. He said in two weeks Dad will no longer receive his salary." The woman's eyes welled with tears, she was afraid for their future and felt helpless.

"What?" How can they do that?"

Sharon walked over to the nearby table and grabbed a tissue from the box. While she dabbed at her eyes, she explained. "Your Dad is considered AWOL, so the city council decided they couldn't justify paying his salary. We have until the end of December before the checks stop being deposited."

The girl's eyes opened wide. "Mom, what are we going to do? How are we going to live?" And like her mother, Bridget also began to cry.

"I don't know yet, Honey. We'll get by, we have some money in the bank. Heck, worst case scenario, I'll go back to work," she sniffled. That quick answer seemed the right thing to say. At least for now.

Staring at her mother for a moment, Bridget suddenly stiffened and threw her arms up in despair. "I can't take much more of this, Mom. I can't." The girl turned and ran up the stairs to her room.

Sharon sat on the couch and grabbed a fresh tissue. Looking around the room, she suddenly saw each piece of furniture, every photo and painting, every knick-knack and memento that made this house their home. She never imagined that one day she might not be living here. She never thought she'd be in danger of having the house taken from her. Now that possibility, as well as other issues, flooded her mind like a month-long monsoon rain. Insurance, mortgage payments, utility bills . . . Bridget's college education. Oh, God, please, what am I to do?

Getting up from the couch, she began pacing around the house. She went from room to room, cataloging each item in her mind. She knew it was irrational, but she tried to put a price on each piece of furniture and appliance. *The truck, I can sell the truck. No, that's Eric's pride and joy. Oh, what am I saying . . . Eric's gone!*

Walking into the kitchen she took in the room. *The butcher block table is worth $500, that would help with an insurance payment.* Her head spinning, she walked past the table to the corner cabinet where Eric kept his liquor. While memories of birthday dinners and holiday celebrations at that very table played in her mind, she began to reach for the cabinet.

~~~~~~~~~~

The odd-looking duo walked north on State Street, dodging the holiday shoppers along the way. "Where are we going?" Eric asked the Professor.

"We're going to Lower Wacker Drive, it parallels the river." The Professor stopped at the curb, waiting for the light to turn green. "Are you noticing anything as we make our way to Wacker?"

Eric looked around. "Well, I see all the shoppers and tourists, and I see the stores decorated for the holidays."

"What else?"

Taking another glance as the light changed, allowing them to cross the street, Eric responded. "There's a lot of traffic—cars and busses."

"Hmm," exclaimed the Professor, shaking his head. "You are new, aren't you?"

"What?"

"If you're going to survive on the street, you have to be aware of everything that's going on around you. For instance, look at the people walking by. What are some of them doing?"

"Uh, shopping?"

The Professor grabbed Eric by the coat sleeve and stopped him. "They're eating, dammit! Lots of them are munching on something, and some of them won't finish their food completely which means they will probably toss what's left in the trash."

"Oh . . . right." Eric hesitated. "Wait . . . you mean, you actually go

THE YEAR WITHOUT CHRISTMAS

in the trash and pick out the food someone threw away?"

The pair started walking again. "That's right. Sounds disgusting, doesn't it? But I'll tell you something, when you haven't eaten in a couple days and don't have a dime to your name, half a hamburger is like manna from Heaven."

"Oh, my God. Professor, I don't know that I can do that."

"Yeah, I know, I didn't think I could either until the hunger pains got so bad that I swallowed my pride and found something more substantial."

Eric digested what the man had just told him. *Could I do it?* He wasn't sure, but it would be a while before he'd have to make that decision. He still had a little money left. "Professor?"

"Yes?"

"I still don't get it; you're a smart guy, a university professor. Why are you homeless?"

They were about a block away from their destination.

"It's a long story, my friend, but the short version is I got caught embezzling some money from the school. I had some family problems, built up a lot of debt that I couldn't satisfy. Being the head of the History Department at the University, I had access to funding and grants. Bottom line: I got caught after a major audit was conducted. I served a couple of years in prison."

"Did you lose your home? Is that why you're on the street?"

"No, I still have that. My wife and son still live there."

They turned the corner on State and Wacker and headed toward a stairway leading down to the river.

"So what happened? Why didn't you go home?"

Reaching the top of the stairway, the Professor paused. "I was a felon, Eric. I couldn't go back and teach, which was the only thing I ever wanted to do. More importantly, I couldn't face my family. I had humiliated them. We were well-respected in our community, active in our church . . . we were living the good life."

"Did your wife kick you out?"

He shook his head. "No, once I got out of prison I went to a halfway house for a while. I met up with one of the guys you met at the vacant lot. He had been homeless several times in his life. We shared our stories and became friends. Once we were released, I decided to give it a go on the streets. Aaron's a big guy . . ."

"He sure is," Eric interjected.

"Yeah, he's got my back. His size keeps me safe; nobody messes with me when Aaron's around."

"But what about your wife and son? Don't you want to be with them?"

The Professor rubbed his forehead and took a deep breath. "More than anything in this world. But I haven't the courage yet to face them. Maybe one day. C'mon, let me show you something."

They made their way down to the river level. Eric looked around. On one side of the walkway they were standing on was the Chicago River. Chunks of ice floated by like Lucite chips. On the other side was Lower Wacker Drive. It was a dark and somewhat winding narrow thoroughfare, separated by concrete columns. On the far side of the street was a sidewalk several feet above street level.

"Be careful, we're going to cross to the other side." The two companions waited for the traffic to clear and then darted across. They walked up five steps to the sidewalk where the Professor pointed to his right. "Down there, about one hundred feet."

"By that box?" Eric asked.

"Yeah, c'mon." When they arrived at the spot the Professor had pointed out, he stopped Eric. "Feel the heat?"

"Yes."

"That's coming from the hotel that sits above us. These are heating exhaust vents, and on the coldest nights during winter, finding a box and sleeping in front of this vent may be the only thing that keeps you from freezing to death."

"What about the cops, do they hassle you here?"

The giant fan kicked in, making the noise even louder than the traffic passing by. "No. On frigid nights, they actually show some compassion," shouted the Professor. "I guess they know they'd have more stiffs to take to the morgue if they chased us away."

Eric thought about the handful of homeless people he had chased away from businesses in Websterville. He'd locked up a couple of them, just so they could get out of the cold and get something to eat. Now, it was his turn. Would his brothers in blue be as kind?

Looking at the box, Eric asked the Professor. "Where do you get a box like that?"

"That's the hard part. On sub-zero days, every homeless person downtown is checking the alleys for big boxes they can put up against a heating grate. Sometimes you've got to fight for one."

Crap. I don't know if I can do this.

The Professor waved his arm. "C'mon, we've to get back up on top and head a few blocks north. I've got one more place to show you."

About ten minutes later, Eric and the Professor were at the intersection of State and Hubbard Streets. The Professor turned right and walked about half a block, stopping in front of an old limestone building. Looking up, the Professor said, "Here we are, The Chicago Lighthouse Mission. You many need to stay here at some point if you are going to live on the streets."

Eric looked up at the three-story façade. "Looks like some kind of old municipal building, maybe even an old police station."

"Very good, my friend. This is an old turn of the century district station. It was called the Hubbard Street District. Twenty years ago, they converted it to a homeless shelter. Let's go inside."

They walked up the marble steps, worn down from decades of traffic to a glassy texture. Once inside they encountered a huge cherry wood desk that was used by the police desk sergeant to check in prisoners; now it served as a check-in desk for those in need of shelter, clothing and food. A middle-aged bearded man looked up as they entered. "Hi, Professor!"

"Hi, George. Just stopping in to show my new friend your marvelous facility."

"Good to see you, as always, Professor. You know where everything's at, feel free to give your buddy the tour."

"Thanks, by the way, this is Eric," he replied, pointing to his friend.

The man gave Eric a mock salute. "Hi, Eric, nice to meet you. The Professor knows this place inside and out, he's a good man. Listen to what he tells you if you want to survive living on the streets."

Eric waved back at the man. "Thanks, I'll do that."

The two men walked through the facility, the Professor pointing out the rooms used as dorms for families, men and women. "They try to keep families together if space permits, and obviously, they segregate the men and women to prevent any incidents."

Websterville had no city homeless shelters. Cops either locked up the homeless or took them to the local churches that took care of the few individuals who were homeless. Eric had never seen anything like this, nor had he ever imagined that he might actually avail himself of the services they offer.

As the Professor finished the short tour, they walked back out to the street. "I'm going to make an educated guess and say you've never stayed in a shelter."

Eric nodded. "You're right."

"Well, it looks rather tame now, but on days when the temperature is freezing, or a blizzard is dumping a ton of snow on the city, this place is a mad house. In fact, it gets so crowded that they have to turn some folks away."

The two men began to make their way back to the vacant lot. "What happens then? What happens if you're cold and hungry and they can't take you in?"

They turned on to State Street as the Professor answered. "Luckily, the mission has a couple of vans they send out during the night to several locations that I'll show you later. They provide sleeping bags, blankets and food."

"Wow, these folks are life-savers."

"Exactly. I found out about them during my first winter on the streets. Some old-timer took me aside, just like I'm doing with you, and showed me the ropes. No one can make it out here on their own, Eric, all of us need each other to survive."

As the two men walked the streets back toward their own little piece of the city, Eric was lost in his thoughts. *Can I do this? Am I strong enough?* As they passed a family looking at a Christmas display in a department store window, Eric's thoughts drifted toward his own family, particularly, his grandson, Brian. A single tear rolled down his cheek. *I can't . . . I can't.* He pulled the bottle from his jacket pocket and took a drink. *I'm sorry, I just can't.*

29

No passion so effectually robs the mind of all its powers of acting and reasoning as fear.
—**Edmund Burke**

Sharon reached for the corner cabinet where Eric kept his liquor. She rarely used this cabinet for a couple of reasons. First, she wasn't really tall enough to reach the second shelf where the bottles were kept. Being 5'3" sometimes limited her activities around the kitchen. However, the real reason for not going into this cabinet was that she was not a drinker. Oh, she'd have an occasional drink of wine if they were dining out with friends, or even a glass of champagne on New Year's Eve. But she knew how destructive alcohol could be. She had watched helplessly as Eric's father slowly became a slave to drink. Now, the same thing was happening to her husband.

She stood on her tiptoes, grabbed the first bottle and took it down. Unscrewing the cap, she went over to the sink and emptied the contents. When the last drop from the bottle disappeared down the drain, Sharon went back to the cabinet and found several more bottles. Barely able to reach them, she pulled a chair over and stood eye level with the enemy. There were at least five more bottles on the second shelf, and a couple more on the one above it. *Oh my God, it's worse than I thought.* She quickly removed all of the liquor from the cabinet and began pouring it all in the sink. The fumes from the alcohol made her nauseated. Not so much from the actual smell, but from what it represented. It made her sick to think about how these beverages had ruined her life with Eric. *No more. I will no longer allow any alcohol in this house. Never again.*

When the last bottle had been drained, she gathered the empties into a shopping bag and brought it out to the trash. A thought occurred to her that perhaps Eric may have alcohol stashed away elsewhere. Like a child on a treasure hunt, Sharon focused on ridding her house of all things alcohol. She went from room to room searching for any cans or bottles that may have eluded her, looking in drawers and on bookshelves, but she found nothing. Tired from her completed task and the emotion connected with the destruction that Eric's drinking had caused her family, she went over to the sofa in the family room.

With a sigh, she gathered her hair aside and lay down. When she did, her eyes were drawn to a nearby photo on the wall. It was a picture taken two years ago, a picture of her and Eric. She was seated and Eric hovered above her, his arms wrapped around her, symbolically protecting her from anyone or anything that might try to harm her. Their life had been so comfortable then. She thrived in his shadow. Their son, Mark, was married, and Bridget was a sophomore in high school. As their children grew older, the couple began to do more things together than ever before. They became closer; their love seemed to reach new heights, both physically and emotionally. Theirs was a love story, one she thought would never end.

And now . . . Sharon was at a place she couldn't even comprehend. *How? Why? Eric, please, don't do this to me. Don't leave me.* She turned away from the photo, her vision blurred by tears. She felt cold. Alone. There was no one to comfort her. The fear of the unknown was terrifying. *What's going to happen to me? I can't make it on my own. Eric, if you love me, please, please come home.*

~~~~~~~~~~

Bridget's cell phone rang. She rolled over on her bed toward the nightstand and picked it up. The caller ID indicated it was from her girlfriend. Bridget wasn't in the mood to speak with anyone after what her Mother had just told her. She tossed the phone on the floor without answering it.

Somehow, her life had gone from great to horrible overnight. She thought she'd be a shoe-in for a college scholarship, but after her disastrous championship performance, that didn't look like it would happen. Now, with Dad's salary no longer coming in there was no way she could afford to go to college. She'd probably have to get a job working as a cashier at the Farmers Market Grocery. *Who's going to hire a kid with no degree?*

THE YEAR WITHOUT CHRISTMAS

Her mother said she would get a job? *Yeah, right.* Her Mom didn't have a college degree either. She had stayed home with the kids while Dad earned the paychecks. Now look where she was—almost 50 years old with no skills. Well, at least none that anyone would pay her for.

Dinnertime was approaching. Bridget felt her stomach rumbling, the emptiness filling her with mixed emotions. She was hungry, but the ability to say no to food gave her the control she needed to manage her life. Getting up from her bed, she grabbed the water bottle from the dresser where she always kept several handy. She finished half the bottle in one drink and then began to take off her clothes. Standing naked in front of the mirror on the back of her bedroom door, she examined her reflection. It was working; her weight was dropping. Her hip bones were beginning to show, as were her ribs. She still felt fat, however, as she pinched a fold of skin from her abdomen. *Stay focused, you'll get there.*

She walked over to her closet and began to put on her running clothes. The sun had dipped below the horizon, the cold dark night began to overtake the landscape. She knew to add an extra layer of clothing to keep warm. Heck, lately she was cold just sitting around inside doing nothing. Experience told her that once she got out the door and the cold wind hit her, she'd feel like she was dressed for summer, but she'd warm up after a couple of miles. Between the sweat from the effort of running, and the anticipation of the weight she would lose, running was probably the only thing that fortified her. Tonight, she would try to run for two hours—that should dull the pain.

Finished dressing, she walked down to the first floor. Good, her mother was sleeping on the couch, and hadn't prepared dinner. Bridget crept out the back door being careful to gently pull it shut. As she ran down the driveway toward the street, she let her mind wander, wishing that one day she could just continue to run until all of her problems were far, far behind her. It didn't seem like a fantasy a young girl with a promising future should have, but it was Bridget's reality. *Dad, are you ever coming home?*

~~~~~~~~~~

It was dark by the time Eric and the Professor returned to the empty lot. Aaron was the only person standing by the fire barrel.

"Hey, Brother," the Professor shouted to Aaron, over the noise of the El train. "All alone?"

The big man nodded. "Yeah, you might say me and the boys had a little disagreement. They got pissed an' took off."

Approaching the barrel to warm up, they saw the fire was almost out. "Hey, what's up with the fire?"

"Ain't nuthin to burn. That's what got me pissed. I went lookin' for somethin' to eat, and when I come back, those two idiots had used our sleepin' boxes for the fire instead of goin' to look for somethin' else to burn."

"Mine, too?"

"Yeah. They burnt it all . . . lazy bastards."

Aaron bent over and picked up his stirring stick. He put it in the barrel and began stirring and shifting the remaining ashes. When he did, a beautiful shower of sparks floated from the container and flew above the dirt lot like a meteor shower.

"Aaron, let's go. We've got to find some more boxes to sleep on tonight, otherwise we'll freeze to death."

"What about me? Shouldn't I go with you?"

The Professor shook his head. "No, Eric, you stay here and guard our stuff. Don't let anyone take that shopping cart, we're going to need the clothes and sleeping bags we keep in it to get through the winter."

"Okay. Good luck."

The Mutt and Jeff-looking pair made their way toward the nearby alley, hoping to strike gold in one of the many dumpsters behind the businesses. Although they were nasty and difficult to get in and out of, the dumpsters offered an array of items the homeless could utilize to stay alive.

Eric was glad he didn't have to go with the two men. He was tired from walking most of the day. Since he'd arrived in Chicago, a good part of each day was spent on his feet, either walking or just standing around the fire barrel trying to keep warm. As a cop, he was used to driving his beat car around most of the day, only getting out answering calls or checking on suspicious vehicles or people.

His strength wasn't what it used to be either. He no longer had a regular fitness regime. His only goal each day was to stay warm and drink. Speaking of which . . . Eric reached into his pocket for the half pint whiskey bottle he kept there. He unscrewed the cap and took a drink, allowing the amber liquid to slide down his throat. Closing his eyes, he savored the warmth it created and appreciated that it dulled his senses. Eric didn't want to feel anything or think about anyone.

As he brought the bottle up to his lips for a second drink, someone grabbed his arm. "Hey, what . . . ?"

"Take it easy, Man. Wanna share some of that with us?" The man wore an old Army field jacket and cargo pants that were at least two sizes too large.

Eric saw three men standing in front of him.

"Yeah," said another man, wrapped in a big parka with a hood. "We're thirsty. Whatcha got?"

Not wanting any trouble, Eric answered. "There's only a couple of mouthfuls left, but you can have it if you want. Here." Eric handed the bottle to the Army man.

The man took a drink. "Ahh, that's good stuff." He handed the bottle to the third man, who appeared to be the oldest of the trio and who had a cane. He finished the last of the bottle and then threw it into the barrel.

"What else you got, besides whiskey?"

Even though his brain and reflexes had been dulled by alcohol, Eric's instincts told him there was trouble afoot. "Hey, guys, I don't have anything. I'm homeless just like you." As he said that, the three men surrounded him.

"You got any money, homeless man?"

"Yeah, you can afford whiskey, you must have some money," said the parka man. "Give it to us."

Eric turned around several times, weighing his options. He couldn't possibly beat all three of the men, and if he ran they'd probably take the shopping cart. As odd as it seemed, Eric felt he owed an allegiance to Harold and Aaron and decided to stand his ground.

"Gimme your money!" Parka man shouted. And as Eric turned his attention to him, he felt a blow to the back of his head. The old guy with the cane struck him a second time, causing Eric to drop to one knee. The man in the Army jacket kicked Eric hard in the ribs, knocking him to the ground. The last thing Eric remembered was the men swarming around him like ants on a piece of candy.

While Eric lay unconscious on the ground, the fire belched one last time, surrendering its heat to the cold Chicago night.

30

Friends show their love in times of trouble.
  —**Euripides**

The two men made their way back to the vacant lot. They had found what they were searching for about three blocks away, behind a furniture store: two large cardboard boxes and the remnants of a wooden skid. Aaron quickly broke the pallet down into manageable pieces that could be carried, while Harold folded the cardboard and lugged it.

As they exited the alley adjacent to the vacant lot they called home, they saw the fire barrel. "Where's Eric?" The Professor asked his companion.

"That him on the ground?"

"What?"

Quickening their pace, they arrived at the barrel moments later. Eric lay motionless, his knit cap showed evidence of blood at the back of his head. The Professor knelt down beside him. "Eric," he said, shaking his friend. "Eric, wake up. Wake up."

Eric stirred. Reflexively, his hands went up to protect himself. "Easy, it's me, Harold." The man took hold of Eric's arms, calming them. "What happened?"

Blinking, Eric took a moment to get his bearings before he answered. "Uh, three guys, they surrounded me . . . robbed me."

Aaron immediately looked over toward the shopping cart that held their sleeping gear. "Cart's still there; looks like we're okay."

The Professor glanced in that direction and nodded, "Good." Looking back at Eric, he asked, "Can you get up?"

Getting help from the Professor, Eric sat up. "Oh, man. My head is killing me." He put his hand behind his head to rub the spot that was giving him pain and came away with blood on his hand. "One of them had a cane. He hit me from behind." Quickly putting his hand in his pants pocket where he kept his money, Eric exclaimed, "Crap, they took all the money I had left."

"Damn," Aaron chimed in,"we're back to drinking the cheap stuff,".

"Try to stand, Eric." Harold grabbed his two hands and prepared to help him to his feet.

"Ow!" Eric let go and grabbed his side. "My ribs . . . I think the guy who kicked me may have broken them."

"We need to get you to a doctor, but it's about a ten minute walk from here. Do you think you can make it?"

"I don't know, Professor, let me try to stand." Getting to one knee, Eric slowly got to his feet. "Hold on to me," shouted Eric, "I'm feeling a little dizzy." Both men grabbed him.

"Just give me a second to clear my head." He stood supported by his two friends until he felt steady enough. "Okay, you can let go." Trying to take a deep breath, Eric felt the pain again in his side. "Yeah, I should see a doc, but listen, I don't have any money or ID."

"That's okay. There's a walk-in clinic close by that's run by volunteers from the University of Illinois. You don't need any money; they take care of folks like us."

"Okay, Professor, but let's go nice and easy."

"No problem. Aaron . . .?"

"I'm gonna stay here and get the fire goin' and keep watch on our stuff."

"Okay. See you later."

Eric put his arm around the shoulders of the smaller man, and the two street people headed toward the clinic. "I can't thank you enough," Eric told him, as they shuffled along.

"I told you, Eric, no one makes it on their own out here. At some point you have to trust someone enough to allow them to help you."

"I'm workin' on that."

~~~~~~~~~~

Eric, Sweetheart, it's okay. It was an accident. You were only doing your job. You can't leave . . . we need you. Despite her pleas, Eric continued to walk away, not even stopping to wave or say goodbye.

Sharon awoke with a start, almost falling off the couch. *Oh, God, please bring him home.* She sat up and looked over at the clock above the mantel. Dinnertime, but what was the sense in preparing anything for her and Bridget. Her daughter seemed to exist on water and crumbs. Truth be known, Sharon no longer had much of an appetite either.

Nevertheless, the woman was intent on keeping her life as normal as possible while waiting for Eric to come home . . . or be found. She didn't want to think about that last possibility. She had convinced herself that as soon as he somehow reconciled himself with what happened, he would be back. *He has to come back*. Running her hands through her hair, she went to the bottom of the stairs and yelled, "Bridge, what would you like for dinner?" No answer. "Bridge!" She yelled louder.

Not getting an answer, Sharon walked into the kitchen and looked over at the hooks near the back door. Bridget's running jacket was missing—she was out running again.

Okay. She went to the pantry and surveyed the contents. "Hmm . . . maybe pasta. She loves that," said the woman to no one in particular. Sharon set about getting the ingredients together and began to prepare the meal. An hour later, Bridget came in through the kitchen door.

"Oh, hi, Mom. You were asleep when I left, I didn't want to wake you so I went for a run."

"That's fine. Um, Bridge, can I ask a question?"

"Sure, Mom."

"Now that the season's over, do you still have to train so hard?"

The girl knew where this was headed, and she didn't want to go down that road. "I'm not training; I'm actually running to relax. When I'm out running, it allows me to de-stress and to think more clearly."

Sharon turned down the flame on the sauce she was preparing. "You're sure that's all it is?"

"Yeah, why?"

"I just want to make sure you're not injuring yourself. It seems you're gone for longer than usual sometimes."

Bridget pulled off her jacket and hung it up. "No, nothing like that. Running just helps me get through the day."

She didn't buy it, but Sharon wasn't about to alienate her daugh-

THE YEAR WITHOUT CHRISTMAS

ter by belaboring the point. She did, however, want the girl to know that her actions were being watched. "Bridge, tomorrow is Christmas Eve."

"I know," she answered, as she went to the sink for a glass of water. "How could I not know? The Christmas tree is taking up half the family room."

Her mother continued. "So, tomorrow Mark and Erin have invited us to their house for dinner. Afterward, we'll have Brian open the gifts we bought him."

Smiling, Bridget put down her glass. "He's going to be so excited. I think four-years-old is the perfect age for a child at Christmastime. The whole Santa thing is so new and mysterious to them."

Sharon nodded. "You're right. I remember when you were that age and we used to take you to the department store downtown to sit on Santa's lap. You were in awe of the fat man with the white beard."

Nodding, the girl was lost in thought for a moment. "Yeah, that was pretty cool for a while . . . until I found out what a sham it was."

"Those were the days," the mother remarked. "Your Dad used to cuss every Christmas Eve when he had to spend hours putting your toys together. He used to hate to see the boxes that said: 'Some assembly required.'"

Bridget laughed. "Yeah, he told me later that he was glad as I got older and only required things like electronic gadgets and clothes."

For a moment there was silence as they were both lost in the memory of the man who made their holidays so joyful.

Sharon broke the silence. "Bridge, remember when we brought the food to the homeless shelter on Thanksgiving?"

"Yeah, that was pretty cool. I enjoyed doing that."

"Well, obviously this year's Christmas is going to be difficult, so I thought we'd do the same thing—I'll prepare some dishes to take along and we'll spend the day at the shelter."

The girl took a long drink of water before responding. "Good idea, Mom." She finished her water. "Mom, I've been thinking. What if Dad is some place where there's a shelter, and he's depending on the people there to feed him? I mean, he doesn't have his wallet or anything. What if Dad is homeless?"

Just the thought of her husband in that type of situation pained her. Her eyes beginning to well up, she looked at her daughter.

"Honey, I guess that's a possibility, which is all the more reason why volunteering at the shelter is the right thing to do."

Bridget put her glass in the sink. "I'm going to take a shower."

"Okay, dinner's ready whenever you are."

Frowning, her daughter answered. "I'm not too hungry after that run."

"Bridge . . . don't fight me on this."

"Yeah, whatever," said the girl, as she walked out of the kitchen.

Sharon pulled out a chair and sat at the table. *What if Eric is homeless? I hope he's safe, wherever he is.*

31

Christmas is a holiday that persecutes the lonely, the frayed, and the rejected.
—**Jimmy Cannon**

Eric rolled over on his piece of cardboard as the sun began to illuminate the Second City. The reflection off of the EL train from the bright yellow fireball in the sky woke him, along with the train's ever-present din. His homeless companions were already up and standing at the fire barrel, passing a bottle back and forth. As he struggled to get out of his sleeping bag, he felt a sharp pain in his side where the doctor at the clinic had taped his bruised ribs. The back of his head was still tender after three stitches had closed the wound there. A couple of minutes later, Eric joined his friends.

"Merry Christmas, Brother!" The Professor greeted Eric.

"What?"

"I said Merry Christmas. Today is Christmas."

Aaron nodded and handed the bottle of wine to Eric. "Here ya go, Bro. Get yer heart started."

He grabbed the bottle, took a swig, and then handed it back to the big man. "Thanks. Merry Christmas to you both . . . I guess."

The Professor seemed to be a bit more upbeat today than normal. He smiled and looked upward. "Sun is shining; temperature's rising . . . it's gonna be a good day in the Windy City."

Eric frowned. "I don't get it."

"What?"

"How can you be so happy? Last time I looked, we're homeless." Eric accepted the bottle from Aaron and took another drink. "We're livin' on the street."

"Yeah, I know that, Eric. I've been out here a lot longer than you have," the Professor answered. "You have to understand something, my friend. Life is what you make it. Each of us makes our own choices. When you do, those choices come with their own set of consequences. I don't know your story, but as for me, I choose to live 'off the grid.'"

"What does that mean?"

"Off the grid? It just means I'm tired of society's rules. I don't care to comply with some bureaucrat's policy that says I must have an address, an ID, and I have to use and pay for electricity and water. I'm just tired of it all. I get what I need from city agencies and volunteers, as well as scrounging around and pan handling."

Eric looked over at Aaron. "What about you. Why are you out here?"

The big man shrugged his shoulders. "I guess I'm just different . . . don't fit in a lotta places. Been to prison a couple times. I don't like to follow rules. I like it out here, I can do what I want."

The three men stood silent for a while as Eric stood thinking about what his companions had just told him.

The silence was broken by the Professor. "Eric, what's your story? Why are you out here?"

Eric felt his skin begin to flush beneath his growing facial hair. He was reluctant to disclose to anyone the real reason he left home. Feeling on the spot, he answered. "I got in some trouble, and, uh, I just couldn't take it anymore."

Aaron looked at him. "You got in trouble with the poh-leece?"

"Yeah," Eric nodded.

"Lots of folks out here are in that same boat, Eric." The Professor smiled as he spoke. "I understand where you're coming from, but I'll tell you something. Sooner or later that problem will catch up to you and you're going to have to resolve it, one way or another."

"Yeah, I suppose you're right about that."

"Hey," Aaron said to the Professor. "When do you want to head over to the shelter?"

"We should probably get going soon. The line will be long today."

"What are you talking about?" Eric asked the Professor.

"It's Christmas, man, big dinner today. Time to get warm and fill our bellies with some great hot food."

The big man stirred the fire. "Yeah, everybody gonna want a piece o' that today. You gotta get there early."

THE YEAR WITHOUT CHRISTMAS

Christmas. Sharon and Bridget, home without me . . . lonely . . . wondering where I'm at. As Eric thought briefly about going home, he suddenly remembered Al and Sandy Giordano. *Their Christmas, ruined . . . by me . . . their son, gone forever.* His eyes filling with tears, he decided. *I'm better off where I'm at.*

~~~~~~~~~~

Last night was wonderful. Last night was horrible. Sharon poured herself a second cup of coffee. Christmas Eve at her son's home should have been the beginning of her favorite holiday, one she looked forward to each year. But without Eric, it was like going to a concert and not being able to hear the music. Little Brian only mentioned Papa once, when she and Bridget arrived. "Where's Papa?" The little boy asked Sharon. *Where indeed?* After that initial question, her grandson turned into a typical little boy. "Can we open the presents now?" He repeatedly asked until, finally, it was time. Once they were opened and Brian had an opportunity to play with each one, he fell asleep in his mother's arms.

"He tires easily," Erin told Sharon. The doctors tell me the chemo has that effect on everyone receiving the treatment. *Why call it chemotherapy? Why not just call it what it is—poison?* Sharon hated the fact that she was powerless regarding Brian's health. While the child was home from the hospital, she felt like she was intruding if she stopped in. Sometimes Brian was asleep, other times he was sick or cranky from all his meds. *Lord, please, cure him.*

The only thing she felt positive about was prayer. She had been praying since she first got word of Brian's leukemia. Because she'd been praying for her grandson and her husband, Sharon felt like she had never been closer to God. *Was this His way of getting my attention?*

Finishing her coffee, she got up to put her cup in the sink. Her stomach growled, but Sharon wasn't in the mood to eat. The thought of food reminded her of the argument she had with Bridget last night on the drive home from Mark and Erin's house. Her daughter had barely touched the dinner that Erin had spent so much time preparing. "It wasn't fair to Erin for you not to eat," she told Bridget. "She's has her hands full taking care of Brian, and yet she took the time to have us over for dinner. It's just not right."

Her daughter claimed she wasn't feeling well, but Sharon saw through that flimsy, often given excuse. By the time Sharon was pulling into their garage at home, neither person was speaking with the other, except for Bridget telling Sharon that she should go to Mass by herself in the morning. And that's what Sharon intended to do. She would go to Mass and ask God to please heal Brian, and bring Eric home. Afterward, she would go home and finish preparing the food she was taking to the shelter. It's what she would want someone to be doing for Eric, if he was homeless.

~~~~~~~~~~

The line outside the homeless shelter snaked around the corner. "Hey, Professor, this ain't bad. Only waited about an hour." Aaron smiled as he inched his way closer to the steps.

"Yes, sir, I can smell the gravy and biscuits already, Aaron. Merry Christmas!"

Eric looked at his companions. *Why are these guys so happy?* The trio made their way up the stairs and inside the hall. Eric breathed in the odor of pies baking in the kitchen ovens. His mouth watered, and suddenly a smile appeared on his face as he and his buddies jostled with the others to get one of the vacant seats at the many tables set up in the shelter's dining hall.

"There's three over there!" The Professor shouted to Eric and Aaron, as he scurried in that direction. The three men settled into their chairs and waited patiently.

"What's next?" Eric asked the Professor.

"Now, we simply wait. They won't start serving until every chair is taken. Then, volunteers bring out plates of food. Everyone gets the same thing, that way no one fights over the food or the portions."

Before long, all fifty seats were occupied and a woman with long gray hair and wire-rimmed glasses stood before the group. She clapped her hands twice to get everyone's attention before she began to speak. "Today is a special day; today is Christmas. Some of you I recognize as regular visitors to the Lighthouse Mission. Others are first-timers. Regardless of whether you have been here before or not, just know that we are here to help you any way we can. Today's wonderful feast is possible because of so many people who volunteer their time, energy and products, to ensure every needy person receives a complete meal. Enjoy your time here. And now, Father James Callahan will bless the meal."

"When do we eat?" Eric whispered.

"It's their procedure, pray first, eat later. They're big on spirituality here . . . like to try to convert folks to Christianity. They get visiting ministers here all the time. I've never seen this guy before."

Father Callahan was older, maybe 70 or so, reddish-gray hair thinning in front with a widow's peak. He walked with a slight bend in his back as he strode to the front of the room. The priest began by making the sign of the cross. "In the name of the Father, and of the Son, and the Holy Spirit, Amen. Dear God, we thank you for Chicago Lighthouse Mission and the extraordinary people who work so hard to take care of those less fortunate. We ask that you bless this meal, as well as those men and women who have come to enjoy your heavenly bounty. Amen."

Some of the diners offered their own "Amen," and with the formalities over, an army of volunteers marched out of the kitchen with Christmas meals balanced on both their arms and hands. The tables quickly filled with individual plates, each overflowing with Turkey, mashed potatoes, ham, green beans and corn. Baskets of bread and plates of butter adorned each table. Pitchers of water and carafes filled with coffee were provided as well.

"Man, this is great," Aaron said, looking down at his plate while cutting another piece of ham. "I love Christmas."

Eric hadn't eaten like this in weeks. As he quickly ate the food and drank a glass of water, he began to feel a pain in his stomach. He looked over at the Professor who was taking his time eating his portion. "I'm not feeling too good."

Looking down at Eric's almost empty plate, the Professor answered. "Yeah, well, when you devour your food like that, there's a good chance you're going to feel sick. Your stomach's not used to being full, my man. Take your time. Pour a cup of coffee and relax, let the digestion process begin."

Aaron didn't seem to be having any problem at all. In fact, he reached across the table and grabbed an unfinished meal from a man who had walked away. "Mmmm . . ."

Eric grabbed a plastic cup and poured some coffee. Taking a deep breath, he forgot about his ribs and felt the sharp pain again.

"Damn." Still uncomfortable, he got up. "I'm going to find a restroom."

The Professor pointed. "Out the door, to the left."

"Okay, thanks." Eric made his way to the Men's Room and locked himself in one of the stalls. Thinking about his life on the street and how he had relieved himself while living out there, sitting in a real bathroom felt luxurious. He lingered for a while and then went to the sink to wash his hands. He took a look at himself in the mirror and saw someone who resembled Eric, but wasn't quite like the Eric he remembered.

Pulling off his cap, he continued to gaze at his image, looking at his long unkempt hair and beard. *I look like crap . . . feel like it too.* He washed his hands. *Wow, hot water. It feels so good.* He cupped his hands and rinsed his face. The water helped him to feel better, a bit stronger. He dried off and walked out the door. As he headed back to the dining hall, the priest who had blessed the meal was walking toward him.

"Hi, Father."

"Hi. Merry Christmas. Did you get enough to eat?"

Eric nodded and rubbed his stomach. "Probably too much. That's why I hit the rest room."

"I understand," said the priest. "What's your name, son?"

"Eric."

"Eric, you're not from around here, are you?"

"Uh, no."

"You haven't been homeless very long either. I get the sense that something is bothering you. Something has happened that has caused you great pain and sorrow."

He looked down at the floor before answering. "Father, I, uh . . . Yeah, I've had some problems that are probably best left alone."

"Really? You think your problems are so big that they can't be fixed?"

"Kind of. Yeah."

"You're Catholic, aren't you?"

Eric nodded.

"I can tell. And like many of us, when we sin or we do something that we think can never be fixed, guilt takes over our reasoning."

Does this man know me? "Hey, listen, Father, I'm not really in the mood for a lecture right now. If I need you, I'll come and see you. Okay?" Eric walked past the priest and rejoined his two buddies. He had a strange feeling about Father Callahan. Somehow, their paths might cross again.

32

He that cannot forgive others breaks the bridge over which he must pass himself; for every man has need to be forgiven.
—**Thomas Fuller**

Taking off her coat, Sandy Giordano hung it in the front hall closet and then walked back to the kitchen. "Al?" She saw her husband sitting at the table. "Merry Christmas!"

"Hi, how was church?" He responded, cooly.

"Packed. It was the usual holiday thing—people who don't go to Mass all year show up and make a big deal of it on Christmas." She folded her arms. "I wish you would have come with me."

Al turned the page of the morning paper and then took a drink of coffee. "Yeah, sorry, but I'm not there yet. With Gene gone, I'm not exactly in the holiday spirit."

Sandy went to the cabinet, got a cup, and poured herself some coffee. "Me either, in fact it broke my heart to see so many families there, but I think we have to start dealing with our new reality." She sat down at the table with her husband. "I saw Sharon in church."

"Yeah?"

"She was seated up toward the front, alone, no family members."

Al closed the newspaper and looked at his wife. "Listen, Sandy, I don't have any bad feelings toward that woman, other than the fact that when I see her it brings back memories of 'that night.'"

Nodding, Sandy took a drink. "I know, but I feel sorry for her, Al. None of this is her fault, and now she has big problems with her husband missing and her grandson sick with leukemia."

"What, and we don't have any problems?" her husband quickly remarked.

"I'm not saying that, Al, my pain is as real as Sharon's. This morning, when I woke up, I didn't want today to begin . . . not without our son. It's the worst Christmas we've ever had. However, I can't let it ruin 'us,' we have to be strong for each other. I can't bear the thought of losing another loved one."

Al looked at his wife, took a deep breath and then let it out. "I know. I don't ever want to relive anything like those first two weeks after his death." His shoulders sagging, Al's eyes began to well up. "I wished it had been me that was killed that night. I . . . I didn't tell you but . . . I . . . I thought about killing myself the first time I visited Geno's grave."

His wife went to him and wrapped her arms around her husband's shoulders. "Oh, Honey . . . "He turned to her and put his arms around her waist, pulling her in tight as they both cried tears filled with sorrow, but also cleansing tears, representing love and need.

"Al, we have to get past this. We have to talk to each other so you never have those thoughts again. Please promise me you'll let me know your feelings. Honey, I need you so much."

Sharing his secret with her, he felt relieved. "I promise I'll try. I guess I just need more time."

"Me too, Honey, but we have to help each other. We can't do it individually. We have to work together. I need you now more than ever."

Moments later the couple let go of each other and Sandy sat down in her chair. She looked over at her husband and he stared back. Through the silence, they heard each other and grew stronger.

~~~~~~~~~~

Sharon was busy putting together the dishes she was bringing to the shelter. Mostly vegetables, some cooked, others raw. Yesterday she called the woman in charge of the Christmas meal. "They need healthy meals whenever possible," she told Sharon. "We'll give them some sweets too—pies and cakes—but they'll get a good portion of nutritious food first. Bring your donation in as early as possible, and if you can stay for prep and serving, you'll make my day."

That's exactly what Sharon intended to do. She would stay as busy as possible, not allowing herself time to think about her own situation. Her visit to the shelter on Thanksgiving strengthened her resolve to help as often as possible. She never realized how many people were in need of simple things like food and clothing, stuff most people took for granted. When Bridget mentioned that perhaps Eric was homeless, Sharon made up her mind to be a regular volunteer.

She had all of her supplies lined up on the kitchen counter. *One last thing to do.* Bridget had not yet come down from her bedroom. Sharon needed to check on her before she left. Walking up to her daughter's bedroom, she knocked on the door before going inside. Bridget lay on the bed in her pajamas with her iPod, ear buds in place, staring at the ceiling.

Seeing her mother, the girl pulled the chords from her ears. "Hi, Mom."

"Good morning; Merry Christmas."

"Yeah, Merry Christmas," she answered, with a forced smile. "Sorry about the argument last night."

"That's okay," the woman replied, as she sat down on the bed. "We're both dealing with some pretty horrible stuff."

The girl nodded in agreement.

"I went to Mass this morning . . . "

"I know; I heard you leave."

"Bridge . . . I know your world is upside down, your future uncertain. You're worried about Dad and Brian, and so am I. But I'm worried about you, too. I don't want you to get sick, or lose focus on what you need to do to be a success."

The girl looked at her mother. "Mom . . . "

"Wait, hear me out. I'm not going to lie to you, Sweetheart. I don't know what's happened to Dad, and I don't know what we're going to do starting next month without his police department check. But here's one thing I do know. Together, we are going to get through this problem. One way or another, we're going to continue to live as we always have, so that when your father comes home he'll have the same loving home he had when he left."

"What about Christmas, Mom? What's the sense in having the tree up with the presents underneath?"

Sharon grabbed her daughter's hand. "We'll have Christmas when Dad comes home. Whether it's sooner, or later, we'll wait, and the tree will stay up. If it's a year without Christmas . . . or longer," she said, as a tear rolled down her cheek, "we'll wait."

Bridget sat up and hugged her Mother. "I understand. It's just so hard not having Dad here. I didn't realize how much I loved him until he was gone."

"That's okay," Sharon said, as she rubbed Bridget's back. "Your Dad knows you love him, and when he gets through with whatever's keeping him from being with us, you can tell him how much you love him."

"Okay, Mom," she sniffled.

Grabbing a tissue from the nightstand, Sharon dried her eyes and stood up. "I'm off to the shelter. I'm probably going to be gone most of the day. Do you want to come with?"

"Uh, yeah, can I jump in the shower real quick?"

"Sure. Make it fast. I'll start loading the car."

"Okay, Mom. I love you."

Sharon bent over and kissed her daughter's cheek. I love you too."Walking down the stairs to the kitchen, the woman thought, "This might not be a bad Christmas after all."

33

Worry does not empty tomorrow of its sorrow.
It empties today of its strength.
   —Corrie Ten Boom

It was a week into the new year and Sharon began to seriously worry about how she and her daughter would live without Eric's police department salary. Although they didn't live paycheck to paycheck, like they had during their first few years of marriage, Sharon knew they hadn't saved enough money for them to live indefinitely without some kind of income. Mark's education had put a sizeable dent in their savings. Catholic high school and then four years at Michigan State University had been expensive. And even though their son had worked while he attended school, it was hardly enough to cover the cost of his room and board on campus.

It was mid-morning. Bridget was at school and Sharon was busy preparing a large pot of chicken noodle soup. The size of the recipe would last them a couple of days at least, and would save Sharon some grocery money as well. Lately, she began to plan her meals with a more frugal approach. But she also knew the soup was one of Bridget's favorites. Sharon could ill afford to make meals her daughter wouldn't eat.

Standing at the kitchen counter, she glanced out the window facing the side driveway. She had not been outside yet, but she could tell by the fog on the windows that the temperature was in the single digits. She shivered at the thought of being out in the cold. *Was Eric out in it somewhere?* She was about to walk over to the thermostat to turn the heat up, but thought better of it. Instead, she went to the front hall closet and put on a sweater. "Can't afford higher heating bills," she thought.

The kitchen phone rang. "Hello . . ."

THE YEAR WITHOUT CHRISTMAS

"Mrs. Doyle? This is Chief Williams."

"Hi, Chief."

"I was thinking about you over the holiday. I know this Christmas could not have been a very joyful time for you and your family."

Sharon pulled out a kitchen chair and sat down. "Yes, it was a difficult week for us."

"I'm sorry. We are all praying that Eric will be located quickly. If you recall, I notified you that the city council decided to suspend your husband's police salary while he is in an AWOL status."

"Yes, Chief, you told me."

"Well, I went back to them yesterday, pleading your husband's case . . . trying to get the council to change their mind on the matter."

Sharon took a deep breath and slowly released it. "And . . ?"

"Unfortunately, they refused to reconsider. However, I did get them to agree to continue to pay the city's share of your health insurance as long as you continue paying the monthly co-pay."

Bowing her head, she gave thanks. "Chief, thank you, that will be a big help."

"You're welcome. The council agreed to continue his insurance until next year, after that I'm afraid you'll be on your own."

"Well, hopefully, things will change for the better before that happens."

"I hope so," said the chief. "One more thing. I spoke with our department therapist, Dr. Sally Lake. Our EAP program won't cover an employee and his family unless that employee is on active duty with the department. However, I spoke with the doctor and she's agreed to see you for three sessions—no charge."

"Thank you, Chief, that's very kind of you. By the way, any word on my husband's whereabouts?"

The chief paused for a moment. "No. I wish we had some clues about his disappearance, but he seems to have vanished."

Now it was Sharon's turn to pause. She had hoped when she heard the chief's voice that he was calling with news about Eric.

"Mrs. Doyle, are you there?"

"Yes, sorry. Thank you so much for your help. At least one problem is solved with your generous offer to continue Eric's health insurance."

"Well, I wish I there was more I could do for you. Call me if you have questions about anything related to your husband's status."

"I will. Goodbye, Chief."

Now, how do I earn the money to pay the copay, mortgage and utilities?

~~~~~~~~~~

"Gonna be a cold one tonight. Hawk's gonna be bad."

Eric had learned the "The Hawk" was a Chicago slang term for the wind. Being from nearby Michigan, Eric knew about the wind chill factor, how it made the temperature seem even colder than it was if one's skin was exposed. But the Chicago wind in the winter seemed relentless. It was everywhere, and came from all directions. Frostbite was a common malady for homeless people. That and freezing to death.

"What you wanna do, Professor? We gonna find a heat grate or a buildin'?"

The unlikely trio stood around their fire barrel, backs to the wind. "I'd rather stay around here, if we can find a building to get inside somewhere. Otherwise, we'll have to take that long walk to Lower Wacker. We'll be frozen before we even get there."

"Yeah, might not even be any spots left," said Aaron.

"What about the shelter?" Eric did a little dance trying to warm his feet up as he stood by the barrel.

The Professor shook his head. "It will be jammed tonight and they'll give families priority. Aaron, can you take a look around the area and see if you can find a place for tonight?"

The big man nodded. "Sure thing. Give me sumpthin to do." He dropped his fire-stirring stick on the ground and took off toward the EL tracks. "Be back in a while."

A gust of wind whipped up the snow in the vacant lot, causing a white mini-tornado. "Damn!" The Professor grabbed the stick off the ground and began stoking the fire. "Eric, it's getting low. Go around the corner and get some trash from a dumpster. We've got to keep the fire going until Aaron gets back."

"Okay," Eric replied, and headed in the direction of the closest alley. He pulled a pint of wine from his pocket and took a long drink. Temporarily warmed, and focused on the directions from the Professor, Eric's mind drifted toward home. *Hope the furnace is working,*

Sharon gets cold easy. Stopping at the first dumpster he encountered, Eric slid open the sliding door. *Let's see what we got.*

~~~~~~~~~~

"Al, I need a favor." Sandy Giordano shut the door quickly, trying to keep the cold weather out. "I've got a catering job tonight at the Elk's Club, but my part-timer called in sick. Do you think you can give me a hand tonight?"

Having just come home from working the day shift, Al was not in the mood to go out again. "Aw, Sandy, I just got home. I froze my ass off today—three traffic accidents and a lost kid. I was out of the car most of the afternoon."

"C'mon, Al, you know I wouldn't ask if I wasn't in a real bind."

He let out a huge sigh. "Okay. What do I have to do?"

Sandy smiled and walked over to her husband and gave him a kiss. "Thanks, Baby. I'll need you to help load the van and then drive it over to the club and unload it. Melissa and I will take it from there."

"Doesn't sound too bad, except it's so damn cold. It's supposed to hit below zero tonight."

Sandy laughed. "Don't worry, Dear, the van's heater works quite well. Besides, with you there tonight I've got someone to keep me nice and warm."

"Yeah, well, I guess it beats sitting home alone. Hey, whatever happened with what we discussed concerning hiring another employee?

"I want to," she replied. "I just need to sit down and write the ad and get it in the paper."

"Well, that all takes time so you need to get on it."

"I will. In fact, I'm thinking hiring one full-time person and another part-timer."

"Wow," Al whistled, "that would give you six employees. You're turning into a corporation."

Sandy busied herself at dining room table, looking at the mail her husband had brought in. "Hey don't laugh. If business continues the way it has been, maybe we should incorporate."

Al waved his arms. "That's way above my pay grade. I'm just a simple cop. You need to talk with a lawyer about that."

"I thought you hate lawyers."

"Not all of them—just the defense lawyers."

"Oh, Al . . ." She chuckled. "C'mon, give me a hand in the kitchen. We'll grab a bite before we head over to the business."

"Okay."

"Al?"

"What?"

"I love you."

34

PTSD is a whole-body tragedy, an integral human event of enormous proportions with massive repercussions.
—Susan Pease Banitt

Sharon parked her car in the lot of the Professional Building downtown. Getting out she began to shiver as the cold wind blew under her coat, replacing the warmth the car's heater offered. However, she wasn't only shaking from the cold. She was anxious about meeting with the therapist. She had visited the doctor before to discuss Eric's diagnosis, but now she was here for her own well-being.

Sharon had never needed to see a therapist or counselor . . . until now. Dr. Lake was pleasant enough during their first meeting, but Sharon still felt some trepidation. Would the doctor tell Sharon the reason Eric left was due to Sharon's lack of understanding? Or did he leave voluntarily? Maybe he was kidnapped in a robbery or something. As she approached the side door of the building, she checked herself. *Stop with the questions, you're driving yourself crazy.*

The door to the doctor's suite was ajar and Sharon walked in. "Hello, Dr. Lake?"

"It's good to see you again," the therapist replied, getting up to greet Sharon. "C'mon in, please. May I take your coat?"

"Actually, I'm kind of chilled. Would you mind if I left it on for a while?"

"Not at all. Please, have a seat." Dr. Lake directed Sharon to an arrangement of chairs, separated by a table. "I just made a fresh pot of coffee. May I offer you a cup, Mrs. Doyle?"

Sharon nodded. "That would be great, and, please, call me Sharon."

"Okay. Black, right?" The doctor asked as she poured two cups.

"Yes, I'm surprised you remembered."

Returning to her chair, Dr. Lake set the coffee on the table.

"Thank you, Doctor."

"My pleasure."

"No, not for the coffee. I meant, thank you for offering your services. I'm afraid I would be hard pressed to afford you otherwise."

"You're quite welcome, and it's actually a service I provide to family members when an officer is involved in a critical situation, such as the one your husband was involved in. Frankly, I was surprised when the city council decided to withhold his salary."

Sipping her coffee, Sharon nodded. "It's definitely going to change our lifestyle."

"Indeed, but maybe I can offer some suggestions on ways to get through this crisis." The doctor crossed her legs and leaned forward a bit in her chair. "From all I know about your husband, he was a model police officer—never in trouble, the recipient of several awards for valor and outstanding police work. His professional life was exemplary."

"You're right," Sharon added. "Eric and his partner, Al, were senior officers who most often led the department in arrests."

"I can believe that." Dr. Lake paused. "Let me ask you . . . how was your home life? Did Eric have any problems separating his job and his private life, or was he always on duty so to speak?"

She shook her head. "No, Eric knew to leave the job at the station. Once he was off duty, he was a typical husband and father. Don't get me wrong, he was very proud of being a cop, but he didn't allow it to interfere with family."

"That's good to hear, Sharon, and it also explains the radical reaction to the shooting incident. Share with me again Eric's behavior after Al's son was killed."

Sharon took a sip of coffee and set the cup on the table. "Well, he was obviously depressed about what happened. But he didn't want to talk about it with me, which is unusual because we always share everything. Then he began to isolate himself from all of us—even his grandson, Brian, whom he dearly loves. In fact, Brian is suffering from leukemia and I sometimes find myself torn between feeling sorry for Eric, and being mad at him for not being here for our grandbaby."

"Oh my. How is Brian doing?

"He's undergoing chemo right now—it's not a good time."

"I'm sorry to hear that."

"Thanks. Brian's a tough little guy."

"Good. I can understand your conflicted feelings toward your husband, but you must understand that PTSD changes the victim, causing him to act irrationally. What else has Eric done that seems out of character?"

"He began to drink heavily, even during the day. He had never done that before."

The doctor jotted a few notes and continued. "Did you confront him about his drinking?"

"Of course. It began to interfere with our family life, particularly our teen-aged daughter, Bridget. Eric would forget about important events she was involved in at school . . . even forgot to pick her up after track practices. She became very upset with her father."

"Were the two of them close?"

"Very. I think that's why Eric's drinking and apathy hit Bridget so hard. She felt her father no longer loved her."

The therapist nodded. "Yes, that would be devastating to a child. Last time you mentioned Bridget was running more than usual and wasn't eating much. Any change?"

"I think things are worse." Sharon wiggled out of her coat. "Lately she's been running in the morning *and* at night. She's become quite thin. I'm afraid she's going to make herself sick, but she won't discuss it with me. Whenever I try to talk to her about her eating and exercising, it starts an argument. As much as I'd like to talk with her about it, I don't. I feel like I'm walking a tightrope with her all the time."

"Unfortunately, your daughter's behavior is not atypical. Many young girls, when faced with a situation out of their control, will try to do other things like limit their food intake and increase the intensity and duration of exercise in an effort to control their weight. They see each pound lost as a victory."

"So how do I get her to start eating again?"

"I don't know that you can," the doctor responded, as she walked over to the coffee pot. "More coffee?"

"Yes."

"Your daughter will have to make that decision herself. With any type of addictive or obsessive behavior, the individual has to want to change. Nothing anyone says will cause them to stop."

Sharon stared out the window, watching as the wind blew snow from the boughs of the evergreens. She felt a chill pass through her. *Am I going to lose my husband **and** my daughter?*

"Let me return to your husband. As I told you, he is dealing with PTSD, or Post Traumatic Stress Disorder. Simply put, PTSD is an anxiety disorder that some people get after seeing or living through a dangerous event. Eric's shooting triggered this disorder. We see this occurring most often with members of our military, or anyone who has been a victim of an assault or abuse. But as we learn more about PTSD, we see that law enforcement personnel are also very much at risk.

"Some of the symptoms include flashbacks of the incident and bad dreams. This may cause the person suffering to feel emotionally numb, guilty, depressed or worried. They may lose interest in things and activities. PTSD sufferers may feel on edge, and have difficulty sleeping. They may be quick to anger."

"Doctor, that's exactly what happened with Eric. Before the shooting, he rarely got angry or yelled at anyone. However, before he left, he had angry outbursts at Bridget and me. I thought it was just from his drinking."

"Drinking definitely exacerbates the condition. In fact, studies indicate that people with PTSD often also have problems with alcohol and drug use. This 'self-medication' allows the victim to detach himself from the distress caused by the disorder."

Taking a drink of her coffee, Sharon sat forward. "So in your opinion, do you think my husband's condition will ever improve? Is the PTSD the reason he left?"

The therapist took a breath and sighed. "I can't say conclusively that Eric left because of the PTSD disorder, but combined with his alcohol abuse I will say that it's likely he left because he felt guilty and depressed. Oftentimes, when people are suffering from anxiety disorders, they view the very people they love as part of the problem. Rather than cause more disruption and destruction in those relationships, the victims will decide the simplest solution is to leave."

Sharon put her hands to her mouth. "Do they ever return?"

"Only if they truly want to, and only when they've hit bottom."

THE YEAR WITHOUT CHRISTMAS

~~~~~~~~~~

The long shadows of sunset painted the vacant lot as the three nomads struggled against a cold Chicago wind.

"Hey, Professor, we gotta get inside somewhere. Tonight's gonna be too damn cold to sleep out here." The big man tore up the remaining cardboard boxes and stuffed them into the fire barrel.

Harold looked like a windup toy soldier as he marched in place, trying to keep his feet warm. "Yeah, I agree, Aaron. Do you have any suggestions?"

"Can we go to the Mission?" Eric asked.

"Uh-uh, that's only for when we really have a bad night," Aaron answered, as he stirred the fire.

"He's right," the Professor added, as a gust of wind blew his slight frame backward two steps. "We can't wear out our welcome there. It gets a lot worse out here than what we have tonight."

"Let me try again an' see if I can find a place," the big man said. "I'm gonna check that office building behind Sophie's. Place just closed up a few weeks ago, I saw them moving out a bunch o' desks and what not."

"Okay, hurry back. The fire's not going to last much longer."

"Aaron started walking away but turned back to Eric. Hey, let me take the bottle along."

Eric took the bottle of vodka from his jacket pocket, took a drink, and then handed it to Aaron. "Save some for me."

"Hmmph." Aaron took off towards Sophie's.

Eric stepped closer to the fire. "Professor, I don't know if I can't make it through the winter. It's only January and I'm cold and hungry most of the time."

The Professor smiled as he continued his warming dance. "You'll make it. I felt the same way my first year on the streets, didn't think I'd survive. However, I did, and I learned from the people out here that you have to take advantage of your surroundings. Know where the warming shelters are, where the missions are at . . . take advantage of people's generosity."

"Yeah, I guess you're right. It's just that being homeless wears you down. It's like we're always searching for something—food, cardboard and stuff to keep us warm."

Laughing, the Professor asked Eric, "What would you do if you weren't searching for those things? Those very activities are what's helping to keep you alive. Do you think you can just sit in a corner all day and drink? You'd be dead in no time."

Eric thought about that. "I guess you're right. I guess one has to do something, but it's like we do the same stuff every day."

"Yes, we do. It's a choice we made when we decided to leave our pasts behind. You can always change your situation; you can leave this life and go back to your former one. That is, if you didn't damage it beyond repair."

As the wind swirled around the two companions, it fed the fire causing it to consume its fuel. With only a few flames barely visible, the big man returned. "Got a place, let's go."

Eric walked over to the building alcove and retrieved the trio's shopping cart containing their sleeping bags and other homeless accoutrements. Ten minutes later, they arrived at a back door facing a dark alley lined with dumpsters. Aaron turned the knob and eased the door open. "Didn't hear no alarm when I broke the glass. Not much left inside, so I guess they figure it ain't worth protectin'."

Entering the dark interior, Eric stepped on the shards of broken glass lying on the floor. Crunch. The sound and feel of the glass crushing beneath his shoe ignited his memory, vividly recalling the night he had stepped inside the warehouse in Websterville. In an instant, he was back in the moment. He scanned the room for suspects, and held out his hand as if he was holding his police pistol. From the corner of his vision, he saw movement across the room.

"Stop! Police!"

Startled, Aaron froze momentarily and then turned around to look at Eric. "Fool! What's wrong with you? Shut yo mouth 'fore you get us locked up."

Sweating despite the cold, Eric looked down at the floor and shook his head briskly as if trying to clear his mind of the unwanted images residing there. His heart raced while he followed his homeless friends deeper into the darkened bowels of the building. "Aaron, give me the bottle."

35

First the man takes a drink; then the drink takes a drink; then the drink takes the man.
—Japanese Proverb

The bright sun felt good on Eric's face and made the forty degrees seem more like sixty. There was a time when it seemed like March would never arrive. Eric's first winter living on the streets of Chicago had been challenging to say the least. He was tempted to abandon his plan on several occasions and return to his family. That is, until his memories of "that night" reminded him of why he had left. Although tired and noticeably thinner, he somehow felt a sense of accomplishment about having it made it through the winter.

Eric was hungry. Searching through his pockets he found he had less than one dollar in change. He felt the vibration in his stomach as it growled, warning him that he needed to eat. The Professor and Aaron were gone. Eric hadn't seen them in two days. They sometimes took off together without a word about where they were going or when they'd return. Theirs was a strange relationship, one that proved the axiom that opposites attract. Although not sure, Eric suspected the Professor had some type of condition and that Aaron acted not only as the man's bodyguard, but also ensured he got any treatment he needed.

Eric hadn't had a drink in more than a day. Panhandling had been spotty lately, and besides, he didn't feel like walking all the way over to State Street where most of the office workers and shoppers would be. *Might as well try Sophie's.* Minutes later, he opened the front door of the café and sat down at the counter.

"That who I think it is? My, my, ain't seen you in forever. How you been?"

Eric smiled. "Yeah, it's me, Sophie, and I'm hungry."

"I bet you is; want some coffee?"

"Sure."

Sophie went to the percolator and poured a cup for Eric.

"Here you go, Darlin'." The woman turned and went about preparing breakfast items for the few customers in the restaurant, but continued talking while doing so. "Didn't recognize you at first with that hairy face. And look like you lost weight. Street been tearin' you up."

Eric sipped the steaming brew and unbuttoned his jacket. "Yeah, guess that livin' on the street will do that to a person."

Sophie plated an order of eggs, bacon, and toast, and then carried it around the corner to a man seated in one of the booths. "Here you go, Darlin', enjoy." Coming back around to the stove, she broke a couple of eggs and grabbed several strips of bacon. She looked over her shoulder at Eric. "I know you didn't come here to talk, you'se hungry. I'll fix you what you had before."

"Sophie, I . . . uh,"

"Hush, Darlin', I know. You ain't got no money. Don't you worry about it."

In minutes, Eric had a plate filled with eggs, bacon, hash browns and toast in front of him. Breathing in the aroma, he closed his eyes and conjured up an image of his own kitchen. He could see Sharon sitting across from him, asking if she could get him anything else. And there was Bridget, standing at the counter in sweats, just in from a run, drinking a glass of orange juice.

"Hey, thought you was hungry!"

Eric's eyes snapped open. "Uh, yeah, I am. Sorry Sophie, I was just thinking about something."

"Yeah you was—you was thinkin' about what use' to be. Don't get all up in your head, it'll drive you nuts." Sophie went over to the sink and began to wash some dishes. "Hey, where Harold at?"

Taking a bite of his toast with butter slathered all over it, Eric savored the taste before answering. "I don't know. He and Aaron have been gone for a couple of days.

"Hope he's okay with his heart and all."

"What's that, Sophie? His heart?"

"Yeah," the big woman replied. "Professor don't talk much, but one day in here he told me he got a bad ticker . . . had a couple heart attacks and was in the hospital. Aaron looks out for him, makes sure he gets to a doctor when Harold's not feelin' good."

Eric took a forkful of eggs. "I didn't know."

"They a crazy pair but they good for each other. Aaron watches over the Professor, and Harold keeps Aaron from goin' off. That big man got anger problems."

Several minutes later, Eric had all but finished his breakfast and was draining the last of his coffee. "Sophie, you're an angel. That was the best meal I've had in a long time." Eric dug in his pocket and pulled out all of his change. Placing the coins on the counter, he began to zip his jacket. "I'm afraid that's all I can give you."

The big woman smiled. "Darlin' I know you ain't got no money. Even if you did, you gonna spend it on booze, not food." She scooped up the change and handed it to Eric. "Here, you need this more than me. Sophie ain't gonna go broke anytime soon. The Lord takin' care o' me cause I'm takin' care o' some o' His."

"Thank you." Feeling somewhat refreshed, Eric made his way out of the restaurant. He walked to the corner and looked toward the vacant lot, then turned around and looked in the direction of State Street. Turning his face up to the sun, he thought, "It's a good day for begging after all," and headed toward State. Sophie was right—he needed money for alcohol.

~~~~~~~~~~

Returning home from school, Bridget walked through the kitchen door and hung her coat on the hook behind it. Hearing the TV in the family room she called out, "Mom?"

"We're in here."

Curious, the girl went to see who was with her mother. "Brian!" She shouted when she saw her nephew sitting on the couch next to her mother. "How are you?" Bridget hurried over, picked the boy up, and began to snuggle and kiss him. "You look so good."

The little boy smiled and hugged Bridget. "Doctor said I'm better."

She kissed him once more and then put him down. Brian wandered over to the Christmas tree that was still standing and grabbed one of the presents. "Can I open?"

Bridget looked at her mother. "No, Sweetheart," Sharon said, "I told you that we'll open all the presents when Papa comes home. Put it back." Frowning, Brian set it back under the tree and went back to the couch to resume watching cartoons.

"So, how did the test go today?"

"It was easy," Bridget replied as she removed her shoes. "I think I'll go for a run while the sun is still out."

"Wait a minute, I want you to see something." Sharon grabbed a piece of mail from the table next to the couch and handed it to her daughter. "This came today from the University of Illinois in Chicago."

Taking it from her mother, Bridget eyes grew wider as she looked at it for a moment, but then set it down on the coffee table."Probably bad news," she quipped. "We both know that I can't afford to go there now, not after my performance at the regional meet. Just toss it in the trash." She grabbed her shoes and socks and ran up the stairs to her room.

"Bridge . . ." Sharon picked up the letter and opened it. While the cartoons played on the TV for Brian, Sharon read and re-read the contents of the first page. Wiping a tear from her cheek, Sharon stood up and made her way to the stairs. She glanced back at Brain. "Nana will be right back. I have to tell Bridget something."

She made her way to her daughter's room and knocked gently on the door. "Bridget?"

"What?"

"Can I come in; I need to show you something?"

The girl walked to her bedroom door and opened it. "What is it, Mom, I need to change clothes?"

"Read this," Sharon said, handing the letter to her daughter.

Taking the letter, Bridget began to read it. She took a few steps back and sat on her bed. After a minute, her eyes began to well with tears. Bridget looked at her mother. "Mom, they're offering me a partial athletic scholarship."

"Yes, one that will pay your tuition." Sharon smiled and wiped away more tears.

"But, Mom, we can't afford room and board for me in Chicago. And anyway, how will I get there? I don't have a car."

"Don't worry, we'll work it out. I can get a job and . . . you can take dad's truck to school. It needs to be driven anyway."

Bridget sprang from the bed and hugged her mother. "Mom, I can't believe this. I'm going to college!"

"Yes you are." Sharon said as she hugged her daughter. "Yes you are." Sharon let go, and as she left the room, she looked over her shoulder and said, "Get your run in now, Mark and Erin will be joining us for dinner when they come to pick Brian up."

"Okay, Mom. Love you."

"Love you, too." Sharon made her way back to where her grandson sat contentedly on the couch watching a big yellow bird. *Thank you, Lord.*

36

We think sometimes that poverty is only being hungry, naked and homeless. The poverty of being unwanted, unloved and uncared for is the greatest poverty. We must start in our own homes to remedy this kind of poverty.
   —**Mother Teresa**

Sharon stood in the bulk food aisle at the supermarket. Tomorrow was her day to volunteer at the homeless shelter, something she had been doing every week since Thanksgiving. At first, her decision was purely due to an uneaten holiday dinner she didn't want to go to waste. However, it soon turned altruistic as she grew to be more concerned for anyone suffering hard times. She identified with their plight, even though she herself still lived comfortably. As she had an opportunity to spend time with various individuals, she engaged them and discovered each person had suffered personal tragedy of one kind or another. Sharon felt a kinship with the residents of the shelter, and in a strange way, she somehow felt she was helping her husband by helping those who could not help themselves.

Bending low to grab two large cans of tomato sauce, she heard her name. "Sharon?" She stood up and saw Sandy Giordano standing in the aisle next to her. Setting the cans in her cart, Sharon answered, "Sandy, um . . . hi."

"Hi." Sandy answered, while looking at Sharon's nearly overflowing cart. "Having company?"

Sharon hesitated for a moment, not realizing the woman was perplexed about the amount of food Sharon had in her cart. "Oh, yeah, it's not for us. I volunteer at the homeless shelter downtown and help cook dinner once a week. Sandy, I . . ."

"Oh, how nice of you. Listen, I . . ."

The women spoke simultaneously; each stopped and smiled as

they realized what they had done. Sharon steeled herself and wondered if now was the time to offer an apology. Stiffening as if anticipating a blow, she continued. "Sandy, I hardly know where to begin, or what to say, except that I'm so very sorry about your son. We . . . I . . ." Sharon stopped and looked down.

Sandy gathered her thoughts. "Thank you. It's been difficult for us without Geno. We took his death very hard."

"I'm sure, I mean, your only child."

"Yes, we were both very bitter at first. In fact, the first few weeks afterward I thought our marriage was over. Al and I couldn't even be in the same room together without arguing."

"I'm sorry, Sandy. This ordeal has been hard on all of us."

The woman nodded. "I know, Sharon. I have to confess that after our son's death, I blamed you as much as I blamed your husband. Whenever I saw either of you around town, I did my best to avoid you both. But I was wrong, I was acting more from the ache in my heart, rather than anything else. Now I realize that what happened that night was a tragic accident, and that Geno contributed to it by his own actions."

Sharon felt her tension dissipate. "Thank you, Sandy. You don't know how relieved I am to hear you say that. I've been wanting to talk to you for so long about what happened."

"Me too. I saw you at Mass on Christmas and wanted to say something to you then, but . . ."

Smiling, Sharon stepped forward and hugged the woman. "That's okay. I'm glad you stopped me today, I feel much better now. And speaking of Mass, I want you to know that I'm praying for you and Al every day."

Sandy nodded. "It must be working, we're beginning to get back to some sense of normalcy. Sharon, your husband . . . I . . . is there anything I can do?"

"Unless you can find him, no, not really. But thank you for asking."

"You and Bridget are good people. I hope Eric somehow finds his way back from wherever he is."

"Me too. It's pure torture not knowing what happened to him."

"I'm sure. Well, I've got to pick up a few items and get back to work. I'm glad we had this talk," she said, as she moved her cart forward.

"So am I, Sandy. Thank you."

~~~~~~~~~~

Sharon set the salad on the table and went to the counter to fetch the low-cal dressing she'd made. "C'mon, everyone, it's time to eat," she yelled toward the family room.

It was Friday, and the kids were once again visiting, something Mark thought was more important now more than ever with Eric still missing. Erin picked Brian up off the floor where the little guy had been playing with a collection of toy cars Eric kept at the house for him. But before his mother picked him up, Brian grabbed a small police car to bring with him to the dinner table. He held it up in front of him. "That's Papa," he said.

"Yes it is," Erin replied.

Once everyone sat down, Sharon turned to Mark. "Son, will you say grace?"

"Sure, Mom." Mark recited the blessing and added, "And please keep Papa safe."

"Amen," everyone said.

Sharon began passing the bread and sliced pork roast, potatoes, onions and carrots around the table. "Erin, when is Brian's next doctor visit?"

"Next week."

"Are they checking the bone marrow?"

"No, the doctor wants to make sure his white blood cell count is normal after the chemo." Erin put a carrot on Brian's plate.

"I don't like carrots," the boy cried.

"You have to eat just one, okay?"

Brian looked at Sharon. "Nana, do I have to?"

Looking at her daughter, Sharon shrugged. "Tell you what, you eat half and I'll eat the other half—deal?"

The little boy smiled. "Deal."

"Nana . . ." Erin shook her head. Her mother-in-law had a special way of dealing with Brian, something Erin needed to take advantage of at times. She took a bite of bread. "I'm hoping everything looks good. The doctor said that more than half of the children with leukemia are cured with standard chemotherapy treatment, but we have to stay vigilant."

Mark set his glass down after taking a drink of water. "Mom, I know this is probably none of my business, but what are your plans now that dad's salary has been discontinued? I'm worried about you and Bridge," he said, looking at his sister. "She told me the good news about the scholarship at U of I, but room and board in Chicago is going to be pretty steep."

"I know, and I'm trying to get myself together and anticipate the costs. Dad and I have some savings and investments, and I'm going to get a job. We'll be okay for a while."

Bridget interrupted. "Mom, I've been thinking that maybe I should just go to community college for a while. That way I can stay home and help out, you know, get a job . . . at least until Dad comes home."

"No, Bridget, you're going to Chicago. You have a fantastic opportunity in front of you, and it would be a sin for you not to take advantage of it."

"I think Mom's right, Bridge," Mark offered. "U of I Chicago is a great school, plus you'll be competing in track at the college level. They're an NCAA school."

Bridget sat silent for a moment. "I don't know, Mom, I just don't feel right about the whole thing, especially leaving you alone."

Erin forced the last bite of carrot into her son's mouth. "Good job!" She said, clapping her hands. She looked at her mother-in-law. "You won't be alone, Mom. Brian and I will be visiting you so much that you'll probably get sick of seeing us."

"Never happen." Sharon smiled at her grandson.

"Mom, don't hesitate to ask for help if you need it. You and Dad have helped us so much already, it's only right that we should help you when you need it. That's what Dad would want me to do."

Sharon began to well up with tears. "I know, Son. I promise I'll let you know if I need you."

Bridget moved the food around on her plate. *Why am I putting Mom through this? Doesn't she have enough to worry about without me adding to her burden?* "I, uh, I'm full," Bridge announced, as she stood up. She took her plate and set it on the counter.

"Bridge, you hardly ate anything."

"I had a big lunch," she told her mother, and then finished her glass of water. "Besides, I don't want to stuff myself, I'm meeting a friend later for a run."

Mark and Erin look quizzically at Sharon as Bridget went up to her room. "Just leave it alone . . . "

37

When faith is lost, when honor dies, the man is dead.
—**John Greenleaf Whittier**

It had been more than a month since Eric last saw the Professor and Aaron. Sometime within the first week of their disappearance, Eric returned to the vacant lot after panhandling to find the shopping cart with the sleeping bags and several clothing items missing. He wasn't sure if his two friends had come by and taken it, or if another homeless person had. Regardless, Eric felt he should stay at the lot for a while just in case his friends returned. However, after waiting weeks it seemed that would not likely happen.

April would be ending soon, which meant the fire barrel would no longer be as important for his survival. Sure, the nights were still chilly, but he found that even without a sleeping bag the cardboard kept the chill off his body. However, he did miss the warmth and comfort of his quasi-cocoon. Before setting out to find a new place to call home, one that would also shield him from the rain, he decided to stop at the mission to see if he could get something to eat and perhaps, a sleeping bag or blanket.

On the walk over to the mission, it began to rain. At first, Eric ducked into a couple of doorways hoping the rain might stop. But when it appeared it would likely last for some time, he decided to endure being wet for the sake of getting to the shelter and hopefully, a warm drink. Turning the corner, he spotted the Lighthouse Mission and immediately thought that it was indeed a lighthouse. Soaked, he bowed his head from the drizzle and walked toward the light and up the front steps.

As soon as he got inside, Eric glanced over at the old police desk. George was sitting in his usual spot, overseeing everything. He looked up when he heard Eric enter. "Hey, good to see you again my friend," George greeted him. "Man, you look soaked. We can take care of that and get you warmed up."

Eric smiled. "Thanks." He took off his jacket. "Can I hang this here?" He asked, going over to where a row of hooks had replaced the FBI Ten Most Wanted posters.

"Sure."

Eric walked over to the desk and for a moment, he visualized how this old police station must have been when it was still active. With the desk sergeant seated high above the officers and everyone else coming through the front door, it was laid out much like a courtroom. The sergeant, acting as the judge, easily identified the good guys from bad guys, and no one had to guess who was in charge. "Uh, George, do you think I might get some coffee?"

"Of course, but you know the drill. I have to check you first to make sure you don't have any alcohol." He came down from his position and quickly checked Eric's pockets for bottles. Finding none, George pointed to the double doors that led to the large dining hall that used to serve as the squad room. "Go ahead, there's a big pot of coffee inside and some sweet rolls that a woman from the bakery down the street brought in. They're a day old but they'll stick to your ribs and fill you up."

"Thanks, George." Eric headed toward the doors and stopped short. Looking back, he asked, "George, have you seen Aaron or the Professor lately?"

George's smiled disappeared. "I thought you knew about Harold since you used to hang together."

Puzzled, Eric replied. "Knew what?"

"The Professor's dead. Aaron brought him here about a month ago when the Professor started complaining about chest pains. He collapsed soon after he came in. We called 9-1-1 right away, but by the time they got here the Professor had died."

Eric's breath caught in his throat. "He died? What, what about Aaron?"

George shrugged his shoulders. "Don't know. When the ambulance people finally stopped working on the Professor and were about to take his body away, Aaron became angry with them. He accused them of not responding quickly enough to save his friend. The cop who responded along with the ambulance tried to calm Aaron down, but Aaron continued to yell and eventually shoved the cop. The officer arrested him; I haven't seen Aaron since that day."

Stunned, Eric stood silent. *That explains why I haven't seen either one of them.*

"Don't take it too hard," George told him. "Being homeless is a tough life—no health care or proper nutrition takes its toll on the body. If you already have a health problem, living on the streets can kill you. That's just a fact of life."

Eric nodded. "Yeah, I guess so. I'm sorry to hear about the Professor, he taught me about a lot of things."

"He was a good man."

"Yeah," Eric agreed. Pushing through the double doors, Eric made his way over to the big aluminum coffee maker. He grabbed a Styrofoam cup and filled it with the steaming brew, then opened a large box and chose a sweet roll. He brought his selection and his coffee over to one of the long folding tables, away from the handful of others who were there at the mission for the same reason. Taking a sip from his cup, he jerked it away from his lips. "Damn." The hot liquid burned his tongue.

"Let it cool; what's your hurry?" Eric heard a voice from behind him, and then a man in a black suit sat down next to him. "May I join you?"

Eric looked closely at the man. "Oh, it's you," he said, quickly placing the voice with the face. "You're the priest I met here on Christmas Day—Father Callahan."

"Right. Good memory, Son." The priest took a drink of his own coffee from a ceramic cup. "You look a bit down in the dumps, want to talk about it?"

Eric took a bite of his sweet roll. It tasted great, except that his tongue was still stinging from the hot coffee. "Uh, I just found out a friend of mine passed away."

"Oh, I'm sorry to hear that. How can I help you?"

"I don't need any help, unless you can give me a blanket or something." Eric took another bite.

The priest laughed. "A blanket is all you need? That's not a problem, but I was hoping you'd ask for something a bit more spiritual."

Eric glanced at the priest, but kept silent.

The two men sat quietly for a moment, before the priest broke in.

"Do you have any family?"

"Father, I don't mean to be rude but I'm really not in the mood to talk right now. If you can get me a sleeping bag or something, I'll be very grateful. Otherwise, I'd just like to finish my snack, dry off for a while, and then I'll be on my way."

The priest stood up. "Sure, Eric, I'll tell the staff to get a sleeping bag for you." Father Callahan walked toward the door leading to the supply room. Before going through it, he turned toward Eric. "Your family misses you, especially, your grandson." Then the priest disappeared through the door.

"What?" Eric took a second to digest what the man said. *He called me Eric. Did I tell him my name? And how does he know I have a grandson?* Eric got up and immediately went into the supply room. A woman was working behind the counter, sorting items of clothing. A sleeping bag sat on the counter off to the side. "Where's the priest?"

"Who?"

"The priest who just walked in here, Father Callahan."

The woman gave Eric a quizzical look. "You're the only one who just walked in, and I don't know any Father Callahan." She stiffened and took a couple of steps backward, trying to stay as far away from Eric as she could.

"Hey, I'm not crazy. I saw a priest walk in here just a second ago." Eric pointed to the sleeping bag on the counter. "I asked him to get me a sleeping bag."

"You, uh, you can have it—go ahead—take it."

He walked up to the counter and grabbed it. Looking around the room, Eric saw that the door he came in through was the only way in or out of the supply room. *Where did he go?* The woman stood frozen, not sure what Eric might do.

Sensing her fear, Eric put the sleeping bag under his arm. "Sorry to bother you. I must have been wrong about the priest." He backed away and left the room, returning to his seat in the dining hall. *Am I losing my mind?*

Eric stayed at the shelter for several hours while his clothes dried and he warmed up. As he sat drinking his coffee, he tried to make sense of what happened today. Father Callahan's appearance and subsequent disappearance troubled him. Was he losing touch with

THE YEAR WITHOUT CHRISTMAS

reality, or was it an illusion created by his drinking?

The Professor's death shocked him, not that he didn't think homeless people died, but more from the standpoint of the man being a type of mentor in the strange world of living on the street. Harold had taken Eric under his wing, schooling him on how to survive in a culture that most often is not welcoming to those who are homeless.

Scratching his beard, Eric remembered how the Professor had warned him about letting his beard get out of hand. "Folks don't like scruffy looking people. If you keep yourself clean and shave every so often, they're more likely to be compassionate and offer you food or money. The shelter will let you clean up. They have plenty of disposable razors and toothbrushes. If you're close to a park, use that public restroom to wash up."

The Professor was a font of knowledge about being homeless. Eric thought about the time they were searching for cardboard. One afternoon he and Harold were walking down an alley when Eric slipped into a loading dock area to relieve himself. "What are you doing?" The Professor asked.

"Gotta pee."

"Not here. If somebody sees you and complains, the cops will either give you a ticket or arrest you. Most citizens who do the same thing get a warning; we aren't that lucky. The police don't have much tolerance for the homeless using the streets as a bathroom." After that lesson, Eric always searched for a gas station or fast food restaurant when he needed to use a bathroom.

One day Eric and the Professor were in a fast food restaurant. Earlier, they had each panhandled about ten dollars and decided to get a hamburger and coffee. After finishing their meal, Eric decided to use the rest room. Several minutes later, Eric came back to the table where the Professor was sitting. "Eric, just before you came out of the bathroom, some kid about fourteen years old came out."

Puzzled, Eric said, "Yeah, the kid was in the stall when I went in, but he finished his business before I finished mine."

The Professor shook his head. "Bad move. You want to keep your distance from children, in fact, avoid even speaking to them."

"Why?"

"They're trouble. All they need to do is make an allegation that you touched them or said something inappropriate and you'll find yourself in jail. Hell, even if you're found not guilty, that accusation will stay with you forever. And if you don't beat the charge . . . well, I don't need to tell you what happens to child molesters in prison."

As a cop, Eric never gave any thought to how the homeless in Websterville survived from day to day. Now, he was learning firsthand what it was like. "Don't stay in one place too long," the Professor admonished. "I can't tell you exactly how long is too long —maybe more than a few hours is a good rule of thumb. Anything more than that invites trouble and may result in the manager of the place banning you."

I'll miss you, Harold. Eric stood and took his plate and cup to the nearby trashcan and dumped them. Picking up his sleeping bag, he made his way back toward the desk area. "You leavin' us?" George asked Eric as he went to retrieve his jacket.

"Yeah."

"Rain let up, but I don't think it's done for the day."

Eric reached into his jacket pocket and felt the pint bottle he had left in it. *Good, George hadn't searched his jacket.* He set the sleeping bag down and slipped into his jacket. "I'm planning on staying dry."

"Good luck with that," George said, as Eric walked out the doors leading to the street. Looking toward the lake, he saw a covered underpass that would be perfect for the time being. At least he'd stay dry if the rain started up again. As he approached the area, he looked at the street sign: Lower Michigan Avenue. "Michigan," he said aloud, and then pulled out his bottle and took a long drink.

38

What we would like to do is change the world-make it a little simpler for people to feed, clothe, and shelter themselves as God intended for them to do.
—**Dorothy Day**

Sharon and Bridget put the rest of the dried dishes away. "That should do it," Florence said, as she moved beside them and retrieved their wet dishtowels. As one of the shelter's supervisors, Florence had grown close to Sharon and her daughter. "I love Fridays," Florence offered the two women. "You both have brought a little bit of sunshine to this place. I appreciate your help, and I know the residents have grown fond of you as well."

"Thanks," Sharon replied.

"Mom, I'm going to visit with Shelly for a while."

Sharon gestured toward one of the couches in the common area. "The young girl with the long hair and the baby?"

"Yes, she kinda looks like she wants to talk."

Sharon smiled at her daughter. "Good idea, Bridge."

She walked over and sat next to Shelly and her two-year old son, while Sharon stayed in the kitchen. "What's her story?" Sharon asked.

"Another sad one, I'm afraid. She came in several weeks ago, said she had no car and no place to go. We took her in and had her fill out the usual paperwork providing us with some background information. It seems her husband is in jail on a two-year auto theft charge. The couple had been living with the husband's mother, but Shelly told me the mother is on drugs and gets violent."

"That's not a good environment for the child."

"No, it's not."

"How about the girl's parents? Why doesn't she stay with her own folks?"

Florence nodded. "Good question, but she told me her mother is dead and she never knew her father."

"Wow," Sharon sighed. "That poor girl."

Florence walked over to the large industrial refrigerator and took several dishes out. "Sharon, can you help me put together a stew for tomorrow?"

"Sure." The two women busied themselves as they continued their discussion.

"Shelly and her little boy really belong in a women's shelter, not here. Unfortunately, Websterville is a small town and hasn't yet seen the 'need' for one, as they put it. Some of the other residents have shunned Shelly, saying she doesn't help enough around here."

"You mean, like cleaning?"

"Yes, everyone is expected to help out and do their share in keeping the shelter clean. The problem for Shelly is that taking care of a two-year-old is a full-time job, especially here. Some of the older people don't want to be bothered by kids."

Sharon started to prepare a broth, while Florence cut up leftover meat and chopped vegetables.

"The rules here only allow for a two-four week stay. Shelly's got about another week before she becomes ineligible to remain here."

"What about the baby?"

"Doesn't matter; there are no exceptions, otherwise we'd have folks living here forever. We try to accommodate everyone without enabling their situation."

Setting the large pot on the stove, Sharon turned on the burner. "Where can they go? I mean, she certainly can't go back to the mother-in-law's."

"I have some feelers out to a couple of churches, but after the holidays most of their charitable funds are depleted."

The two women worked silently for a while, before Florence spoke. "Sharon, do you think you might be able to help?"

"How? I uh, I don't know. I'll have to think about it. In fact, tomorrow I'll go see our pastor and find out if he has any ideas."

"Okay." Florence answered, as she dumped a large helping of vegetables into the broth Sharon had prepared. Get back to me as quickly as you can."

THE YEAR WITHOUT CHRISTMAS

Thirty minutes later, Sharon and Bridget were driving home from the shelter. "Hey, Mom?"

"Yes."

"Can I use the car tomorrow afternoon?"

"Sure, what for?"

"I was talking with Shelly about her stay at the shelter . . . she needs to get away from it for a bit. I thought I would take her and Marco to the mall."

"Marco, is that her child's name?"

"Yes. I thought we could just hang out, get some ice cream or something."

"That's a great idea, Bridge. I'm sure Marco will enjoy getting out of that place, too."

"Thanks, Mom. Shelly seems really depressed about things. I think a trip to the mall is just what she needs."

"I agree." As she continued the drive home, Sharon thought her daughter's interest in helping others might be just what Bridget needed as well.

~~~~~~~~~~

"Thanks for taking us, Bridget. We've been cooped up in the shelter the past few weeks. And with the weather getting nice, it's good to be out of there for a while; I feel almost normal again." Shelly was carrying Marco as they walked into the Websterville Mall.

"Hey, let's get one of those little car-looking carts to push Marco in," Bridget said, as she walked toward a row of strollers for rent.

"Good idea, sometimes he feels like he weighs a ton. Anyway, he likes those carts."

As the girls continued deeper into the mall, Bridget turned to Shelly. "When I picked you two up at the shelter, it looked like you had been crying."

Shelly hesitated before answering. "Yeah, I had an argument with one of the residents. This older guy keeps after me to smoke some weed with him."

"I thought drugs and alcohol weren't allowed at the shelter."

"They're not, but this guy somehow keeps a few joints handy. The thing is, I know he wants more than to just share a joint, if you know what I mean. I told him I'm not interested in him, that I just want a place for me and Marco to be safe."

They stopped in front of a coffee shop. "So what did he say?"

"He got all insulted, said he could make my time at the shelter more pleasant if I was nice to him. I told him to forget about it. So he got mad and threatened me, said I better watch my back."

Bridget's eyes became wide as saucers. "What? Did you tell Florence?"

"No, the worst thing you can do when you live in a shelter is to draw attention to yourself. It's best to stay in the background if possible, keep things to yourself and try to get along with everyone."

Bridget shook her head. "Unbelievable. I guess I don't know as much about that place as I thought I did. Hey, let's get a coffee—my treat."

"Mmm, sounds good. I want some kind of foo-foo latte or frappe or whatever it's called."

The girls walked inside and continued their discussion. They took their drinks to a table in the corner of the coffee shop. Shelly reached into her bag and brought out a sippee cup for Marco. "Here you go, apple juice for my best guy." The child eagerly grabbed the cup from his mother and sat contentedly, sucking on his juice.

"Looks like he has his drink of choice," Bridget commented.

"Yeah, he loves his juice. The problem is, I don't know how much longer he'll be able to enjoy drinking juice every day."

"What do you mean?"

"Florence told me I only have one more week to stay at the shelter before they discharge us. There's a limit to how long anyone can stay."

"That's crazy," Bridget said, as she set her coffee down on the table. "What are you going to do; where will you go?"

"I don't know. If I can make it for three months somewhere, I can go back to the shelter for another month." Shelly looked down, avoiding Bridget's gaze. She rubbed her eyes for a moment and then took a deep breath. "I know I can't go back to my mother-in-law's, it's not safe. I think I have enough money for a few nights at a cheap motel, after that I guess Marco and I will just wing it."

"What about your church?" Bridget asked. "Can they lend you some money for an apartment?"

Shelly stirred her drink. "I don't belong to any church."

THE YEAR WITHOUT CHRISTMAS

Bridget sipped her coffee while she watched Marco in the stroller as he finished his juice. The little boy reminded her of her own nephew, Brian, whom she couldn't imagine living on the street. She looked at Shelly. "Listen, there must be something we can do. Let me talk this over with my Mom, she'll have an answer."

"That's kind of you. I hope your Mom can help, but at least winter has passed. If we have to, we can make it for a while . . . at least until I'm eligible to go back to the shelter."

"C'mon, let's take Marco over to the children's play area for a while."

"Okay."

As they pushed Marco past the stores and toward the center of the mall, Shelly turned to Bridget. "I wish I was in your shoes right now."

"Yeah?"

"You have a great family, your Mom cares about you, and you're getting ready to go to college—something I never had a chance to do."

"You can still go," Bridget quickly added.

"How? My husband's in jail; I don't have any family, and I have Marco to look after."

They arrived at the play area and Bridget watched as Shelly took Marco out of the stroller. She wished she had an answer to Shelly's question, but she didn't.

~~~~~~~~~~

Several hours later, Bridget dropped Shelly and her baby back at the shelter and then continued on her way home. She walked in and found her mother cleaning in the family room, a Saturday ritual for as long as Bridget could remember. "Hi, Mom."

"Oh, hi, Bridge. How did it go with Shelly?"

"Pretty good. We had some coffee and talked for a while. Later, we took Marco over to the play area. That little guy has a lot of energy. By the time we left he was out cold; he slept all the way to the shelter."

Bridget watched as her mother picked up the presents under the tree so she could vacuum the rug. "Mom, c'mon, are we really going to keep the decorations up? It's spring already."

Sharon set the gifts on the coffee table. "Yes, we are, and quit asking me about it. I am not taking them down until your father comes home."

"Okay, okay." Bridget didn't see things the same way her mother did. She wanted her Dad home as much as her Mom did, but keeping the house decorated for Christmas was stupid. "Mom?"

"Yes?"

"Shelly told me the shelter is kicking her out in one week. She has no place to go, and only a handful of money to stay at a motel for a couple days. Is there anything we can do, maybe see if our church can help out?"

Putting the last package on the table, Sharon walked over to the vacuum cleaner. "Funny you should ask. While you were gone, I took Dad's truck and went to see Father William."

"And . . .?" Shelly asked, expectedly.

"He told me the church donates to the shelter on a regular basis, and that our parish does not have any extra funds to help out individuals who aren't actually residents of the shelter."

Hoping her Mother had a solution to the problem, Bridget's spirits deflated and she plopped down into a nearby chair.

Leaning on the vacuum, Sharon continued. "Catholic Charities in Detroit is probably best able to help her out, but the Pastor said it could take weeks to get the paperwork in place and actually get Shelly and the baby off the street."

"That sucks!" Bridget said, with a sour look on her face. She crossed her arms and sank into the chair, throwing her legs over the arms.

"Wait a second, before you get upset . . . I think I have a plan to solve this dilemma, but only if you are completely on board with it."

"What is it, Mom?"

Taking a seat on the couch, Sharon explained. "I might be out of my mind suggesting this, and I could very well regret what I'm about to say, but . . . after I spoke with Father William, I went inside the church to pray. While I was in the midst of praying for your Dad, and for a solution to Shelly's problem, it suddenly occurred to me that *I was the answer.*"

Bridget wrinkled her brow, "What, how are you the answer?"

"Well, after spending time in the shelter with men and women who are less fortunate that we are, I began to think about other ways

THE YEAR WITHOUT CHRISTMAS

in which I might be able to help."

"We help feed them every week, Mom, what more can we do?"

"I know," Sharon said, putting her palm up toward her daughter. "Let me finish. As I was praying over what I could do to help Shelly, it became clear that she needed someone."

Confused, Bridget shook her head. "I don't get it."

"Shelly doesn't have a mother; I can try to fill that void for her—if only for a while—I want to invite her to stay with us until she gets back on her feet, or until her husband gets out of jail."

Silence. Bridget pondered what her Mother had just told her, and then broke out in a wide smile. "Holy cow, do you mean it? I mean we hardly know her . . . well, I mean, I guess we do, but, yeah—living here with us—sure."

"It seems like the right thing to do," her Mother explained. "We certainly have the room, and in a couple of months you'll be graduating high school and will be home for the summer before going away to college. I expect that you will help out."

Sitting up in her chair, Bridget nodded. "Yeah, it'll be cool having a little kid around. And when Brian comes over to visit, he'll have a playmate. Let's do it, Mom!"

"Okay. In the meantime, let's get the spare bedroom ready for our new guests." Sharon and Bridget went upstairs to the spare bedroom to make sure everything was in place. Watching her daughter dusting the furniture in preparation for their anticipated visitor, Sharon knew she had made the right decision.

39

Our national drug is alcohol. We tend to regard the use any other drug with special horror.
—**William S. Burroughs**

Eric ducked out of the incessant Chicago rain and began to explore the world beneath North Michigan Avenue. He noted it wasn't as busy as Lower Wacker Avenue, the other underground street the Professor had shown him. Traffic here was sparse, but there were more trucks making deliveries to loading docks, which made it noisier. That was fine, at least it was dry.

Walking a block in either direction searching for a spot to hunker down, Eric spotted some cardboard lying on the cement. *Someone's already claimed this spot.* Nevertheless, he decided this would be a good place to wait for the rain to end and to finish his bottle of vodka. He had been nursing the bottle all day, knowing he was short on money and would probably have to either buy a cheap bottle of wine, or go panhandling again. The rain made his decision easy: he'd buy a bottle of cheap wine.

"Hey, whatcha drinkin'?"

He looked up to see a woman standing next to him. Dark complected, her long hair worn in a ponytail, she had a thin weathered face with lines etched in it like growth rings in a tree. He read her age to be somewhere in the late forties. Her baggy clothes hid her figure, but Eric guessed she was probably lean, judging from her hollow cheeks.

"Who wants to know?" Eric responded.

"Easy big fella," the woman said, as she backed up against the wall and slid down next to him. "I'm Doreen; who are you?"

"Eric."

The woman extended a gloved hand. "Pleased to meet ya."

THE YEAR WITHOUT CHRISTMAS

Eric shook her hand. "Same here."

"Ain't seen you 'round here before, but it looks like you been on the street for a while." Doreen jutted her chin toward the bottle Eric was holding. "Can I get a taste?"

"Uh, sure," he said, handing the bottle to her.

Doreen took a healthy drink. "Mmm, that's good, 'cept it's almost gone. You got any more?"

"Nah, that's it, I'll have to buy a bottle somewhere."

Hearing that, the woman's face brightened and she moved closer to Eric. "Say, can you buy a bottle for me, can ya buy me a 40?" The woman leaned into him, and reached down between his legs. "I'll take care o' ya."

"Whoa! What are you doing?" He pushed her arm away.

"What? You don't like women?"

"No . . . I mean, yes, but I'm not looking for what you're offering."

"Sorry, man, I thought it would be a fair trade. I do that for some of the guys out here, makes 'em feel better, if ya know what I mean."

"I'm sure you do, but I'm not interested. What's a 40, anyway?"

"Man, you are green. Olde English, man, malt liquor, the big bottle—powerful stuff."

"Oh, yeah, malt liquor. I think I've got enough for a bottle of beer. Where can we get it?"

The woman stood up. "C'mon, grab your sleeping bag and follow me. There's a liquor store right up those stairs," she said, pointing to a set of stairs across the street. "You're gonna like OE."

As the couple walked up the stairs, the woman asked, "What about weed, do ya smoke?"

"Marijuana? No, I don't do drugs, they're illegal."

"Ha!" She laughed. "So is being drunk in public, but it don't look like that bothers ya."

Eric didn't have an answer for that. He'd always thought people who did drugs were weak and stupid. He'd locked up his share of addicts and alcoholics. Now he was learning first hand that there wasn't much difference between the two. "Yeah, I guess you're right."

In minutes they were inside the liquor store. Doreen led Eric to the cooler where the single bottles of malt liquor stood in straight lines like soldiers in formation. She opened the door, picked out a bottle of OE, and brought it to the counter. "Hey, Pauli."

The aging, bald cashier put down his newspaper and got up from his stool, "Hi Doreen. That it?"

"Yep." The woman turned toward Eric. "Pay the man, my dear."

Eric pulled a handful of change from his pocket and counted out two dollars and thirty-nine cents, and then put the remaining few coins away.

The cashier put the bottle in a brown paper bag. "Here you go. See you next time."

"For sure." Doreen grabbed the bottle as Eric reached for it. "C'mon, I'm gettin' thirsty." They retraced their steps and quickly resumed their positions on the cardboard underground. She unscrewed the cap and took a long drink. "Ah, damn that's good. Here you go, Sweetie," she said, handing the bagged bottle to Eric.

He took a drink and then nodded. "You're right, this is good."

"Yeah, it's a little stronger than regular beer—gives ya a better buzz." The woman put the bottle up to her lips. "Ow, damn!"

Eric looked at her. "What's the matter."

She rubbed her cheek. "This damn tooth o' mine's been botherin' me sometimes when I drink somethin' cold. I'm gonna have to see the dentist tonight."

"How are you going to do that? Dentists cost money."

"Nah, they got 'em on the bus."

Puzzled, Eric asked. "What bus?"

"Oh, yeah, you're green. I forgot. The city puts a bus out at night; they call it the night ministry. Actually, it's pretty cool—got doctors and dentists, shrinks and church folks. Heck, they hand out free stuff, man, like socks and blankets and all kinds o' donated food."

"Hmm, that sounds good."

"Yeah, they think they're helpin' us out, but what they're really doin' is helpin' us buy a bottle or a joint, since we don't have to buy or own food if they give it to us for free."

"Take me there."

"I will, but they only come 'round at night like after seven. Let's finish our 40 and take a nap, then I'll show you where the bus sets up." She took another drink, wincing at the pain in her tooth. She handed the bottle back to Eric. "You sure you don't want me to do ya?"

"I'm sure," he said, taking a drink. "Anyway, I'm married; I couldn't do that to my wife. Just show me where this bus is at tonight and we'll be square."

"Okay, but you don't know what you're missin'."

"Whatever," he shot back. *I do know what I'm missing.*

~~~~~~~~~~

Sharon opened the door to the spare bedroom. "Here's where you and Marco will be staying while you're here.

Shelly walked into the room carrying her son. She looked around for a moment and then turned to Sharon. "Oh my God, this is beautiful. I've never had a room like this before," she gushed. Sitting on the bed, she put Marco on the floor. "A TV . . . ?"

"Yes, you have your own TV with cable, and there's a bathroom right across the hall."

"Mrs. Doyle, this is so over the top," she went on. "I don't know how to thank you."

"We'll worry about that later. Right now, why don't you and Marco get settled in."

Bridget rolled the woman's suitcase into the room. "Here's your stuff, Shelly. I hope we didn't forget anything at the shelter."

"I didn't have much to begin with."

Sharon walked over to the small toddler bed against the wall. "Marco should be fine sleeping here. Our grandson, Brian, sleeps in it whenever he visits, but I'm sure he won't mind if you borrow it for a while." She walked over to the dresser and opened the bottom drawer. "There's an extra blanket and pillow in here if you need it. Why don't you and Bridget visit for a bit while I start dinner?"

"Can I help? Before Marco was born, I worked at a restaurant and helped out with the cooking."

"Not today, but I'll keep that in mind." Sharon walked over to the door and was about to close it, but stopped. "Ladies, we'll have to make sure we keep the doors closed so Marco doesn't fall down the stairs. And I'll dig out the gate we used when Brian was younger."

"Got it, Mom."

After the door closed, Shelly lifted her suitcase and put it on the bed. "Might as well get unpacked."

"Need help?" Bridget asked.

"Nah, like I said, I don't have much."

Bridget watched as Shelly unpacked several articles of clothing for her and Marco, as well as some baby bottles and toiletries. "Ya know . . . if you need anything for Marco, we probably have it, what with my nephew, Brian, and all. Sometimes he stays here for days."

"That's good to know. Thank you."

"Yeah, and you'll probably fit into some of my clothes."

Shelly sat silent for a moment and then looked at Bridget and wiped away a tear. "I . . . I don't know what to say. You and your mom, I mean, I hardly know you guys and you take me in like I'm family. Why?"

"It's actually my mom who decided to ask you to stay with us, but it's a long story."

"Can you talk about it?"

Bridget shook her head. "Not yet, but I will, eventually."

"It's about your Dad, right?"

"Yeah."

"I don't mean to be nosey, but I mean, you haven't ever mentioned him. Not even last Saturday when we spent the whole afternoon together. Is he . . . I mean, did he pass away?"

Now it was Bridget's turn to wipe her eyes. "Kind of. We'll talk later." She turned and went for the door.

"Where are you going?"

"I want to get a run in before dinner." She opened the door and hesitated before leaving. Turning toward Shelly, she said, "I'm glad you and Marco are here. I think it's going to be good for all of us." Then she closed the door behind her.

Shelly picked up her son and held him in the air above her head before giving him a kiss. "I think we're going to be okay. I think we finally have a chance at making it."

40

Man is born broken. He lives by mending. The grace of God is glue.
—**Eugene O'Neill**

An ambulance screaming through the nearby intersection caused them to stir. The empty bottle lay between Eric and Doreen, evidence of their tenuous linkage, as the two began to awaken from their alcohol-induced sleep. Through tiny slits, Eric saw the red lights from the emergency vehicle bouncing off the concrete walls and pillars. "Al, I didn't mean it," he screamed ". . . I thought he was a burglar. Al, please, you gotta believe me!"

As Eric began thrashing about on the ground, his latest homeless companion, Doreen, sat up, startled. "Hey, what's goin' on? Wake up!" She reached over and shook Eric. "Hey, it's okay. Wake up."

Opening his eyes completely, Eric looked at Doreen. "What happened?"

"Damned if I know. You were goin' nutty or somethin'. What the hell's wrong with you?"

Eric sat up and rubbed his face. He looked across the street and got his bearings, remembering where he was. "Nothing's wrong; just a bad dream."

"Man, your head's screwed up."

He looked sideways at her. "Yeah, whatever." Standing up, Eric felt his head pounding and momentarily lost his balance. "Whoa, that forty-ouncer was pretty good."

She nodded in agreement. "I told ya, Man." Doreen stood up. "Wanna head over to the bus?"

"Yeah, let me get my sleeping bag," he said, reaching down for it.

"Man, don't be luggin' that crap around with ya. C'mon, you can keep it with my stuff down the street." Eric followed the woman for a block until they came to a cutout in the wall. "Here," she pointed to an area with an open folding gate in front of a door. "Used to be a freight elevator, but nobody uses it now. I keep my stuff here."

Eric looked at a large cardboard box and a tarp spread on the ground. "Doesn't anyone steal your things?"

"Uh uh, people know this is me. They know they're in for a ass-kickin' if they take any o' mine. I got folks lookin' out for me."

He set his sleeping bag next to the box. "Okay, if you say so." Eric felt his stomach growl. "Let's head over to the bus you've been talking about. Maybe I can get something to eat."

Doreen gestured with her head and then said, "This way."

Minutes later, they were in front of the iconic Wrigley Building on North Michigan Avenue. Stunning white floodlights lit its ivory façade, making it and the surrounding area as bright as a sunny day. A large white and blue bus with the words, "Night Ministry" painted on each side was parked in the turnaround in front of the massive structure. About a half dozen other homeless folks were milling around the several tables containing coffee and food that were set up next to the bus. Still others were leaving after receiving clean socks and blankets. "This is it, Man, I'm goin 'in. I gotta have them look at this damn tooth."

"Okay, I'll be out here getting something to eat." Eric watched Doreen enter the side door in the middle of the bus as he walked over to the table containing sandwiches and cookies. A female volunteer smiled at him.

"Hello, can I offer you a sandwich and something to drink?"

"Yes, please."

The woman handed Eric a sandwich wrapped in cellophane. "Here you go. How about something to wash it down? I have coffee, hot chocolate or water."

"Coffee's fine. Thanks."

She poured Eric a large Styrofoam cup of coffee and handed it to him. "Enjoy."

Eric noticed a couple of concrete benches along the railing that paralleled the Chicago River. He headed over to one with his food and coffee. As he ate his sandwich, he noticed the normally congested, noisy streets were somewhat subdued at night. *Mostly shoppers* he thought, figuring most of the daytime crowds were workers

THE YEAR WITHOUT CHRISTMAS

who were all probably back at home by now.

Taking a bite of his sandwich, he thought about his own home, remembering how Sharon always had dinner prepared for the family. Whether Eric worked the day shift or one at night, his wife ensured there was always a meal available for him. Sitting outside, eating on a bench in a strange city, he realized how much he'd taken his family for granted. These last months living on the street had been difficult to be sure, but the lack of contact with loved ones, both physical and emotional, proved even tougher than the harsh living conditions.

His thoughts drifted to Sharon . . . her kiss "hello" whenever he came home. Her kiss goodnight, the embraces he shared with her. Remembering the easiness and comfort of being together, caused his eyes to moisten. *What have I done?* He hung his head.

"Eric? I think that's your name." A man in dark clothing extended a hand, as Eric raised his head. "Father Callahan," he said, taking Eric's hand and shaking it. "From the shelter, remember?"

Eric looked up and recognized the man immediately. "Yes, I remember." He took a drink of his coffee. "I can't seem to shake you, Father, you're everywhere."

"Well, not exactly," the priest replied with a big smile. "I volunteer every so often on the night ministry bus. People need more than food and clothing to survive." The man moved to the end of the bench. "Mind if I sit down for a moment?"

"Suit yourself."

The two men sat in silence while Eric finished his sandwich. When he had finished, the priest turned to him. "Son, I've seen a lot of things in my day, some of them good, others that were horrible. I've helped and prayed with people who've been victims and perpetrators of some pretty terrible acts. And I've learned that despite the things people may have done or had done to them, there's only one answer to their problem."

"What's that?"

"One word: forgiveness. I don't mean others have to forgive you for what you've done. Rather, you must forgive yourself. Without forgiveness, guilt will drown you just as the water in that river will if you're foolish enough to jump in," the priest said, motioning over his shoulder at the deep, dark Chicago River.

"If you talk with some of the others who are living out here on the street, you will discover that they didn't just one day run out of money or lose all of their possessions. Homelessness didn't just appear out of the blue one day. Many of them had an event occur in their lives that was so devastating that they had to run away from it."

Eric sat up straight. "What's that got to do with me?"

The priest stared at him and then said softly, "Why don't you tell me?"

For an instant, Eric was prepared to confide in the priest, just as he had confided in other priests when practicing his Catholic faith and confessing his sins. But as he was about to talk about his reason for leaving home, the vision of his partner, Al, leaning over his dying son, flashed in Eric's mind. Shaking his head, he finished his drink and got up from the bench. "Father, I can't do this right now." Eric walked over to the table by the bus and refilled his coffee.

"Care for anything else?" The woman asked.

"No, but thanks for everything." Eric turned and glanced back toward the bench where he had been sitting with the priest. The priest was no longer there. He turned back to the volunteer. "Where did Father Callahan go?"

"Who?"

"The priest, Father Callahan. He was just sitting over on the bench; we were talking about . . . "

"Is he a friend of yours?" The woman asked.

"No, he works on your bus, he's a priest."

Shaking her head, the woman gave Eric a quizzical look. "We sometimes have a member of the clergy who volunteers with us, but we don't have one with us tonight. Can I get one of our counselors to speak with you?"

Confused, Eric turned left and right, searching the street and bus area for any sign of the priest. *Where the hell is he?*

"Sir?"

Eric looked at her for a moment and then walked toward the river. He went to the rail and stared down at the water as it rushed under the bridge spanning Michigan Avenue. *He was here; I talked to him . . . I know I did. Dear God, I'm going insane.* And for a moment, Eric was tempted to jump.

~~~~~~~~~~

THE YEAR WITHOUT CHRISTMAS

"Where have you been, I called your cell?"

Al Giordano walked into the kitchen through the garage service door. "I decided to stop at the cemetery and visit Geno's grave before coming home."

"Oh." Sandy had only visited her son's grave twice while accompanied by her husband. It wasn't comfortable for them, as each had their own way of grieving. Their ritual had become one wherein each person spent time alone at the site, thus giving the other freedom to talk aloud to their boy if they were so inclined. It seemed this was Al's favorite way of communicating with Geno. She understood he wasn't trying to shut her out, but rather he needed to express himself by having a conversation with his departed son.

"The flowers you planted look real good. Geno would like them."

"I know," she said. "I was there a couple of days ago. Whenever I visit, I bring a water bottle and water the plants."

Al emptied his pockets of his wallet and police ID, and then slipped off his pistol and placed it on the top shelf of the cabinet above the phone. "Hey, guess what? Joe Gandurski got a call about a disturbance at the county welfare office downtown. You won't believe who he ran into while he was there."

"Who?"

"Sharon Doyle."

Sandy turned around from the stove where she was preparing dinner. "Sharon?"

"Yeah, Sharon Doyle, and she had some young woman and a toddler with her."

"Hmm. I wonder what's going on?" Sharon asked. "I know she's been helping out at the homeless shelter. Maybe the woman was one of the residents."

Al opened the refrigerator and pulled out a can of beer. Popping the lid, he pulled out a kitchen chair and sat down. "Nah, Joe talked with Sharon after he was done handling the guy who was causing the commotion. She told Joe that the woman and her kid were living with them because the shelter was kicking them out on the street." Al took a drink of beer. "I'll bet Sharon's hurting for money if she's at the welfare office. Heck, she's probably applying for food stamps for her and Bridget."

Sandy frowned and resumed cooking dinner. *That poor woman, she can't seem to catch a break.*

"So, did you get that ad in the paper for the two new employees?" Al asked, as he sipped his drink.

"I faxed it to the paper this morning."

"Good, springtime means a lot of prom and graduation parties. You're going to need the extra help."

Sandy set her spatula on the counter and walked into the den where they kept their computer.

"Where are you going?"

"I'm sending another fax to the paper—I'm cancelling the ad for the time being." Sandy answered, as she walked past Al.

"What? Why?"

As she sat down at the computer to compose the fax, she answered him. "I think I know someone who just might need a steady job. I'm going to call Sharon Doyle and see if she wants to work for me."

"Sharon . . . working for us?" Al remarked. "Are you sure about this?"

"I'm positive," Sandy said, as she began to type the fax.

41

A man seldom thinks with more earnestness of anything than he does of his dinner.
　—**Samuel Johnson**

　The family gathered around the kitchen table for Sunday dinner. Sharon was busy taking the rolls out of the oven. She set them on stovetop. "Shelly, can you put these in a bowl and then set them on the table?"
　"I sure can," she replied. She grabbed a bowl from the cabinet above the counter and began taking the rolls off the hot baking sheet. Breathing in the aroma of the freshly baked dough, she closed her eyes for a second and remarked, "Mmm . . . these smell so good. "
　"I know," Erin chimed in. "I could eat the whole tray. Does Marco like dinner rolls?"
　Shelly nodded. "For sure. We haven't had many opportunities to eat them, but whenever we do, I put a pat of butter on each half and he goes at them like he hasn't eaten in days."
　"Brian's the same way. He's really been a fussy eater since he's been sick, but hot buttered rolls are still one of his favorites."
　Shelly finished putting the rolls in a serving bowl and set them on the table. She looked into the family room where the two boys sat on the floor in front of the TV, watching a movie. "Didn't take them very long to become friends," Shelly said with a smile.
　Erin agreed. "I think your stay here with be beneficial for both of them."
　"Mark, can you come in here and carve the roast?" Sharon set the roast on a cutting board, along with the knife Eric always used to slice the meat. She could have done this job herself, but she felt it was important to involve everyone in the dinner preparation, if even in a minor way.

Mark came into the kitchen, pulled Sharon aside and whispered, " You're sure about Shelly, right? I mean what do you know about her?"

"She's fine, Son. She's had some bad luck in her life, but she's a good person. I asked the Chief to check her out for me."

Smiling, Mark hugged his Mother. "I should have known."

"Bridget, can you pour the milk for the little ones?"

"Yes, Mom."

Placing a bowl of mashed potatoes on the table, Sharon announced, "Okay, everyone, dinner's ready. Bridge, can you get the boys in and bring them to the table?"

Bridget went into the family room and shut the TV off. She picked Marco up and then took Brian by the hand and led him into the bathroom where she washed their hands and then her own. Then, they moved into the kitchen where she handed Marco to Shelly and then helped Brian into his booster seat. "Here you go," she said, as she got him situated, and pushed his chair in close to the table.

Everyone took their seats and Mark blessed the meal, as had become the custom in his father's absence whenever the family ate dinner together.

"Bread, Mommy?" Marco asked, grabbing his mother's arm and pointing to the dinner rolls. Shelly looked over at Erin who was buttering a roll for Brian. "I told you he loved them." She grabbed one and began preparing it for her child.

As everyone passed the plates of food around and took what they wanted, Sharon looked around the table. "I have some news I'd like to share with all of you," she announced excitedly, a large smile appearing on her face. "I have a job!"

"Really?" Bridget asked. "I didn't even know you were looking for work. I mean, you said you were going to need a job, but . . . "

Mark interrupted. "Mom, where? What will you be doing?"

Sharon put her fork down. "To tell you the truth, I'm as shocked as you all seem to be. Sandy Giordano called and offered me a job with her catering company."

"Sandy? You mean Dad's old partner's wife, that Sandy?" Bridget asked, incredulously.

"Yes. She said she was about to place a help wanted ad for two additional part-timers because her business has been growing, but she decided to ask me to work full-time."

"I wonder why," Mark said. "I guess she was the last person I expected to want to help you out."

Sharon gestured. "I know. I was shocked when she called, but after we had a brief conversation at the supermarket some time ago it seemed the tension between us had dissipated. I think she knows we're struggling with your Dad missing."

"Well, are you excited?" Erin asked, as she wiped gravy from Brian's face.

"Yes . . . yes I am. I think having a job will help in a lot of ways, not to mention that we need the money—particularly with Bridget headed for college shortly."

Shelly looked down at her plate. She felt guilty knowing Sharon was struggling financially with her husband gone. And now she had two more mouths to feed, hers and Marco's. Shelly didn't know what to say. *How am I ever going to thank this woman for what she's done for me?* "Sharon, I can help out too; I can get a job, at least during the summer until Bridget leaves for school. That is, if she'll baby-sit Marco."

"I don't know, Shelly. Let's see how things work out before we make any more changes. We'll be fine with the food stamps you're getting. That will help out quite a bit."

"Okay, but I want to do my share here. I want to earn my keep."

"I know you do, and believe me, with me working every day I'm going to need you to take care of things around here, like cooking and cleaning." Sharon smiled at Bridget. "Bridget has never really embraced housecleaning, as I'm sure you gathered from looking at her room."

Everyone laughed, including Bridget.

"Okay, Sharon. I don't mean to be a broken record, but I am so thankful that you've taken me and my son into your home."

Sharon smiled. "I know you are." Sharon picked up the platter of meat. "More roast beef, anyone?"

~~~~~~~~~~

Spring eventually turned into summer and Eric found himself on the move every couple of weeks. His brief exposure to the homeless woman, Doreen, proved to be more of a burden than a help. The woman drank much of his liquor, but never offered him anything in return, except sex—something Eric cared not think about, particularly with Doreen. The only useful thing Eric was able to gain from Doreen's homeless experience was the existence of the night ministry bus. He quickly learned the bus's schedule—where and when it stopped. He relied on the ministry primarily for food, which sadly had become just one meal per day.

Eric discovered more places to panhandle, and found that the hotels on Michigan Avenue proved to be most lucrative. Whenever he saw busses parked out in front of them, Eric knew there was a convention in town. Conventions meant tourists with money to spend. They weren't shy about putting five or ten dollars in his cup, especially if Eric worked the corner late at night when the bar-hoppers were returning to their rooms. They knew exactly what Eric was going to do with the money—buy booze—and they didn't care.

However, everything did not always run smoothly. On more than one occasion, Eric was told to move along by cops on the beat. Eric was inclined to do as they said. After all, he himself was a cop and he respected the job they had to do. But there was one time when a particular convention brought some high rollers into Chicago. This group showered Eric with money, some giving him fifty and twenty dollar bills. When the beat cop came around to chase Eric off the corner, Eric did so but returned to the same spot after the cop left.

Thinking the coast was clear, Eric resumed panhandling until the cop walked up behind him. "Hey, I thought I told you to move along?"

"Yes, you did, Officer. I, uh . . . well, I don't really have any place to go, and to be honest, I need the money these good people are willing to share with me."

The officer frowned. "You don't have any place to go? Well, I've got just the place," he said, as he grabbed his radio. "I-6-3 Foot to Central, can you send a wagon to the Hilton on Michigan? I've got one for the drunk tank."

"10-4, on the way."

Eric was terrified. He knew that if he was arrested with no ID, he would be routinely fingerprinted. He didn't know if there was a missing person report out on him or not, but he didn't want to risk finding out. "Please, Officer, I'll move. I'm sorry for coming back after you told me to leave. Can you give me another chance? I'm begging you."

"Why? Why should I give you another chance?"

Eric wanted to tell him that he was also a cop, but at the last second decided not to risk it. "Sir, I have problems, as you can see. I don't want to bore you with them; you've probably heard every story in the book. But I promise you that if you let me go, you'll never see me at this hotel again."

The cop looked Eric up and down. "Well, I guess so. There's something about you . . . you're not like most of the other homeless people out here. It's almost like you don't belong here." The cop stroked his chin while he thought about the decision he was about to make. "Okay. You promise you'll stay away from here and I'll let you go."

Smiling, Eric extended his hand to the cop and then quickly pulled it back. He remembered the advice the Professor told him about cops not being comfortable shaking hands with street people, too many diseases. "Sir, I promise. Thank you so much."

"Okay. Hit the bricks. You caught me in a good mood tonight."

"Yes, Sir. God bless you," Eric said, and then turned and walked away. He travelled several blocks toward the lakefront where he found a bench to lie down on. The traffic noise, such as it was this late at night, lulled him to sleep. However, with his pockets flush with panhandled money, Eric slept fitfully, worried that someone would rob him during the night. Although worn out, he welcomed the sun as it sprang from the blue waters of Lake Michigan.

Checking his pockets after he stood up, Eric was relieved to find everything in place. He walked across the park to use the restroom and then headed back toward Wabash Avenue where he knew a cut-rate liquor store was located. *Time for breakfast.*

After making his purchase, Eric took his bottle with him across the street and sat on a flower planter near the curb. Taking a healthy drink, he watched as people scurried along the street, ducking into buildings here and there, as they tried to make it to their offices on time. As he put the bottle up to his lips, about to take another drink, a woman walked by pushing a baby stroller. Eric looked at the young child, "Brian!" he shouted. The woman gave Eric a strange look and quickened her pace.

Eric shook his head and let out a deep sigh, his thoughts drifting toward his sick grandson. *Oh, Brian, I hope you are well.*

42

A single sunbeam is enough to drive away many shadows.
   —St. Francis of Assisi

Sharon concentrated on wrapping the leftovers, while Shelly and Bridget visited with the residents of the shelter. Her commitment to volunteering at the shelter had grown stronger as the months passed. She felt a bond with these strangers, in the sense that each of them had a piece of their lives missing. For Sharon, it was her husband, Eric.

Although she received the same answer each time she called the chief to inquire about any new information regarding Eric's disappearance, she was not about to stop. Her desire to find him never weakened. She continued to drive around town hoping to spot him. Several weeks ago, while searching for a parking spot at the mall, Sharon saw a man who looked like Eric get out of a car and walk toward the entrance. She threw her own car in park, and jumped out. "Eric!" She shouted at the man as he continued walking. He failed to turn around until she ran almost on top of him. "Eric!" She cried out again. Startled, the man turned to see who was yelling at him. "Are you okay, lady?"

Discovering that the man was not her husband, Sharon's racing heart slowed. "Sorry," she mumbled, "Thought you were someone else." Dejected, she walked back to her car and drove home, no longer in the mood to shop.

After she finished placing the leftover dishes in the refrigerator, Sharon joined Shelly and Bridget in the common area. Shelly and Marco were near the toy corner, where Marco and two other youngsters were engaged in setting up and knocking over plastic bowling pins. Bridget sat on one of the couches talking with another teenage girl.

"Ladies, I think we should head home," Sharon announced. "I have to work in the morning."

"Okay, Mom," Bridget answered. She said goodbye to the girl she had been talking with and then shook hands with several of the others. Shelly gathered Marco and his things and the group went out to the parking lot, got into Sharon's car, and headed home.

"That was a great meal," Shelly told Sharon. "I think since you've been working at the catering business, the homeless have been eating better than they've ever eaten in their lives."

"Yes, Sandy has been a terrific boss. We used to throw away many of the uneaten meals until I suggested donating them to the shelter. I have to hand it to her, she has really embraced the homeless."

"I think you're spoiling them, Mom."

"You think so, Bridge?"

"Yeah, I mean, they're eating things like Chicken Cordon Bleu and Prime Rib . . . in a homeless shelter. Who does that?"

They all laughed.

"It is weird," Shelly added. "When I was living there, we had meals like beans and franks, grilled cheese, mac and cheese—real simple stuff."

"Okay, okay," Sharon said, as she stopped for a red light. "I know it's unusual food for a shelter, but it's free. I'm just thankful we can provide them with a good, nutritious meal once a week." She resumed driving when the light turned green. "And, I must add that I am very proud of the both of you for your continued dedication to volunteering there." She looked over at Bridget, who was sitting in the passenger seat. "I think the fact that you spend time talking with some of the teenagers, really helps them adjust to their new lifestyle."

Sharon looked in the rearview mirror at Shelly who was sitting next to Marco's car seat. "And you as a former resident of the shelter, Shelly, I think instills hope in those who wonder if they'll ever get back on their feet again."

"I agree. I think they all need to know that there is hope." She paused. "At one point, I was without hope until you stepped in and gave me a helping hand."

Sharon smiled. "I think you've helped me as much as I've helped you."

Shelly shrugged. "If you say so. Anyway, I'll be helping much more when Bridget leaves for college next month."

Glancing sideways at her daughter, Sharon asked her, "Are you excited?"

"Umm . . . kind of. I mean, it's Chicago and all, lots of new things to see and do, but it's the big city. I just hope I can find my way around without getting lost."

"Well, you'll have Dad's truck. It has a GPS in it."

"Mom, I don't even know how to turn the darn thing on, much less how it works."

Laughing, Sharon answered, "Don't worry, I'll teach you before you leave."

"You better, otherwise I should probably leave for college right now. It's going to take me forever to find my way."

As she pulled the car into the driveway at home, Sharon thought about Bridget's upcoming college years. Although she was happy her daughter was going away to a wonderful school, she couldn't help but feel sad as well. With Eric still missing, and Bridget away at school, she would be without any family at home. Besides, she still worried about her daughter's eating habits. The girl continued to run twice a day. Now that the warm weather was upon them, it seemed Bridget's night runs were becoming longer. Sharon hoped the infamous "freshman 15" phenomenon she heard about would happen to Bridge. She could stand to put on the weight.

Of course, Shelly and Marco would be at home to keep her company, but they weren't real family and they would only be there for a while. When Shelly's husband was released from jail, Shelly would have to leave. Sharon was not going to risk having a felon living in her home.

Sharon's other concern was her grandson, Brian. His leukemia was still in the treatment stage. While he was in remission, the doctors couldn't say whether or not the chemo was going to cure him. So much to ponder, so many problems.

~~~~~~~~~~

Sandy and Al Giordano paid the check and left the restaurant. "That was a superb meal," Sandy commented.

"Yeah, my steak was done just the way I like it. You know, I hate to admit it, but ever since you hired Sharon things have improved

THE YEAR WITHOUT CHRISTMAS

between us. It seems we have more time together now. You used to be gone twelve or more hours a day. Now, you come home at a decent hour."

The couple walked to their car and got inside. "I know what you're saying. Sharon's been great; she's a quick learner, not only in the kitchen, but on the business side."

Al fumbled in his pocket for a toothpick as he drove out of the restaurant parking lot. "The only downside is that you don't bring home the leftovers from the catering jobs anymore."

"Well, after Sharon confided that she volunteered at the homeless shelter in town, and I saw her loading a shopping cart with food she bought with her own money, her appeal to donate leftovers to the folks at the shelter was a proposition I couldn't refuse."

Al turned on the radio and hit the station for the Detroit Tigers baseball game. They drove for several miles in silence before Sandy broke in. "Al, what are you thinking? You've got that look, and you're not talking. That usually means there's something on your mind."

He took the toothpick from his mouth and threw it out the window. "You know me, don't you?"

"I should, after being married to you for twenty years."

Silence.

"Al? What is it?"

After a few moments, Al turned off the radio. "I, uh . . . I was just thinking about the last time me and Geno went to the ballgame." Al wiped away a tear. "It was this same time last year. He was so happy, so full of life."

Sandy's eyes welled up with tears. She reached in her purse for a tissue, and then reached over and held her husband's hand. "It's okay, Honey, it's okay. He knows we loved him. What's done is done, we can't change anything." She dabbed her eyes. "Thankfully, we have good memories like the one you just shared. We'll always have them. Always."

Al turned the corner of the block to their house and pulled in their garage seconds later. Before they got out of the car, Al turned to his wife. "It still seems like a bad dream, like I'm going to wake up some day and Gene will be standing there."

Sandy nodded. "I know, Sweetheart. I dream about him too, but more importantly, I'm focusing on us. We only have each other now.

I need you more than ever, and I'm here for you, whatever you need, I'm here. We'll get through this, eventually." She leaned over, took his face in her hands, and said, "I love you Al." She kissed him, and stroked his hair. "We'll be okay."

They left the garage hand in hand and walked into their dark, quiet home.

43

This city now doth, like a garment, wear the beauty of the morning; silent bare, ships, towers, domes, theatres and temples lie open unto the fields and to the sky; All bright and glittering in the smokeless air.
—**William Wordsworth**

Despite her trepidation about driving to Chicago in her father's truck, Bridget had no trouble finding the campus. Her mother's instruction on how to operate the truck's GPS system proved to be invaluable, although after making the journey, Bridget was convinced she could have done quite well without it. The University of Illinois at Chicago was a huge campus. A few miles from the downtown area, its location off the interstate made it easy to access. The UIC athletic complex was expansive, the likes of which Bridget had never experienced. Her hopes for a successful track season were high.

Bridget's roommate, Tasha, was also attending UIC on an athletic scholarship. From the inner city, Tasha was a treasure trove of information regarding where to go and what to avoid. Her gregarious nature and bubbly attitude caused Bridget to bond with her quickly, and after a month of living together, they became not only roommates, but also good friends.

"I've got to get going if I'm gonna make that eight o'clock class," Tasha said, as she hurriedly threw several books in her backpack. "See you at lunch?"

Still lying in bed, Bridget rubbed her eyes and responded. "Yeah, I'll be there; only one class for me this morning—the big lecture hall at ten."

"Biology?"

"Yeah."

"Eww, I hate that class," Tasha answered. "I'm gonna need some help to pass that one."

"No problem." Bridget sat up in bed. "Science and math have always been my strong points. We'll get you through it."

"You promise? I can't let my GPA dip below 2.5 if I'm going to stay on the basketball team."

Bridget smiled. "I promise."

Her tall roommate rushed out the door. With a couple of hours to kill, Bridget decided to wander over to the cafeteria for coffee. She put on her sweats, grabbed her phone and meal card, and then headed toward the cafeteria. Along the way, she came to the Triangle, a pedestrian intersection where the student union posted flyers of upcoming events and other notices on a large three-sided kiosk. Bridget stopped to take a quick look. One item caught her attention. She created a memo on her phone, and then continued on her way.

Several hours later, her lecture over, Bridget walked back to the cafeteria for lunch. Wandering over to the area where most of the athletes ate, she spotted her roommate. "Hey, Tash, what's goin' on?"

"Oh, hey, girlfriend. Nuthin' much. Just chowin' . . . fuelin' up for b-ball practice in a couple hours. How 'bout you?"

Bridget put her backpack down and sat across from Tasha. "Dull morning so far. Bio was the same; Mr. Ashad talked mostly to the blackboard, as he wrote things so small that only those kids sitting in the front row were able to read what he scribbled."

"I hate that!"

"Yeah, me too. Hey, I was looking at the kiosk at the Triangle and saw a notice for something called The Night Ministry."

Tasha took a bite of her burrito. "What's that about?"

"I don't know for sure, but it's supposed to be a bus with some kind of city-sponsored services that takes care of the homeless."

"You thinkin' about volunteerin'?"

"Yeah, I'm thinking about it," Bridget answered. "I kind of miss working with the homeless."

Finishing her burrito, Tasha dug into her side order of rice and beans. "You should probably do it. Listening to you talk about workin' at the shelter in your town, I mean . . . you got a talent for that."

Bridget smiled. "Yeah, I think I'll probably do it. It's at night so it won't interfere with school or track."

Tasha finished her meal and stood up.

"Where are you going?"

"I need one more burrito, and, hey . . . you better get one yourself, girlfriend, you runners are too damn skinny."

Bridget followed her friend to the serving line. "I'm in the mood for a salad."

Tasha shook her head. "Man, you eat like you're a rabbit or somethin', you better put some meat on those bones 'for someone mistakes *you* for homeless."

Bridget laughed, grabbed a plate, and then headed toward the salad bar. *I'll check out The Night Ministry, someone probably needs my help.*

~~~~~~~~~~

Now that fall had begun, the nights were becoming cold once again. The tree-lined lakefront in Chicago reminded Eric of Lake Webster in his hometown. With the kaleidoscope of colors painted by the falling leaves on the grass, it created a picture-perfect scene. That is, if you weren't homeless. Sleeping outdoors on the lakefront on summer nights had been comfortable and convenient. The park benches and public restrooms provided for most of his needs. During the day, he strolled over the several blocks to Michigan Avenue to panhandle. When he had enough for a bottle, he drifted back to the lakefront and drank until he passed out.

At some point Eric had lost, misplaced, or had his sleeping bag stolen. It hadn't really mattered—until now. He hated the approaching cold weather, particularly after his first winter in Chicago. He remembered the harsh wind and snow. *Probably have to go back underground . . . need another sleeping bag too.* The Lighthouse Shelter or the Night Ministry bus would probably give him a sleeping bag and some clean socks and underwear. Still existing on one meal a day, Eric's weight was dangerously low. Truth was, he really didn't have much of an appetite anymore. Some days he didn't even think about food.

As much as he hated to, he began to make his way to the shelter. He could take a shower, shave, and change into some clean clothing. Unless the priest showed up. Eric was still puzzled about Father Callahan. *I know I'm not imagining things. Hell, I talked to the man, even shook his hand.* But why didn't anyone acknowledge that the priest worked there? It was a strange situation, one that bothered him. The priest seemed to know what was in Eric's heart. No matter, he needed to get to the shelter, and if the priest was there, Eric would . . . well, he didn't know what he'd do.

Two hours later, Eric arrived at the shelter and stepped inside. "Hey there, young fella. What can we do for ya?"

Eric hadn't been at the shelter all summer. He expected to see George at the front desk. "Hi, uh, George doesn't work here anymore?"

"Nah, George has some medical issues. He decided working here wasn't helping him get better so he quit volunteering last month."

"Oh, that's too bad. Anyway, I thought maybe I could get cleaned up and get some things while I'm here."

"Sure." The man came around the desk. "You know the drill; I need to make sure you don't have any alcohol—got to check all your pockets."

Eric put his arms straight out to his side. "Sure, no problem."

The man checked Eric's jacket and pants. "Okay, you're all set. Go on back and see the volunteer in the men's dorm. He'll take care of ya."

"Thanks." Eric went through the swinging double doors into the large dining room. He looked around, searching for the priest, but only saw homeless people. *So far, so good.* He continued to the dorm.

An hour later, freshly showered and shaven, Eric returned to the dining area where he sat down with a sandwich and a cup of coffee. After several minutes, a man approached Eric and sat down across the table from him. "Mind if I join you?"

"Your choice."

The man extended his hand to Eric. "Hi, my name is Anthony. I'm the Pastor at the New Life Church of God. Our church is several blocks away on State Street." He handed Eric a pamphlet. "I'd like to invite you to attend one of our services. We're a small congregation that's Bible-based; I think you'll like our message."

Eric continued to eat. The pastor set the pamphlet on the table in front of Eric. "I promise you that God's word is what will help you conquer the evil in your life, take away your sadness and give you a fresh outlook on your future. Sound interesting?"

"No."

The man sat silent for several moments, not knowing where to go from here. "Well, Brother, may I at least pray for you?"

Setting his sandwich down, Eric looked at the man. "Did Father Callahan send you?"

"Who?"

"You know, the priest who works here."

The pastor shook his head. "No, I mean, I don't know any Father Callahan. Is that what you want, a Catholic priest?"

"Uh, uh, I don't need anyone, especially a priest." Eric put his hand on the man's pamphlet and slid it across the table at him. "Go on now, leave me alone."

Picking the pamphlet up, the pastor stood. "Okay, Brother, God bless you. I hope God helps you find your way."

Eric watched the man walk away and join a group of men at another table. *I don't think God remembers who I am.*

44

Health is not valued till sickness comes.
—Thomas Fuller

Sharon finished putting the trays of lasagna in the oven to bake. Tonight's catering job at the Union Hall was a large event. Sandy needed a helping hand to cook and serve the feast they were preparing. She hired a temp named Cindy from the Manpower Agency in town. "C'mon ladies, let's start getting the side dishes prepared," Sandy called out, as she opened the industrial refrigerator. "Sharon, can you start cutting up veggies for the salads?"

"Sure. Garden or Caesar?"

"They specified garden salads on the order form."

"Gotcha," Sharon answered with a smile.

Sandy handed several bags of vegetables to Cindy. "Here, the side dish tonight is mixed vegetables. Go ahead, rinse everything off, and put them in the sixteen-quart pot. Fill it with water but don't start boiling it yet, I don't want them overcooked."

"Okay."

As Sharon was cutting onions, her phone rang. She looked at the caller ID—it was her daughter-in-law, Erin. "Hello."

"Hi, Mom, I hate to bother you at work but I thought you'd want to know."

"Know what?"

"Brian's been running a high fever so I brought him to the doctor at noon. Turns out he wants us to take him back to Children's Hospital again."

Sharon dropped what she was doing and walked into Sandy's office where she could talk in private. "Why, Erin?"

"The doctor said Brian has relapsed."

Sharon collapsed into the chair by Sandy's desk. "Oh, dear God.

What are they going to do? They can't let him die."

"The doctors hope a stem cell transplant will save him."

"What? A transplant!"

"I know, Mom, I know. Listen, the doctor explained that Brian needs this procedure, his white blood cells and platelets have been dropping. A stem cell transplant should bring new bone marrow into his system."

"I know his white blood cell count has not been good, but this . . . this sounds so extreme. Do you think maybe you should get a second opinion?"

With all of the pressure and worry she'd endured these last months, Erin was feeling frustrated. "Mom, listen, I don't have a lot of time. I'm going to do whatever it takes to get Brian healthy again. We were warned at the beginning that it might come to this, and now it has. By the way, we are all going to need to be tested to see if someone is a match, otherwise we'll have to look for a donor who is not just a good match, but preferably, a perfect match."

Sharon sat silently as visions of her grandchild flashed in her mind. *This can't be happening.* Ever since Brian had been diagnosed with leukemia, it seemed like Erin and Mark spoke to her in a foreign language whenever they explained the child's condition.

"Mom?"

"Yes, Erin, I uh . . . when are you taking him to Detroit?"

"We're just about to leave."

"Okay. I can't get down there today. I have a catering job that I can't walk out on. Let me talk with Sandy and see what I can arrange in terms of time off."

"All right. I'll call you tonight and let you know what room we're in. But listen, there's not much you can do at the hospital. I know your catering job is important, don't jeopardize it. I will let you know when it's absolutely necessary for you to come down."

Sharon grabbed a tissue from the box on Sandy's desk and wiped her teary eyes. "Okay, Sweetheart. Kiss Brian for me; tell him Nana loves him."

"He knows you do, and he loves you too. So do I, Mom, I'm just stressed. I'm sorry if I was short with you. I'll talk to you later. Bye."

Putting her phone in her pocket, Sharon put her head down on her forearms and rested on the desk. *Dear God in Heaven, please heal my baby.* Seconds later, Sandy walked into the office.

"Sharon, what's wrong?"

Sharon lifted her head up and looked at Sandy.

"You're crying. Are you okay?"

She shook her head. "No, it's Brian. He's not doing well—they took him to the hospital."

~~~~~~~~~~

It was almost eleven when Sharon walked through the kitchen door, balancing an aluminum tray of leftover lasagna. "Shelly, you're still up?"

Shelly sat at the kitchen table reading, but looked up when she saw Sharon come in. "Hi, what's that?"

"Leftovers from the job. There are two more trays in the car; would you mind getting them for me?"

"Sure."

A couple minutes later, Shelly walked in with the other trays. "Want the garage door down?" She asked Sharon, as she was about to hit the remote button on the wall with her elbow.

"Yes, please."

Shelly set the trays on the counter next to the other one. "How did it go tonight?"

Sharon took her coat off and hung it on the hook by the door. She turned back toward Shelly. "Decent sized crowd, but they were more interested in drinking than eating. The residents at the shelter will enjoy these leftovers."

Shelly looked at Sharon. "You look worn out, why don't you go up to bed? I'll take care of putting everything away."

Sharon stood in front of the sink, not making a move.

"Are you okay?"

Not answering, Sharon wrapped her arms around herself and began to rock back and forth. She shook her head, no, as tears streamed down her face.

Shelly moved to her and quickly hugged her. "It's okay. Tell me, what's wrong?"

"Erin called," she said between sobs, "they took Brian to the hospital. He needs further treatment, something she called a stem cell transplant, whatever that is."

THE YEAR WITHOUT CHRISTMAS

Holding her tightly, Shelly could feel Sharon's body shake as the woman's painful tears wet her cheek. It was a paradoxical situation, one that made Shelly feel both happy and sad. She was glad she was finally able to comfort the woman who had taken in her and Marco in their moment of need. However, her heart ached for little Brian. "I'm sure they're going to take good care of him. I mean, they wouldn't be doing the transplant if they didn't think it would help him, right?"

"I guess you're right. Erin said the treatment is risky and there's no guarantee it will cure Brian." Sharon answered, as she grabbed a paper towel from the roll on the counter. "It's just too much to bear. If only Eric was here . . ." She dabbed at her eyes as she walked silently out of the kitchen and up the stairs to her bedroom.

Shelly busied herself by rearranging the shelves in the refrigerator to accommodate the leftovers. She finally got everything back in, turned off the lights, and then headed up to her own room. Despite the seriousness of the situation, for some reason, she didn't share the sense of doom that Sharon felt.

~~~~~~~~~~

Sandy began to undress as Al walked into the bedroom. He walked over to her, placing her in a warm embrace and then kissed her.

"You're home on time," Sandy said, returning her husband's kiss. "Must not have been too busy, huh?"

Al sat on the chair next to the dresser and began to remove his shoes. "No, it was pretty quiet. Steve Jones called us again, said his neighbor's snow blower keeps throwing snow over on his property. I don't know what he thinks the police can do about it, but he calls us anyway. How about you? I drove by the hall—parking lot was packed."

"Yes, it was a good turnout. The bartender said he went through a whole keg of beer."

"I bet he did," Al said, as he took off his socks. "Gandurski stopped one of the cars leaving the party. Guy blew a .012; he'll be spending the night in jail."

Sandy finished undressing and put on her nightclothes. "Al?"

"Yeah, Baby?"

"Sharon got a call tonight from her daughter-in-law. Her grandson is back in the hospital, I guess his leukemia is not getting any better."

"I'm sorry to hear that. What are they going to do for the little guy?"

"I'm not sure, she didn't want to talk about it, plus we had the catering job." She walked over and sat on the edge of the bed. "I just feel so bad for Sharon. I don't know how much she can handle."

"Are you going to give her time off?"

Sandy shrugged. "I don't know, I guess I will. If I had a grandson who was ill like that, I'd want to be with him. But at the same time, she really is an asset. I don't know how I managed before she came on board."

Al slipped into his robe and headed for the shower. "How did the temp work out?"

"Cindy? She did a good job," Sandy said, following her husband into the bathroom. "In fact, I took her off to the side and told her I might need her more often if Sharon needs time off to be with Brian."

Al turned on the water in the shower and waited for it to run hot. "You're a good woman, Sandy. I love you."

"I love you, too," she said, as she stood at the sink, washing her face. *I only wish there was something I could do to help Sharon.*

45

Love keeps the cold out better than a cloak.
—**Henry Wadsworth Longfellow**

The November wind made a mockery of Eric's outer clothing, asserting itself quickly with a zero degree wind chill. What had proven in the past to be a prime spot for panhandling, the area near the hotel on Michigan Avenue, was no longer productive. Heads down and hats on, people scurried to their destinations, completely ignoring Eric's pleas for a handout. The party crowd that had generously placed substantial amounts of money in his cup as they returned from celebrating, now hailed taxis rather than walk. At times the stiff wind drowned out Eric's pleas for money as it whipped up, down and around the behemoth buildings.

With less money to spend, his drink of choice quickly changed from one of taste, to one he could afford. The result: the cheap wine he drank last night had left him with a massive headache. Shivering in the cold was not helping his headache go away. Moreover, standing in the wind was not something he could do for very much longer. Wiping his nose on his coat sleeve, he resigned himself to the fact that he needed to visit the shelter. He had to get warm, maybe even take a few aspirins for his hangover and then have a cup of coffee.

Eric started walking toward the shelter, but as he turned the corner off North Michigan Avenue, a gust of wind hit him head on like an NFL lineman, knocking him to the ground. As he fell, he dropped his plastic cup containing the small amount of change he had collected, scattering the money over the sidewalk. Rolling onto his side, he tried to grab the cup, but it quickly disappeared down the street, swept up in the wind. Eric got on his knees, took off one of his gloves, and began retrieving his money.

"Sir? Can I help you?"

He looked up to see a well-dressed woman wearing a fur coat with a hood.

"If you'd like," Eric replied, raising his voice above the din of the wind.

The stranger bent over and helped him collect the last of his coins. She handed them to Eric as he stood up. "Here you are." Grabbing him by the arm, she led him to the entrance to the building they were standing beside. "This is better. Now I can hear you; are you okay? I saw you fall down."

Eric nodded. "I'm okay, just cold."

"I bet you are. Where are you headed?"

"I was going to the shelter to warm up."

"The Lighthouse Shelter on Hubbard?"

Eric nodded.

The woman opened her purse and took out some money. "I know the place; it's over a mile away, you'll freeze before you get there. Wait here." She walked to the curb and hailed the next cab she saw. Opening the passenger door, she spoke briefly with the driver and handed him a bill. She turned around and signaled to Eric. "Come here!" She gestured to him and shouted above the wind.

Eric sheepishly obeyed. The strange woman opened the rear door, allowing Eric to climb inside. "He'll drive you to the shelter; don't worry about the fare, it's taken care of." Before closing the door, she handed Eric a twenty-dollar bill. "Here, I know what you're probably going to spend it on, but it will keep you off the street for a while in this terribly cold weather. God bless you, my friend."

She closed the door and the taxi pulled away from the curb. *My first cab ride . . . and first encounter with an angel.* Minutes later, the driver stopped in front of the shelter. Eric got out of the taxi and had to use the building's railing to steady himself as he made his way up the stairs to the front door. Once inside, he was surprised to see about a dozen people milling around the desk area. *Must be the cold weather.* He began walking toward the doors to go inside when the man working the desk stood up.

"Hey, full house today," he told Eric. "Come here and get a number; when someone leaves, we'll send another person inside. In the meantime you can stay in this area and warm up."

Eric walked over and took the index card from the man. His card

THE YEAR WITHOUT CHRISTMAS

had number nine written on it. Putting it in his pocket, he made his way to a bench along one of the walls and sat down. After about ten minutes, he noticed not one person had left the dining area. *I'm going to be here a while.* Eric slumped down on the bench and began to think about the upcoming holiday.

Thanksgiving had always a big deal at the Doyle house. Sharon began defrosting the large turkey the day before. On Thanksgiving morning, she arose early to begin to prepare what ultimately turned out to be a wonderful feast. It had to be, with the number of people Sharon had to serve. Erin and Mark came over with grandson, Brian. Al, Sandy and their son, Geno were always invited as well. If there was snow on the ground, Bridget always got the sled out and pulled Brian around the neighborhood. Eric's father came over before dinner to watch the holiday football games on TV. He also had the duty of bringing pies for dessert. Invariably, a neighbor or two would drop in, as would several of Bridget's classmates. *I wonder if Sharon's having Thanksgiving this year?*

Eric saw his wife's face through closed eyes. He wanted to fall asleep so he wouldn't think about the pain in his head that he was feeling, as well as the pain he had caused his family because of his disappearance. "Dammit!" He said aloud, startling a man sitting next to him.

"You alright, Bro?"

Eric looked at the man and said nothing. Instead, he stood up and made his way to the door. He put his hand in his pocket to make sure he still had the money the kind woman had given him. Satisfied that it was still there, he went out into the harsh wind. He fought the gusts as all the way to the liquor store, where he bought a cheap bottle of whiskey, and then made his way to Lower Michigan Avenue where he'd be out of the wind. He'd be okay, as long as he didn't run into Doreen down there.

~~~~~~~~~~

"So, how did it go last night? I didn't even hear you come in."

Bridget was busy putting on several layers of clothing to prepare for her morning run around the campus. "Pretty good. I guess we had about twenty-five people come to the bus. Most of them were cold, the wind was brutal all day."

"And now you're goin' out to run? You are crazy, girl. It ain't even winter yet, heck, Thanksgiving's still a week away."

Bridget laughed. "I know, I've heard all the weather stuff a million times. But honestly, the first step out the door is the most difficult. Once you get going and warmed up, the weather isn't a factor."

"You keep tellin' yourself that," Tasha quipped, as she continued to fix her hair, "one day you might even believe it."

Gathering her hat and gloves, Bridget put her hand on the doorknob. "I'll probably be gone for about an hour, so I'll catch up with you at lunch. Okay?"

"Yep, you know I'll be there. I might miss a class, but I ain't never gonna miss lunch."

Out in the hallway, Bridget walked to the far end, passing up the elevators. She walked down the seven flights of stairs and opened the door to the outside. A chilly breeze, but not one that was nearly as bad as yesterday met her. She took off running into the wind so she'd have it at her back on her return home to the dorm.

As she ran, her thoughts drifted to the people she helped minister to last night. While she served coffee and sandwiches to the homeless, she couldn't help but feel sorry for those who were living on the street. Remembering her experience working at the shelter in Websterville, she saw a stark difference in the homeless people there compared to the homeless in Chicago. The conditions for the people on the street in Chicago were almost primitive. Many of them were alcoholics who neglected their health, even though resources like The Night Ministry Bus offered health and dental services at no charge. It seemed they had lost hope, and only did the minimum they needed to stay alive.

Bridget also wondered about some of the men she saw last night. Who were they? Did they have families? And if so, why weren't their families helping them? Or for that matter, why would someone with a family choose not to be with them?

As she picked up her speed, she thought about her own father. Where was he? Why wasn't he coming home, or at least trying to contact them? Was it because he was . . .? No, she didn't want to think about the possibility that her father was dead. She'd done that enough already. But there were many nights that she laid awake in her bed thinking that her Dad couldn't be alive. She'd cry herself to sleep on those nights, heartbroken that the last time she saw her father she told him that she hated him. *Dad, if you are alive, please, come home. I need you.*

She would never give up hope, but as the weeks and months passed by, that light of hope began to dim. In a week she'd be going back to Michigan for Thanksgiving. The trip would be bittersweet. She longed to see her family, particularly, Brian. However, being home made her Father's absence even worse. He was there in every room in their house. Even driving his truck made her constantly aware that she missed him terribly.

On her way back to the dorm, she'd stop at the campus chapel and say a prayer, something she'd been doing since she'd arrived at school. Her prayer was always the same: *Dear Lord, I pray that you will bring my Dad home where he belongs, but if you can't, please protect him wherever he may be.*

~~~~~~~~~~

There she was, Doreen, standing near her alcove and smoking a cigarette. Eric walked in her direction. "Hey, stranger, where you been?"

Eric shrugged. "Here and there. I spent most of the summer at the park near the lakefront."

"Oh, yeah, that's a good spot. Close to the hotels on Michigan." She took a drag on her cigarette and exhaled. "I used to work that area, folks were pretty generous. Wintertime it's too damn cold though. Man, that wind just kicks your ass. I got arrested a couple of times for goin' inside to warm up. Folks don't like our kind invadin' their space."

"I know."

"Whatcha got to drink?"

"Uh . . . "

"C'mon, I know you got somethin', 'specialy it bein' this cold and all."

Eric reluctantly reached inside his jacket and pulled out the bottle he had just purchased."

"Hell yeah!" Doreen screamed and broke into a big smile. "Ain't even opened yet—let's crack it."

He unscrewed the cap and took the first drink, the liquid soothing him as it flowed down his throat.

"Hand it over handsome," she said, putting her hand out. She took a generous drink. "Aw, hell, you done good, sweetheart. Folks over by the hotel musta been good to ya."

Eric took the bottle back. "Yeah."

"Tell ya what, it's a cold night. Why don't you just spend the night with me in my little space here," she said, pointing to the cardboard box in the doorway. "We can share the bottle and keep warm at the same time. I might even give you a little treat."

Weighing his options, Eric realized he needed to stay somewhere warm tonight. The shelter he just left was probably going to be at capacity. "Okay, but I'm just here to keep warm, nothing else."

Doreen took a deep drag on her cigarette. "Whatever, but I ain't never been turned down before. I wonder about you."

As a gust of wind swept underneath the subterranean street, the unlikely couple crawled into their makeshift shelter. Eric climbed into his sleeping bag, creating a cocoon of sorts that would ensure Doreen didn't bother him. Zipping the bag completely closed, he did his best to clear him mind of Sharon and the kids . . . and Thanksgiving.

46

*Love reckons hours for months, and days for years;
and every little absence is an age.*
—**John Dryden**

Sharon wound the cord to the vacuum cleaner, placed it on the handle, and then put the vacuum back in the closet. She wanted to keep busy; she didn't want to think about Thanksgiving tomorrow. Her plan to have a family dinner, to the extent that it could be a family dinner without Eric, had been dealt a serious blow when Sandy informed her that she needed help with a catering job at the local Elks Club. The four o'clock Thanksgiving celebration would mean a hefty payday for the business, and Sandy needed Sharon and Cindy to make it a success.

After shutting the closet door, Sharon turned around to see Shelly standing in the family room. "Sharon, I told you that I would vacuum after Marco got up from his nap."

Sharon frowned. "I know, I'm just trying to keep busy and keep my mind occupied."

"Thinking about having to work tomorrow?"

Sharon went over to the Christmas tree that had been up all year and began to rearrange the gifts underneath. "Yeah, that and other things."

"Bridget and I will fix dinner if you'd like."

"No thank you. I want to cook and I've decided we'll have Thanksgiving dinner on Friday instead. Besides, this year it's just the four of us and Eric's Dad. With Brian still in the hospital, Mark and Erin won't be able to make it."

"Can I help you with that?" Shelly asked, as she watched Sharon meticulously take all of the wrapped presents from underneath the tree and then begin to rearrange them in almost the same order.

"No thanks, I like doing it myself." She worked on the project for a couple of minutes, and then stood back to survey her work. "There, that looks about right."

Bridget bounded down the stairs and into the family room, carrying a package.

"What's that?" Sharon asked.

"I bought Dad a UIC sweatshirt from the bookstore at school," she said with a smile. "I hope he likes it." She placed the package under the tree and then sat down on the couch beside Shelly and gave her a hug. "It's so nice to be home again."

Shelly returned the hug. "Thanks, we've missed you. Marco can't figure out why you haven't been here."

"Aww, I missed that little guy."

"And he has missed you, too," Shelly answered." Yesterday, when you came home, he had the biggest smile on his face."

"I know."

Shelly continued. "I think you wore him out this morning when you took him outside to play, he's still napping."

Bridget smiled at looked at her mother. "So what's up tomorrow, Mom? Are we going to have Thanksgiving Dinner?"

Sharon shook her head. "No, Bridge, I'm working and won't be home till later. We'll have our holiday dinner on Friday. You, Shelly and Marco can warm up the beef barley soup I'm making for tomorrow. Okay?"

Bridget hesitated before answering. "Well, if you're not going to be here . . . "Bridget looked over at Shelly. "Let's go to the shelter tomorrow and help serve Thanksgiving Dinner. What do you say?"

Nodding enthusiastically, Shelly replied. "That's a great idea, Bridge. I'm in, and Marco can play with the other kids while we're there. With Brian in the hospital, he doesn't have anyone close to his age to play with."

"Good," Bridget said, as she went to use the phone in the kitchen. "I'll give the shelter a call and tell them to expect us."

Sharon stood staring at the tree, seemingly lost in thought.

"Sharon?"

"Yes, what is it?" Sharon turned toward Shelly, quickly bringing her attention back in focus.

Looking at the present Bridget had just placed under the tree,

Shelly asked, "What happens if your husband doesn't come home, I mean . . . will you celebrate Christmas this year or continue to wait?"

Sharon crossed her arms and hugged herself tightly. "No, Shelly, I won't celebrate until Eric is here to celebrate with us. I don't care how long it takes, but until he's home with me there can be no Christmas."

Shelly heard Marco crying upstairs. "I'd better go get him," she said, and ran up the stairs.

Sharon collapsed in Eric's recliner, as tears flowed freely. *He has to come home. Please, Lord, he has to come home.*

~~~~~~~~~~

Doreen shook Eric again. "Hey, c'mon, wake up!"

Eric poked his head out of the sleeping bag enough to see Doreen sitting up inside the cardboard box that served as their shelter. "What do you want?"

"You been sleepin' most of the day. Let's go get somethin' to drink."

The unlikely couple had finished their bottle last night. Doreen had wanted to get another bottle before the liquor store closed, but Eric decided against that idea. He wasn't sure if it was all the alcohol he drank or if he was coming down with a cold, but he was definitely feeling weak. "No, I'm not feeling real good right now."

"Okay, then give me some money, I'll go and get us a bottle."

He unzipped himself out of his sleeping bag and sat up. "Ow, my head is killing me."

"Yeah, you need a drink, Man. Let me go buy us a couple o' 40s . . . get somethin' strong to knock that headache out."

"Why is it that I always have to buy? Why don't you go get us something to drink with your own money. I'm tired of paying your tab."

Doreen rubbed her forehead. "Hey, Man, you know me. I get what I want by taking care o' dudes like you. It's a even trade. I'd take care o' you if you weren't so damn stubborn about it. What the hell you savin' yourself for anyway?"

I can't take this woman anymore. "It sure isn't for you." Eric answered, scratching his beard. "All you do is take, take, take. Ever since I met you, all you've done is drink my liquor and spend my money."

"You're full o' crap. I offered to trade you sex for your stinkin' booze but you didn't want it."

Eric shook his head. He crawled out from inside the cardboard box and rolled up his sleeping bag.

"Where the hell are you goin'? It's Thanksgiving; I thought we'd get drunk together."

"There isn't enough booze in the world to get me drunk enough to spend another second with you." He turned and walked away.

"You ungrateful bastard! You'll be back; you're nothin' but a loser . . . a bum."

He could still hear her shouting as he turned the corner. *Thanksgiving? Good day to go to the shelter and get cleaned up, get a meal and maybe, even a few aspirins.*

Twenty minutes later, Eric arrived at the shelter, tired and hungry. This time when he was given a number and told to wait, he took advantage of the delay to take a nap on the bench. After about an hour, his number came up and Eric went into the dining area. The tables were beautiful, each one set with pumpkins, cardboard turkey cutouts, and other decorations. Volunteers from the community walked back and forth from the kitchen to the dining room bringing plates stacked high with mashed potatoes, carrots, stuffing, cranberries and, of course, plenty of turkey.

A young girl approached Eric, carrying a plate of food. "Sir, would you care for a plate?"

Eric looked at the high-school-aged girl. She looked to be about Bridget's age. "Yes, thank you."

"Can I get you something to drink?"

For a moment, Eric was lost in his thoughts, thinking he was home as Sharon and Bridget were bringing food and drink items to the table. *Dad, do you want some coffee?*

"Sure, Bridget, thanks."

Puzzled, the young volunteer replied. "Bridget? Uh, Sir, is that a yes? You would like me to bring you a cup of coffee?"

Eric looked at the youngster's face, realizing his mistake. "Yes, please do."

The girl returned shortly with Eric's coffee and placed it on the table in front of him.

"Thank you," he said, taking a drink. "Sorry about getting your name wrong, he said, glancing at her name tag. "Amy. That's a very pretty name. It's just that I have a daughter your age; her name is Bridget. Seeing you reminded me of her."

Amy smiled at him. "Is she . . . I mean, is she homeless too?"

"Oh, no, no, she lives with her mother in a nice house. No, she's not homeless."

"Do you have any other children?"

Eric nodded, "Yes, I have a son. He's married, and I have a grandson—Brian."

"Sounds like a wonderful family," she replied. "How old is your grandson?"

The question gave Eric pause. He had tried to block thoughts of his family and in particular, Brian, from his mind. "He's . . . he's sick."

The young volunteer seemed baffled. "Oh?"

"Yeah, he's, uh, he's four, but he's sick." Eric folded his hands in front of his mouth and stared straight ahead. Tears crawled down his cheeks, disappearing in his beard."

"Sir, are you okay? I didn't mean to upset you. I'm sorry if I said the wrong thing."

Eric said nothing; he continued to stare while thoughts of his precious grandchild sent painful daggers into his heart. *Oh, Brian . . . what have I done?*

~~~~~~~~~~

Bridget removed the tin foil from tray containing the turkey. As the smell of the cooked bird permeated the dining room, Bridget breathed in deep. "Mmm, Mom, this smells so good."

"Thanks, Honey. We're a day late, but everything will taste just as good. Shelly, can you pour the gravy into the serving bowl? Dad, the rolls are ready to come out of the oven. Would you put them in this basket?" She asked, as she handed it to him.

A few minutes later, everyone was eating a wonderful Thanksgiving Dinner, just as Sharon had promised.

Marvin, Eric's father, finished buttering a roll and handed it to Marco. "Here you go, Sonny. Your Mom tells me biscuits are your favorite."

Shelly laughed. "Yep, Marco could eat buttered rolls for breakfast, lunch and dinner."

"I don't blame him. I used to eat my share of them when I was a youngster. Now, I've got to watch what I eat. Seems like everything I swallow goes to my waistline."

Sharon snuck a glance at Bridget. It seemed her eating habits had improved somewhat, but she still looked very thin. *What more do I need to worry about?*

"How did the catering job go yesterday?" Shelly inquired.

"A huge success—Sandy was ecstatic. Her projection on the amount of food she needed was spot on. All we had left were scraps. And the woman in charge of planning events at the Elks Club told Sandy they wanted her to cater their Christmas party."

"That's great, Mom!" Bridget exclaimed. "Oh, wait a minute. Does that mean you have to work Christmas Day?"

Sharon's smile disappeared. "I'm afraid so. I guess I could ask for the day off, but that would really put Sandy in a bind. I can't do that to her after all she's done for me. Without this job, we'd really be hurting."

"I told you I'd help with the bills," Marvin interjected.

"Dad, I know you did. But you're on a pension, you need to stay on a budget."

"Ah, the hell with that. What good is money if you can't help your family out?"

Sharon smiled at him as she reached across and patted the man's hand. "Dad, we'll be okay."

"I know, I just wish there was more I could do. Oh, by the way, I talked with the chief. He told me I could come in Monday and go over Eric's missing person file."

"Really? I'm surprised he's allowing you to do that."

Marvin sat up straight in his chair. "Well, I am retired from the department. Heck, maybe I'll find something the detectives overlooked."

"I hope you do find something, Papa. I don't know how much longer we can go on like this." Bridget hung her head and pushed her plate away.

"I know how you feel, Sweetheart. I miss him too."

The house phone rang and Sharon got up to answer it. "Oh, hi,

Mark. How's Brian doing?" She listened for a few moments and then said, "What? Please, God, no."

Bridget jumped up from the table and went over to her Mother. "Mom, what is it? What's wrong?"

"Our donor compatibility tests came back—none of us are a match."

47

Love is not a volunteer thing.
   —Samuel Richardson

Bridget walked into her dorm room and shut the door. She pulled off her hat and gloves and then set them on top of the heater to dry. Although she was exhausted from the indoor track workout with the team, she nevertheless went for a run by herself afterward. Her long runs outside were even more important to her now, since learning that none of her family was a match for Brian. *How can this be happening? Brian doesn't deserve this.* While she was out running, she was able to separate herself from the urban noise, her school life, and family trouble at home. Running was her escape.

Plopping down on her bed, she untied her shoes and flicked them off with her feet. She went over to her desk, grabbed a bottle of water off the shelf above, and drank half of the contents. As she was about to take a second drink, her roommate walked in.

"Hey, Girlfriend."

Bridget waved with one hand as she raised the bottle to her mouth to take another drink.

Tasha shook her head. "You out runnin' in this weather? It feels like the North Pole out there."

"Yeah, whatever." Bridget answered, in between gulps of water.

"You still in a funk, ain't you? Ever since you came back to school after Thanksgiving break, you just been mopin' around and feelin' sorry for yourself." Tasha took off her heavy coat and scarf and tossed them on her bed. "You still got to live your life no matter what. I know you got problems—your Daddy and that little boy—it's a damn shame about 'em. But look here, what good are you doin' 'em if you don't live each day as you should?"

Tossing the empty water bottle in the trash, Bridget went and lay down on her bed. She threw her arm over her face, trying to hide her tears. "I know you're right, Tash, it's just that I feel guilty," she sobbed.

"'Bout what? What you got to be guilty about? You're doin' what you're sposed to be doin'. Goin' to school, runnin' track. Man, you got nothin' to feel guilty about."

Bridge wiped here eyes. "Thanks, I guess it's like I'm kind of helpless. I mean, I can't help Brian because I'm not a match for the transplant he needs, and my Dad's been gone almost a year. I have no idea where he's at, or even where to start looking for him."

Tasha came over to Bridget's bed and sat on the edge. "Listen, all you can do is be the best at everything you doin'. What would your Momma say if you didn't do your best here? You know she got her own problems without worryin' 'bout you."

"That's for sure. I don't know how she keeps it together. I wish I was as strong as my Mom."

"You kiddin' me? Damn, girl, with all you do with school and the track team, not to mention helpin' me pass biology. You got a full plate. And, hey, you got that homeless bus thing goin' on too."

Bridget sat up and pulled off her running jacket. She looked at her roommate. "Thanks, Tash. I needed that."

"Glad to be of service," Tasha answered, a big grin on her face.

"Okay, time to get showered and then go eat. Speaking of the bus, I'm volunteering tonight."

"See? That's what I'm talkin' about. You got nothin' to feel guilty 'bout."

Bridget grabbed some clean clothes and headed into the bathroom. The Night Ministry Bus had helped her as much as she helped the people it served. The nights she volunteered was when she felt the least helpless, and, truth be known, the closest to God.

~~~~~~~~~~

"So what did the doctor say, Erin?" Sharon stood by the walk-in pantry at Sandy's catering kitchen, talking to her daughter-in-law on the phone. While she talked to Erin, Sharon searched for a bottle of olive oil.

"All we can do now is wait and hope that someone on the list will be a match for Brian."

"How long will that take . . . I mean, did the doctor give you any kind of time frame?" Sharon asked, nervously.

"No, Mom, that's what so scary. We have no idea of when or even, *if*, there will be a match. In the meantime, we just sit and wait."

Sharon spotted the bottle she was searching for and went back to the stove with it. "How's he doing?"

"You know Brian; he's a tough little guy. Even when he's not feeling so hot, he still wants to play, despite his energy level not being what it used to be. I'd like to bring him over and maybe even have dinner with you guys. Mark's working an afternoon shift tomorrow, so we'll be alone. But I have to make sure Marco's not sick. With Brian's resistance low, I don't want to expose him to any germs."

"Of course you can. Marco's fine and he'll be excited to see Brian."

"Funny how things worked out, isn't it?" Erin asked.

Sharon poured a bit of oil into a pan and turned the burner on. "What do you mean?"

"With Shelly and all. It seems like with Dad missing and Bridget away at school, Shelly came into your life at just the right time."

"Hmm, I never thought about it that way. But you're right, she sure has been a big help, and, frankly, having Marco around has helped me keep my spirits up. He's a good little kid."

As Sharon began to prepare an entree at the stove, there was silence at the other end of the phone. "Erin? Are you still there?"

"Yes. I, uh . . . well, are you going to do anything for Christmas this year?"

Putting down the spatula she was holding, Sharon went to the nearest chair and sat down. "Oh, Erin, I just can't. I can't bring myself to celebrate without Eric."

"I know, Mom, but for the kids' sake, can't we do a little something?"

Sharon rested her forehead on her hand and closed her eyes. "I'm sorry, I just can't," she replied, her voice quavering.

"Okay, Mom. I'm sorry I brought it up. I'll see you tomorrow."

"Goodbye."

~~~~~~~~~~

Since leaving the area of Lower Michigan Avenue after having had his fill of Doreen, Eric had been wandering around Upper and Lower

THE YEAR WITHOUT CHRISTMAS

Wacker Drive. This part of the city was farther from the shelter, so Eric hadn't been there in weeks. The much colder weather forced him to stay out of the wind as much as possible. That also meant he hadn't eaten many good meals. Remembering his lessons from the Professor, Eric had lately resorted to trashcans and dumpsters for food.

His panhandling had diminished; the harsh winter meant people either drove their own cars or took the bus or a taxi to stay out of the cold. Thus, there were fewer people to ask for money. Those who took pity on Eric dropped only small amounts of pocket change into his cup. Most times, he had to decide whether to spend the pittance on food or booze. More often than not, he opted for the latter.

Without any money or companions, Eric decided to take a walk to the vacant lot where he used to hang out with the Professor and Aaron. Hoping he might find the big man standing around the fire barrel for warmth, all Eric found was disappointment. The old lot was now a construction site. A chain link fence surrounded the property and protected the construction trailer parked inside. Angry that he had walked all that way for nothing, Eric kicked at the fence, grabbed it and began shaking it while yelling and screaming. A guard dog sprang from underneath the trailer, running and snarling in Eric's direction. Seconds later, a security guard quickly exited the trailer. "Get the hell away from the fence, you bum, before I let the dog out on you."

"Okay, sorry," Eric yelled back at the man and began to walk away. *Looks like I better visit the bus tonight.*

~~~~~~~~~~

It was one of the coldest nights since Bridget began volunteering to work the bus. Standing outside at the table where the Ministry served hot chocolate, coffee and sandwiches, she felt the cold wind slice through her clothing. Usually she could handle the cold weather, particularly when she was out running. The energy and movement involved with exercise kept her body heated. But standing around like this in one place . . . well, it was just brutal.

A woman approached the table. "Can I get some coffee and a sandwich?"

"You sure can," Bridget answered. She poured a cup and then handed it to the woman who took it with her right hand. Next,

Bridget took one of the sandwiches from the box on the table and handed it to her. "Here you go, Ma'am."

The woman made no effort to take the food from Bridget.

"Here's your sandwich," Bridget said, once again offering it to the woman.

Still, the woman made no move to accept the food. Finally, the strange woman put down the coffee on the table, took the sandwich from Bridget, and the put it in her pocket. She then picked up her coffee.

Puzzled, Bridget asked, "Are you okay? I mean your other arm, the left one, is it injured or something?"

The woman slowly pulled her hand out from her coat pocket.

"Oh, God!" cried Bridget.

The woman's gloveless fingers were almost completely black. "I can't hold anything," the woman explained. "It just don't work anymore."

Bridget had never seen a case of frostbite before, but the people on the Night Ministry Bus, as part of her training, had explained what some of the common injuries and diseases were among the homeless. She quickly went around the other side of the table and took the woman by the arm.

"Come with me, let's go inside and let the doctor take a look at that hand."

As Bridget escorted the woman into the bus, a man walked up to the table. Eric waited several seconds, wondering if the coffee was self-serve. Getting impatient, he finally poured himself a cup and grabbed two of the sandwiches. *Must be short on help tonight.* He took them with him and made his way to an office building he had discovered earlier down the street, one that had a deep entrance that would shelter him from the wind.

Eric sat down on the cardboard he carried and began to enjoy the first good food he'd had in a while. Washing the sandwiches down with hot coffee, he felt much better than he had earlier in the day. When he'd finished both sandwiches and the coffee, he decided to get one more cup before the bus went to its next location. He began walking in the direction of the bus, but stopped when he recognized a familiar face: Father Callahan. The priest was milling around the table where the refreshments were served, talking with one of the volunteers. *Not today, Father, go save someone else.* Eric retraced his steps and settled in for the night in his alcove, shielded from the wind. His stomach full, he slipped quickly into a deep sleep.

Meanwhile, Father Callahan continued his conversation with Bridget. "I think it's wonderful that a young person like you can give of her time to help those unfortunate souls who struggle every moment of the day."

"Thank you, Father."

"And where are you from, do you live nearby?"

"Oh, no. I live in Michigan. I go to UIC."

"Do you now?" The priest pointed to the coffee pot. "Can I get a cup of coffee?"

Bridget poured a cup and handed it to the priest.

"Thank you, my dear." The priest took a drink. "Ahh, perfect on such a cold night. Say, I wonder if I might ask a favor of you."

"What is it, Father?"

"Well, I've been working at the Lighthouse Mission over on Hubbard Street, and lately we've experienced a shortage of volunteers. One of the busiest nights of the year is Christmas Eve, and I'm not sure we'll be able to handle all of those who seek our help. Might I ask for your assistance?"

Bridget thought about the man's request for a minute. She had planned to drive home that day, and she was anxious to see Brian. But remembering that her Mother was holding fast to her decision not to celebrate Christmas without Dad, she made her decision. "Father, I wanted to drive home Christmas Eve, but I guess I can wait one more day. Besides, I'd probably be volunteering at our local shelter anyway, so working with you will be fine."

Beaming, the priest replied. "Bless you, my daughter. The Lord blesses those who take care of his children, particularly those who help feed and clothe those who are unable to help themselves. I will see you next week when we will deliver God's message to those who have been unable to hear his word."

"Okay, Father. See you when . . . dinner time?"

"Perfect."

Several people came up to the table asking for hot drinks, causing Bridget to focus on pouring coffee and hot chocolate. When she looked up, the priest was gone. *That's odd, where did he disappear to?*

48

Faith is to believe what you do not see; the reward of this faith is to see what you believe.
— **Saint Augustine**

Eric slept so soundly that the building security guard had to rouse him in the morning. "Hey, Buddy, wake up." The man said, as he nudged Eric with his foot.

Thinking he was about to be robbed, Eric grabbed the guard's leg.

"Hey, what's wrong with you, Man? Get your ass up and move along. We're expecting a big crowd today. Christmas Eve means a lot of last minute shoppers." The man pulled his leg free as he admonished Eric. "But they won't stop here if you're lying in the doorway, so get going."

Suddenly realizing his mistake, Eric got up quickly. "Sorry, I thought you were trying to rob me."

The guard chuckled. "Rob you? What do you have that I might want?"

Eric cast his gaze downward. *You're right, what do I have?*

As he walked out of the alcove, the ice-cold wind assaulted him, stinging his exposed skin like thousands of needle pricks. Tonight would definitely be colder than the ones before, challenging him to survive an hour at a time. If he didn't find a spot near an exhaust grate beneath the city streets, tonight might bring about what had been worrying him: dying in a strange town. Alone. But if that happened, at least his ordeal would finally be over.

It had been a long year for Eric. Living on the street had slowly destroyed him, physically and emotionally. With each passing day, his will to live dripped slowly from his soul like the last drops of water from a sprinkling can. Only a spark remained in his once fiery will, and that ember was slowly losing its heat. Were it not for the memory of his family, Eric would be content if one day he failed to wake up.

As Eric battled a tempestuous headwind on Wacker Drive, he glanced over the edge of the concrete railing that paralleled the Chicago River. Below, huge chunks of ice floated like so many translucent stepping-stones scattered on top of the water.

Eric crossed the street, intent on finding a cardboard box big enough to sleep in tonight. Having left the shelter he'd shared with Doreen meant he was on his own. He needed to search the alleys behind the businesses to find one. A strong gust of wind shouldered him toward the alcove of a coffee shop, like a big brother bullying a younger sibling with superior size and power. In his old life, Eric could have easily withstood that quick shove from Mother Nature. Now, his once muscular frame and considerable strength had vanished, like a magician's trick on a stage. He knew he'd lost weight, drinking more often than eating. He was barely recognizable as he stared at his reflected image in the café's window. He was the "after," in the typical before and after photo of people losing unwanted pounds.

Standing sheltered from the unrelenting wind, he took in the deep aroma emanating from freshly brewed coffee grounds inside the shop. Breathing deeply, his thoughts drifted back home where Sharon made fresh coffee each morning, a practice that had grown comfortable and had created a powerful bond between husband and wife. Their time spent together at the breakfast table was a ritual the couple had created, one that became not only comfortable but also necessary. On those rare occasions when their mornings failed to begin in this manner, it always seemed to make for a somewhat disjointed day.

Awash in those precious memories, a patron exiting the café jostled Eric as he hurriedly opened the door. "Oh, pardon me," the stranger quickly blurted. "I didn't mean to . . ." But as the man took stock of Eric's pathetic appearance, his attitude quickly changed. "Hey, you damn bum, get the hell out of the doorway."

Averting his eyes, Eric responded. "Sorry, Sir, I was just trying to escape the wind. It's so cold."

"Go stand somewhere else."

Eric sank into himself. "Hey, I'm sorry, I didn't mean to get in your way," Eric offered in supplication. "I wonder if you might be able to spare a couple of dollars for some coffee."

"Coffee? You mean booze, don't you? I know how you guys operate. I give you a handout and you head right to the liquor store for a bottle of cheap wine—you're a worthless drunk."

"But..."

"Save it for someone who gives a damn."

A single tear crawled down Eric's cheek, as he stood wounded from the verbal assault. He pulled his hat low over his eyes, not wanting others to see him as the stranger had. *A worthless drunk? I guess I am.* He moved away from the shop and made his way to the street next to the river. He stepped out into the slushy street oblivious to traffic. A bus swerved to avoid hitting him while bellowing a warning with its overpowering horn. *No need to worry about tonight. Why even try anymore?*

He reached the railing and peered down below. The river's reflection mirrored his soul—cold and dark. Mired in despair, he put one leg over the concrete barrier. As he did, he imagined Sharon's tearful face, tears he had caused. He was her pain; he was the problem. His actions had cost him his once perfect marriage, and destroyed a twenty-year love affair that had seemed ironclad.

Eric thought about Brian, his sick grandson. *How could I leave him in his time of need? I'm trash.* Devoid of hope, he lifted his other leg over the railing so that he sat facing the water. In seconds, the pain would end. It was better this way. He wasn't scared, just tired. Life had become too much of a chore. A gust of wind pushed him backward. Off balance and about to fall, he felt someone's arms around him.

"Sir, get down before you hurt yourself!" The voice was strong yet soothing. Eric turned his head to see who had interfered with his plan. To his surprise, an attractive, middle-aged woman stood there. Her hair blew in her face, but it couldn't disguise her concern.

The petite stranger helped Eric off the railing. He offered no resistance. "I've been watching you," the woman shouted above the sound of the persistent wind. "That bus swerved into my car to avoid hitting you. I've been parked at the curb waiting for the police to arrive." Eric looked over and saw both vehicles along the curb.

"Listen, lady, I'm sorry about your car, but can you just leave me alone . . . please?"

"I don't think I can do that," she offered. "Look, it's freezing out here and I'm not dressed for the weather. Why don't you sit in my car while we wait for the police to arrive and make a report?" She grabbed him by the arm and began to direct him to her vehicle.

Eric offered minimal resistance. In his weakened state he was lucky to have been able to get up on the railing. "Lady, thanks, but I . . ."

The woman put her arm around his waist and escorted him to her car. She opened the passenger door, "Here we are, go ahead and get inside." She helped him sit down and closed the door after him, and then she walked across to the driver's side.

"Let me turn up the heat. My gosh, that wind is horrible!"

As he sat inside the stranger's car feeling the heat penetrate his layers of clothing, he heard voices. Glancing down beneath the dashboard, he saw what looked to be an emergency radio. "Hey, what's that about?" he said, pointing to the device.

"That's a police radio."

Looking at the woman, Eric asked, "Are you a cop?"

"No," she laughed. "Actually, I'm a police chaplain."

Eric thought about what was unfolding in front of him. A police chaplain? While he pondered the possibility that perhaps fate may have played a role in saving him, a squad car arrived for the accident report.

"Stay here and warm up," she told him. "I have to give the officer my information, and then we'll discuss our next move. By the way, I didn't get your name."

"It's Eric."

"Okay, Eric. Be back in a jiffy."

A short time later, a gust of cold air roused him as the chaplain returned to her car. "All done. The car's drivable, only minor damage. Now tell me, Eric, how can I help you?" The woman handed him a hot cup of coffee. "Thought this might warm you up. I got it from the bakery across the street."

Eric removed his gloves and put them on the seat. He took the cup from her, the warmth soothing him as he took a small sip. It even brought feeling back to his normally numb hands, as he wrapped them around the steaming cup. "Thank you so much."

"You're welcome. Would you like me to bring you to the local shelter? I know the Lighthouse is going to be packed today—Christmas Eve is a busy time. If I bring you there now, you'll be sure to have time to clean up and be one of the first in line for their special holiday dinner."

Taking another sip, Eric thought that tonight might be a good time to spend the day, and heck, even the night at the shelter. The only reason he'd been avoiding it was because it was too far to walk in the cold weather. But now he had a ride. "Sure, I'd appreciate that."

As the car pulled into busy Chicago traffic, Eric decided the only thing that might ruin Christmas Eve is if Father Callahan showed up, otherwise tonight might be one he would probably enjoy.

~~~~~~~~~~

"Okay, who's ready to go to the shelter?" Sharon said, as she watched Shelly carry Marco into the kitchen.

Shelly grabbed Marco's arm and waved it. "Me, I'm ready." Marco laughed as his mother kept waving the boy's arm in an exaggerated manner.

"I wish Bridget was here to go with us."

Sharon began putting her coat on. "Me too, but I'm happy that she's volunteering at a shelter near the school. We'll see her tomorrow."

"I thought you had a catering job at the Elks."

"I do, but I talked with Sandy and she agreed that I could leave at noon. As soon as I get home, we'll leave for Children's Hospital in Detroit to visit Brian."

Helping Marco on with his jacket, Shelly replied. "I can't believe he's going to be in the hospital on Christmas Day."

"I know, it seems so cruel. But Mark said the doctor told him that it's just a precaution. He wants to make sure Brian stays healthy in case a donor becomes available. He should be released in a couple of days."

The two women loaded several dishes into the car, strapped Marco into his car seat, and then headed toward the shelter. After several blocks, Sharon's phone rang.

"Hi, Mom!" Mark said excitedly.

"Hi, Son. What's up? You sound like you just won the lottery."

"I did."

"What?" Sharon answered, her mouth agape. She threw Shelly a perplexed look.

"You are not going to believe what the doctor just told us. We have a donor for Brian!"

Sharon began screaming, "What? No . . . no way. Oh thank you, God, thank you! Hold on a second. Sharon pulled the car over to the curb and turned to Shelly. "Mark said they found a donor."

"Mom? Stop for a minute, that's not all."

Smiling and crying at the same time, Sharon asked, "Not all, what do you mean?"

"The donor is someone we know."

"Somebody we know—who?"

"Shelly."

Sharon snapped he head around at Shelly. "Our Shelly?"

"Yes, Mom. Our Shelly."

Hearing the conversation between Sharon and Mark, a flood of tears gushed down Shelly's cheeks. She placed her folded hands in front of her mouth and offered a silent prayer of thanksgiving.

"Mark, I'll have to call you back," Sharon told her son, in between sobs."I'm in the car with Shelly."

"Okay, Mom, bye."

Sharon undid her seat belt, leaned over toward Shelly and hugged the woman tightly. "Shelly, how . . . I didn't know you had even been tested?"

Reaching into her pocket, Shelly pulled out a tissue and dabbed at her eyes. "When I heard that your family was being tested to be potential donors, I wanted to help. I took a chance and asked my mother to take me. To my surprise, she brought me in for the test and even paid for it."

"Oh, my God, Shel. Thank you; thank you from the bottom of my heart."

Still crying tears of happiness, Shelly said, "I wanted to help, I wanted to somehow pay you back for all you've done for me and my son. After I tested, I prayed every day that I would be a match, especially after I heard the news that none of your family members were suitable."

Sharon let go of the woman and leaned back in her seat. Running her hands through her hair, she let out a huge sigh. "It's such powerful news, I feel completely drained. Thank you, God."

As both women sat silently, Marco cried out from the back seat— "Can we go play now?"

49

There are only two ways to live your life. One is as though nothing is a miracle. The other is as though everything is a miracle.
—Albert Einstein

Eric felt like his luck was finally changing. After the police chaplain gave him a ride to the shelter, he had taken a shower and shaved. Thanks to the local charities, he even had new clothing—clothes that actually fit his now bony body. After a sandwich and some coffee, Eric slipped into the men's dorm area for a nap. Falling asleep on a bed after so many months of lying on the ground was like enjoying a luxurious spa treatment. He had almost forgotten how good it was to live a near normal life. He did know one thing: he was tired of the way his life had been over the past year. Something had to change.

After sleeping for who knows how long, he opened his eyes and stared at the fluorescent lights shining brightly above him in the dorm room. He thought about the holiday tomorrow, and of course, how his family would be celebrating. Or would they? *I've probably ruined all their holidays, not just this one.* He felt torn between continuing his life on the street, and returning home to face his responsibilities. *What will they think of me? Can they forgive what I've done?* He weighed the pros and cons, thinking about whether or not he'd even have his job if he returned. Then he remembered Brian. *No matter what I do, I will never forgive myself if...*

Turning on his side, he began to weep. What kind of man had he become, and how could he have ever believed that walking out on his family was the right thing to do? Lost in his thoughts, he barely noticed that the lights flickered on and off.

"Everybody up. Dinnertime."

The staff member who had flicked the lights on and off to get everyone's attention, then followed up by stopping by each one of the beds to ensure everyone was awake. "We start serving in ten minutes. If you get in the dining hall now, you'll be assured of a meal. Otherwise, there's a long line of hungry people waiting to come in to eat. You'll have to wait until they all get served."

Eric climbed out of bed and smoothed the covers as best he could. He then wandered into the bathroom and rinsed his face with water. Drying off, he looked in the mirror. His freshly shaven face bore the effects of his year on the street—hollow cheeks and myriad new wrinkles—his homeless experience had definitely aged him. When he exited the bathroom and stepped into the dorm, he came face to face with Father Callahan. "It seems like I can't escape you," Eric said, sarcastically.

Smiling, the priest responded. "Now why would you want to do that, my son? I don't mean you any harm. In fact, it's Christmas Eve, a time to celebrate the birth of our Lord. You do celebrate Christ's birthday, don't you Eric?"

Something was different about the priest tonight. Normally, Eric wanted no part of Father Callahan. Tonight, he was somehow strangely drawn to the man. "Sure, I celebrate Christmas just like everyone else."

"Do you, now? And how will you celebrate the birth of Christ this year, Eric?"

Putting his hands in his pockets, Eric shrugged his shoulders. "I guess I'll just celebrate here."

"Not with your family? Not by going to church and thanking Him for all He's done?"

"All He's done?" Eric shot back quickly. "Look, I don't know if you noticed or not, Father, but I'm homeless." Eric scowled. "I don't think the Lord has done a whole lot for me."

"Is that so? Who is it that caused you to become homeless? Was it the Lord, or did you just decide that you weren't man enough to take care of yourself and your family?"

Eric stiffened. "Hey wait a minute."

The priest shook his head. "Wait a minute? I think I've waited long enough."

"Who the hell are you?" Eric agitatedly asked. "Do you know the pain I've been through?"

THE YEAR WITHOUT CHRISTMAS

The priest put his hand on Eric's shoulder. "Son, your pain pales in comparison to your family's pain. Their hearts have been broken since the moment you decided to leave without a word. Not a day has passed that Sharon hasn't searched for you, praying that you're still alive."

Eric put his hands up. "Stop! How do you know about my family?"

Father Callahan took Eric by the arm. "Come with me into the dining area. I want to show you something."

~~~~~~~~~~

Tasha had gone home yesterday, which meant Bridget spent the day alone. Practically all of the students were gone for the Christmas break. She killed time by cleaning her room and packing the things she would need to bring home for the holiday visit. She got in a long run, making sure she passed by the city Christmas tree downtown. It was beautiful, but made her feel sad at the same time. Unless her father came home, another year would pass without a Christmas celebration in the Doyle household.

As time grew near for her to volunteer at the shelter, Bridget loaded up her belongings in her father's truck. She decided to cut her time short at the Lighthouse and make the drive home tonight. She didn't want to spend another night in the huge dorm alone, and she was anxious to see Brian. Thirty minutes later, she had parked her truck and was walking into the Lighthouse Mission. She strolled up to the person working the front desk. "Hi, I'm a volunteer, I'm here to help with dinner. Would you tell Father Callahan that Bridget is here?"

Clearly confused, the man replied. "We don't have any Father Callahan working here."

Bridget paused. "Hmm, well, maybe he's a volunteer also. Anyway, he asked me if I'd help out tonight."

The man smiled. "I guess he could be a volunteer, but frankly, I've never heard of him," the man said, as he sorted through some volunteer logs. "The good news is that we can certainly put you to good use here tonight. Follow me and I'll take you to the kitchen."

~~~~~~~~~~

Eric allowed the priest to lead him to a table that was located in the far corner of the dining hall. There were only a few seats left, and the area was abuzz with volunteers bringing plates of food to the tables while Christmas music played softly in the background.

After they were both seated, Father Callahan began. "Listen to me, this is important. Don't worry about who I am, or how I know about your family. You have much more important things to think about. The truth is that no problem has ever been solved by running away from it. And no situation has ever been resolved because someone decided to drink it away. The problem is always there, drunk or sober—you can't hide from it."

Eric listened intently as he stared at the man. He heard the priest say the words he knew he needed to hear, and that up until now he had refused to listen to. Sharon, the chief, the EAP counselor, they had all said essentially the same thing, but Eric had shut them out. Instead, he preferred to feel sorry for himself and medicate his feelings with alcohol.

Father Callahan reached across the table and rested his hand on top of Eric's. A surge of energy shot through Eric's body. *Who is this man?*

An intense look in his eyes, the priest continued. "It's time for you to make a decision, my son. You've thought about no one else but yourself, and you've ignored the very people who need you the most. You wife and daughter have cried themselves to sleep on too many nights to count, and your little grandbaby needs his Papa."

Hearing this complete stranger discuss intimate details of his life shocked Eric. His eyes welled with tears and then overflowed. "Father, will you help me?"

Nodding, the priest answered. "That's what I wanted to hear, a request for help. All the time you wasted trying to run away from your demons could have been avoided. All you needed to do was ask the Father for help and He would have answered." He took his hand from Eric's hand and stood up. "Yes, I will help you." The priest began to walk away. "Wait here for a moment."

Trying to sort out what he'd just been through, Eric put his elbows on the table. He folded his hands and rested his forehead on them. His eyes closed, he tried to shut out the noise around him and picture his family in his mind's eye.

A couple of minutes later, his solitude was disturbed by a female voice. "Sir, would you like a dinner plate?"

Hoping the woman would go away if he ignored her, Eric said nothing.

"Sir, are you okay? The woman asked as she placed a hand on Eric's shoulder.

Annoyed, Eric turned his head slightly and looked up at the woman who was pestering him. "Miss, I . . . Bridget! Bridget! Is that really you?"

"Dad, oh, Dad!" She quickly put down the dinner plate as her Father sprung to his feet. They held each other tightly and buried their faces in each other's necks.

"Sweetheart, I've missed you so much."

As he held his daughter, he felt her body convulse as she wept tears of joy. "Dad, what happened? I mean, why are you here . . . how are you here? Didn't you know we were looking for you?"

"Yes, I mean, I figured you probably were, but . . . what are you doing here?"

"I go to college in Chicago, Dad. I was accepted at UIC."

Eric released his hug and took his daughter's face in his two hands. "Wow, I can't believe this is happening," he said, kissing her. "Let's just say I made the biggest mistake of my life, but now, thanks to Father Callahan, I'm ready to make things right. Where is he?"

"Father Callahan?" Bridget asked. "He's not here, the man at the front desk said that he's never heard of him."

Eric let go of her. "That can't be. I was just talking with him a couple of minutes ago. He was sitting right there," Eric said, pointing to the empty chair across the table.

"Dad, he told me to meet him here today, but I haven't seen him."

Scratching his head, Eric looked around at the dining hall. "Do you think he's in the kitchen?"

"I just came from the kitchen—he's not there. He's not even here at the shelter today."

Eric shook his head. "I don't understand any of this, but right now I need to make things right. How can we get home?"

Bridget smiled and pulled a set of keys from her jeans. Hanging them in front of her Father's face, she said, "Your truck is waiting outside."

His face beaming, Eric told her, "Get your jacket, your Mom is waiting for me."

"Okay, and let me stop by the kitchen and tell them I have to leave."

As father and daughter hurried from the shelter and got into the truck, Eric looked over at his daughter as she started the engine. "I can't believe you're here."

The motor turned over and Bridget pulled away from the curb. She reached into her jacket pocket and retrieved her phone. "If it's okay with you, Dad, I'm going to drive straight to Detroit. Brian's in the hospital, but I think the best medicine he can have right now is to see his Papa. I'll call Mom and have her meet us there."

"Definitely."

A light snowfall began to speckle the truck's windshield, but that wasn't what blurred Eric's vision. *I'm going home.*

50

When you look at your life, the greatest happinesses are family happinesses.
—Joyce Brothers

Sharon opened the oven door and placed the two pies inside to warm. "Five minutes should do it," she said to Shelly.

"I don't think there's any rush, the kids are busy watching the Christmas movie," Shelly answered. "They'll probably be ready for pie and ice cream when it's over."

Sharon looked toward the corner to see a dozen or so youngsters sitting on the floor in front of the television. *My Brian will soon be watching movies too.* Sharon smiled as she stared out the window above the sink at the shelter. The phone call from Mark, telling her about Shelly being a perfect match for Brian's needed transplant, was almost like her own transplant. The news rid her soul of dark thoughts, and lit her up inside like a noonday sun on a warm summer day. Suddenly her phone rang, interrupting her dreamy reflection.

"Hi, this is Sharon."

"Mom, it's me."

"Is everything okay, Honey? I thought you were going to call in the morning as soon as you got on the road."

"Well . . . I decided to leave tonight instead. I'm anxious to get home."

Sharon nervously rubbed her neck. "Bridge, you know I hate it when you drive at night. Besides, I thought you were volunteering at the shelter tonight. What happened?"

The girl chuckled. "I was there. In fact, I met someone there . . . someone I became instantly attracted to—someone I decided to bring home with me."

Sharon covered her mouth and said nothing.

"Mom, are you still there?"

"Bridget Doyle, are you serious? You just meet someone . . . in a homeless shelter, and you want to bring him home? Honey, I, uh, I don't know about this."

"Tell her, Bridge, don't' torture her any longer," Eric prodded his daughter.

"Who's that; is that your friend?"

Bridget smiled at her father while she spoke with her mother. "Yes, Mom, it's my friend. Here, say hello to him."

She handed the phone to her father. "Hi, is this Bridget's mother, Sharon?"

Sharon froze. *That voice. It can't be.*

"Hello, Sharon?"

Trying not cry, Sharon gasped for air. "I . . . yes, this is Sharon. You'll have to pardon me, your voice sounds so much like someone I know."

"Someone you know, or maybe, someone you love?" The man asked.

"What are you saying?"

As tears rolled down his cheeks, Eric told her. "Sweetheart, it's me, Eric, I . . . I'm coming home."

Sharon grabbed the kitchen counter to steady herself. "Eric, oh God, Eric, is that really you? Honey, how, why, oh dear. Where have you been; are you okay?"

Eric leaned against the door of the truck, unable to speak. His body trembled as the grief he endured for a year gave way to hope and happiness. He had finally allowed his emotions to pour forth, no longer any need to hide them or drown them in alcohol. He handed the phone to his daughter, and then buried his face in his hands. *Thank you, Father. I am so blessed.*

"Mom, Dad can't talk right now. He's too emotional."

Taking several deep breaths, Sharon asked, "Tell me how this all happened. Is he okay? I have a million questions."

"Easy, Mom, I don't know all the answers yet myself. We just found each other about ten minutes ago, but in the next four or five hours I'll probably know a whole lot more about what happened to Dad."

"Okay, drive safely but get here as fast as you can."

"I will. Oh, he wants us to go straight to the hospital. He said he needs to see Brian. Can you meet us there?"

"If I have to walk the sixty miles to get there, I'll meet you."

"Good, wait for us at the elevator bank on the children's floor. I'll call when we're in the parking lot."

~~~~~~~~~~

Before she knew it, Bridget and her Father arrived at Detroit Children's Hospital. Their drive home was the most satisfying trip Bridget had ever taken. Her prayers had been answered—she had her Dad back. As they got out of the truck in the hospital parking lot, Bridget studied her father's thin frame. "Dad," she joked, "you look like a runner now."

Eric smiled at her. "I sure don't feel like one."

She hugged Eric and said, "Don't worry, Mom's cookin' will have you looking good in no time at all."

"I'm counting on it. C'mon, let's go see her and Brian." They walked hand in hand into the hospital and soon boarded an elevator that would take them to the cancer wing.

As the elevator bell sounded, announcing their stop, Eric took a deep breath. "Here we go, Bridge."

The doors parted and Eric saw Sharon, Mark, Erin and a woman Eric didn't recognize, all waiting for him. Before he could exit the elevator, Sharon rushed inside and wrapped her arms around him. "Eric, you're home. Honey, I missed you so much." They danced and hugged and cried, until the elevator alarm began to buzz and warn them to allow the doors to close. Holding each other tightly, they walked off together.

Eric wiped the tears from his wife's face, but she continued to weep and laugh at the same time. Finally letting her husband go, she took a close look at him. "You're so thin."

"And you're so beautiful," he beamed.

"And you have a lot of explaining to do, Mister," Sharon said, with a serious look on her face.

Before he could answer, Mark and Erin stepped in between Sharon and Eric and trapped him in a huge bear hug. "Dad, we were so worried about you." Eric kissed them both and then looked at Shelly who was standing off to the side. "Do I know you?"

"Dad, this is Shelly." Bridget interrupted. "She and her son, Marco, have been staying with us."

"Oh."

Sharon walked over to Shelly and put her arm around the woman's shoulders. "Yes she has, and she's become a beloved member of our family."

Bridget gave her a mother a puzzled look. She was surprised by her mother's description of Shelly. She was very close to Shelly and Marco, but a "member" of the family?

Sharon continued. "Brian's treatment has not been going well," she said, looking at Eric. "He's been a very sick little boy. Our last hope to save him," she continued, her lips quivering, "was a stem cell transplant. We were all tested, but none of us were a match." Sharon squeezed Shelly. "This young woman took it upon herself to get tested, and we learned yesterday that Shelly is a perfect match."

Eric walked over to Shelly and embraced her. "Thank you for saving my grandson's life."

Now it was Shelly's turn to break down. Tears rolled down her cheeks as she turned away from Eric, trying to hide her embarrassment at the family's show of gratitude.

Eric wiped away his tears with his coat sleeve. "Can we go see Brian now?"

"Yes, Dad. This way."

As the family turned the corner of the elevator bank and into the main hallway of the children's cancer wing, Eric glanced up at a huge painting hanging above the double doors to the entrance. He stopped and stared. "No, it can't be."

"What, Honey?" Sharon asked

"The painting of that priest; I know him."

"Dad, you couldn't possibly know him," Mark said. "That's Father James Callahan, a Catholic priest who cared for children with cancer in the inner city. His work is legendary, that's why they named the cancer ward after him."

"Whatever, but I swear I've seen him—I've talked with him."

Sharon rubbed her husband's back. "Eric, Father Callahan passed away in 1963. You couldn't possibly have seen him."

"Mom, I saw him too. He's the one who asked me to work at the shelter. He's . . . " Bridget eyes opened wide."He's the one who made it possible. He made sure I'd find Dad!"

"I can't believe it, it's so amazing." Sharon shook her head.

"It's true, Sharon. He was leading me to Bridget all along."

She smiled at her husband. "I believe you, and I believe that prayer works. All one needs do is ask and the Father will answer."

Eric looked up at the painting again. "That's what Father Callahan told me. I guess he knew what he was talking about."

The family walked arm in arm to Brian's room, first stopping at the nurses' station for gowns and masks. Eric entered his grandson's room first and quietly approached the boy's bedside. He leaned over and gently kissed the boy on the forehead.

Brian's eyelids fluttered as he woke up and tried to focus on the man leaning over him. In just a few seconds, the little boy sat up and grabbed Eric around his neck. "Papa!"

"Merry Christmas, Brian. I love you."

Sharon dabbed at her eyes with a tissue. *Finally, it's time to celebrate Christmas once again.*

About the Author

John M. Wills is a former Chicago police officer and retired FBI agent. He writes both non-fiction and fiction in the form of novels, short stories, articles and poetry. An award-winning author, John has written eight books and published more than 125 articles.

An avid reader, he also writes book reviews for the New York Journal of Books, and is a member of the National Book Critics Circle.

John has had several award-winning short stories published in popular anthologies: "True Blue to Protect and Serve; Stories of Faith and Courage, Cops On The Street, American Blue: Real Stories by Real Cops," and "Rappahannock Review."

Made in the USA
Charleston, SC
10 September 2013